NO TIME
FOR FEAR

"Wait till he looks the other way, then you hop over the wire."

No Time For Fear

True Accounts of RAF Airmen Taken Prisoner, 1939–1945

Victor F. Gammon

'When caught in searchlights, dodging
flak, there is no time to be afraid'
— An aircrew colleague

**ARMS AND
ARMOUR**

Arms and Armour
An Imprint of the Cassell Group
Wellington House, 125 Strand, London WC2R 0BB

Copyright © Victor F. Gammon 1996

First published 1998

British Library Cataloguing-in-Publication Data:
a catalogue record for this book is available from
the British Library

ISBN 1-85409-434-3 (hbk)
ISBN 1-85409-490-4 (pbk)

Distributed in the USA by
Sterling Publishing Co. Inc., 387 Park Avenue South,
New York, NY 10016-8810.

Designed and edited by DAG Publications Ltd.
Designed by David Gibbons; edited by John Gilbert.

Printed and bound in Great Britain by
MPG Books Ltd, Bodmin, Cornwall

CONTENTS

Preface

Many books have been written on the exploits of war heroes and escape stories, but Vic felt very strongly that the true experiences, personal accounts and memories from men of the Royal Air Forces who were taken prisoner in the European theatre of the Second World War should be brought together and that they needed to be recorded. He set himself the task and dedicated twenty years of his life to this end.

On completing his work, it was found to be too long for one publication and required printing in two volumes.

It was a proud moment when I saw my husband's first book *Not All Glory!* appear on the bookshelves in August 1996, but Vic felt that his task had yet to be completed.

Vic died in January 1997 after a very short illness. At the time of his death he was busy collating and finalising his second volume. During the short time he had in which to realise how ill he was, Vic decided that his tentative title for the new book, *No Time For Fear*, was definitely right – and he left it to me to make sure the book was published.

It was Vic's suggestion that I ask our friend, Calton Younger, for his help and guidance. He not only accepted, but, 'considered it an honour to be asked'.

I am indebted to Cal for his tremendous help in the final preparation and editing of *No Time For Fear*, and for his time, given so generously, on the travelling involved. He has been a great support. I could not have done it without him.

My grateful thanks go also to Cal's wife Dee, who, uncomplainingly, has been left for hours during this busy time.

For any 'Kriegie' omissions, due to my ignorance, please forgive me.

I hope I have justified Vic's faith in me and that he would be as proud of *No Time For Fear* as he was of *Not All Glory!*

Sylvia Gammon

Introduction

The first British servicemen to take aggressive action against the enemy in the Second World War were Royal Air Force flyers. Within 30 hours of the declaration of war, 24 were dead and a sergeant and an aircraftman were taken prisoner. To be actively involved in fighting a war is an experience that will leave an indelible mark on a man for life; to be taken prisoner as well leaves a deep scar. To become a prisoner usually means to have been involved in violent action and to have reached a point where resistance is useless. A soldier often feels an accompanying measure of guilt, despite having fought to his last round. No such feeling assails the airman; his aircraft, the weapon with which he fought, lies burning on the ground. He is disarmed and in a situation from which there is no escape – at least, not at present.

Some 'Kriegies', as men captured by the Germans called themselves, faced prison life with a burning, and sometimes obsessional, desire to escape. Others endured captivity, resigned to live out the war as best they could, arguing that they were supremely lucky to have survived several battles when they could have been killed or maimed; so why tempt fate any further? Between these extremes there were the majority – men who would always assist others to escape and take the chance themselves should it appear. Neither way was easy.

Vic Gammon

"I'm sorry, I can't under-stand a word you say."

—— Acknowledgements ——

The author wishes to acknowledge the help of the contributors listed below and apologises for any inadvertent omissions:

Ron (Ackers) Akerman, R. (Jock) Alexander, W. (Tex) Ash MBE, George Atkinson, Bill Baird, John Banfield, George Barrowman, H. (Batch) Batchelder DFM, Charles Beeson, John (Jock) Bell, Ron Bence, Bill Bennett, Air Vice Marshal D. C. T. Bennett CB, CBE, DSO, Harry Bickell, William (Bill) Bloxham, Stan Booker, Brian (Porky) Booth, George Booth, Cas de Bounevialle, Don (Fritz) Boutle, Mrs J. Bowerman, John (Jack) Boyes, Albert Bracegirdle DFM, Roy (Lofty) Bromley, Stan (Lemmy) Brooks, John (Jack) Broughton, Don Bruce, Ron Buckingham, Alec Burton, Maurice Butt, George Calvert, C. (Ken) Campbell DFC, Percy Carruthers DFM, H. (Bert) Carter, Lt Cdr John Casson OBE, E. (Ted) Chapman, Ken Chapman, J. R. (Nobby) Clark, Allen (Nobby) Clarke, John F. (Jack) Clarke, Len Clarke, Matt Clarke, Reg Cleaver, Bob (Smudge) Coles MBE, E. Hugh Collins, Tom Cooksey, Henry (Roger) Coverley, Stan Croft MBE, Hal Croxson, V. (Bob) Cutts, Ron Damman, Gp Capt. Harry (Wings) Day GC, DSO, OBE, James (Dixie) Deans MBE, H. David Denchfield, John Dennis, A. J. (Tubby) Dixon, J. (Bas) Downing, Bert Dowty, R. (Jack) Dunn, Desmond Dunphy, Wg Cdr L. Edwards RNZAF, Dennis (Pinky) Emes, Douglas F. Endsor, Ron Esling, T. (Phil) Eyles, Ron Fermor, Geoff (Charlie) Fletcher, C. (Wally) Floody, Leslie Ford, John Forward, A. (Fris) Frisby, Denis (Freddie) Fry, Doug (Junior) Fry, W. V. (Bill) Garfield, Bill Garrioch, D. B. Gerrard, Ron Gibson, E. (Goldie) Gold, Bill Goodall, Ken (Marmaduke) Goodchild, W. (Bill) Goodman, Reg Gould, G. Greenfield, John (Gristle) Grimer, Ray Gulliford, A. (Ron) Gunton, Roy (Happy) Hale, E. L. Graham (Knobby) Hall MBE, L. Harcus, Marshal of the Royal Air Force Sir Arthur Harris Bt. CGB, OBE, AFC, LLD, Gerry Harris, W. (Peachy) Harrison, W. (Bill) Hart, Tom Harvey, Benny Hayward, Walter Hedges, Ray (Tin Bashing Tom) Hedley, Peter Hewitt, Bill (Shiner) Higgs, Paul Hilton CGM, Geoffrey Hobbs, Eric Hookings, John E. Howard. Maj. J. (Jimmy) Howe MBE, Frank Hunt, W. Jim (Red) Hunter, Stan Hurrell, W. (Wilf) Hurst, Reverend A. (Jacko) Jackson, Gp Capt. Frank Jensen CBE, DFC, AFC, AE, R. (Johnnie) Johnston, Ivan Kayes, Alex Kerr, Archie King, John Knott, D. H. Lawrence, John Leakey, W. (Bill) Legg, Norman (Len) Leonard, E. (Doc) Libbey, Len (Lindy) Lindridge, Denis Lloyd, Frank Lock,

Dan London, Bert (Rosie) Long, Len Ludlam, Mike Ludlow, George Luke, H. Lloyd Lyne, Jack (Tiger) Lyon, J. Alistair Macdonald OBE, John Mahony, Jack Marsden, Air Marshal Sir Harold Martin KCB, DSO, DFC, AFC, Peter Mason, Air Cdr. H. Massey CBE, DSO, MC, Alan McInnes, H. (Mac) McLean, Phil Middleton, Alex (Dusty) Miller, James (Jack) Mills, Arthur (Arf-a-mo) Minnitt, Reg Moffat, Ron Mogg, Arthur (Chester) Morris, Don Morrison DFC, DFM, Bob (Snowball) Morton, Vic Munnings, John Murrell, Sydney Murrell, Tom Nelson, Wg Cdr G. (Bill) Newby, Reginald (Dick) Newdick, C. (Nick) Nichol, Alec (Nicky) Nicholas, Neville Northover, H. J. Noy, N .F. Oates, Gordon (Oggie) Ogden, Ian Osbourne MBE, S. (Jim) Padgham, Jim Palmer, Norman (Bill) Panter, Geoff Parnell, D. (Jack) Paul DFM, Roger Peacock, Gwilym (Taffy) Peake, John Pickering, Deryck Polley, Leslie Poole, Jack Potter, Phil Potts, Edgar (Eddie) Poulter, Max (Zaba) Rech, Stan Reed, Wg Cdr Ken (Shag) Rees, George Rex, Ian Robb, Mike Roberts, Bill Rolfe, C. (Cec) Room, Eric (Sandy) Saunderson, Ron Scales, E. Scott-Jones, Percy Sekine, Geoff Shepherd, Leslie (Sid) Sidwell, Larry Slattery, Arthur (Smudge) Smith, F. G. Smith. J. (Chip) Sparrow, R. (Bobby) Stark, Maurice (Moggie) Stretton, Marian Jozef (Joe) Stule, Archie Sulston, Johnnie Sutton, Wilf Sutton, Alec Taylor, James (Jim, Schneider) Taylor, W. (Buck) Taylor, Peter Tebbutt, H. (Tommy) Tomkins, Peter Tomlinson, Ken Townsend, R. (Bob) Trett, Ken Trott, Frederick Turner MM, J. (Jim) Verran, Len (Titch) Walker, Brian S. Walley, R. David Ward, Bernard Warren, Doug Waters, Arthur Weston OBE, K St J, BEM, John Weston, W. (Bill) Williams, Alan (Tug) Wilson, Ernest Winfield, Harry Wink, Roy Witham, George Woodhead, George Wright, G. (Wilbur) Wright, David Young, Calton Younger. Special thanks are due to Desmond Dunphy, MIL, for his advice and help with the German language; also to R. (Bob) Anderson and Dave Westmacott for permission to use cartoons from *Handle With Care*.

Vic Gammon

Glossary

Allgemeine Zeitung General newspaper

Arbeitskommando Working party

Aufstehen Get up

British Free Corps An organisation created by the Germans for propaganda purposes, inviting men to join in order to 'take part in the struggle against Bolshevism' and 'condemn the war with Germany', it claimed to be 'a thoroughly British volunteer unit conceived and created by British subjects from all parts of the Empire'

Bürgermeister Mayor

Fallschirmjäger Parachutist

Feldwebel Company Sergeant-Major

Gauleiter District Leader – the highest-ranking Nazi party official below the top Reich

Gefreiter Lance-Corporal

Generaloberst Field Marshal

Hände Hoch! Hands up!

Hauptmann Captain

Heraustretten! Come out!

Herrenvolk Master Race

Hitler Jugend Hitler Youth – the male branch of the German youth movement

'Joe' An agent being dropped by parachute

Lager Camp

Lazarett Hospital

Leutnant Second lieutenant

Oberst Colonel

Oberfeldwebel Sergeant-Major

Obergefreiter Corporal.

Oberkommando der Wehrmacht The supreme command of the armed forces

Oberleutnant Lieutenant

Posten Sentry or Sentries

QDM A homing bearing

Raus! Move it!

Reichsmarschall Special title created for Hermann Göring

Schnell! Quick!

Soldat Soldier

Untermensch Subhuman

Unteroffizier Lance-Sergeant

Völkischer Beobachter *Racial Observer* (newspaper)

Völkssturm The People's Army or home defence unit

Wehrmacht Armed Forces, but usually applied to the German Army by Kriegies

"... and here's a picture of my sister ..."

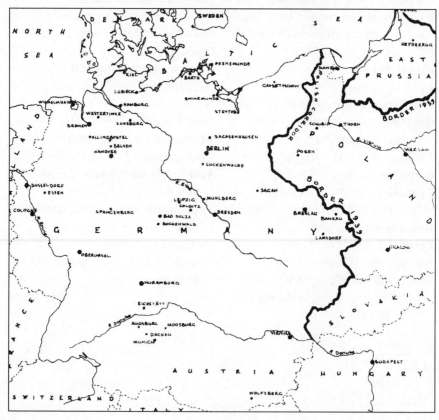

PART 1

1939–1940

DAY OF DISASTER

A furious and frustrated Flight Lieutenant Ken Doran glanced over his shoulder as he set course for RAF Wattisham. Behind his Blenheim bomber lay powerful units of the German Navy, anchored and apparently unharmed, apart from the cruiser *Emden*. A Blenheim had crashed in a fiery explosion on to her foredeck. Other huge maelstroms marked where three Blenheims had dived into the sea at Wilhelmshaven, flames dowsed but the crews dead. Another aircraft lay floating on the water; there was still a chance for those flyers.

Doran and his crew, who had led the attack, had seen their own 500lb bombs bounce from the armoured deck of the *Admiral Scheer* and explode harmlessly in the sea. The attempt to damage the *Kriegsmarine* on the second day of the war had failed dismally and five of the attacking force of ten Blenheims had been lost.

The subsequent award of the DFC did nothing to compensate Doran for the loss of fifteen of his comrades; thirteen dead and two prisoners of war. The prisoners were the first to be taken in the war, Sgt George Booth and AC1 Larry Slattery*.

Both were injured and taken to hospital. Slattery was first to be discharged and Booth was distressed. For the first time he felt alone in an alien land. Eventually, to his astonishment, he was told that Slattery, a talented violinist, had been taken to the local barracks where he had been enrolled as a member of the band. Booth refused to believe it.

When it was Booth's turn to be discharged from hospital, he was told that his departure would have to be on a Friday. His escort, an officer and a sailor, lived near the camp to which he was to be sent and had wangled a weekend leave. Smiling wryly, Booth realised that servicemen everywhere behaved in the same manner.

On a snowy February morning, all those connected with George Booth's case assembled to wish him farewell. As he climbed into the passenger seat of a car, his kit and Red Cross parcels filled the rear seats. Booth was dressed in a strange conglomeration of odd clothes: a French side hat, Polish trousers with a non-matching tunic, a Polish greatcoat

---

* *Not All Glory!*, pp. 11–13

and hospital boots. He clutched a walking stick to steady himself on the icy paths. Somehow, the war seemed unreal to George Booth and he had not taken in that he was a prisoner with an indeterminate future. There was little to indicate fears and miseries that might come.

Booth had not known what to expect of Oflag 9/AH Spangenberg near Kassel. This three-storey, gabled, half-timbered building looked more like a holiday home than a prisoner-of-war camp but the ten-foot-high barbed wire fence surround dispelled any illusion. This was Booth's initiation to the world of 'THE WIRE'. It was to dominate his life for the next five years.

The neat building at Spangenberg was originally the dower house of the castle which sat firmly on the top of the adjacent hill. It had been used before the war as a Hitler Youth and 'Strength through Joy' hostel. Nazi slogans proliferated on every wall.

Life was tranquil and dull for the other ranks and NCOs at Oflag 9/AH, so all accepted an invitation to a church parade and religious service with the officers caged in the castle above. This was a chance to meet new faces and perhaps arrange with the officers for a loan, out of their allowance from the detaining power, to buy a few necessities against IOUs to be redeemed after the war.

Among the officers from the three services were some other ranks serving as orderlies. One of them was Larry Slattery. Booth was anxious to hear his story.

Taken from the hospital at Wesermünde, Slattery had been treated as a VIP. A violin had been bought and he had been installed in the town band based at the *Wehrmacht* barracks. He was told that all he had to do was to work for German Intelligence and then, he was promised, he would be returned to Eire by submarine. Slattery's prompt refusal meant that he hardly had time to pack his few possessions before he was despatched to Spangenberg.

After the service, as the NCOs assembled in the courtyard for their march down the hill, their numbers were infiltrated by an officer who intended to descend to the dower house where he believed escape might be easier. But the party was too small for him not to be noticed. Attempts at escape were still impulsive and opportunist. They had not yet become the meticulously planned and carefully organised operations necessary for any chance of success.

During the first half of 1940, following their stay at Spangenberg, the RAF and Royal Navy men were moved from camp to camp without apparent purpose.

WINTER FLIGHTS

'I tell you, you will be shot down only if you break formation,' declared the sergeant instructor as he demonstrated on a blackboard the deadly crossfire from the tail turrets of three Wellingtons. At the intersection of the dotted lines which represented machine-gun fire, a fighter plane sporting a swastika was disintegrating in a cloud of smoke. The theory did not work in practice, as was proved on 14 and 18 December when seventeen Wellingtons, half of those attacking German shipping, were shot down. Others, badly damaged, crashed on return to base. Fruitless attempts were made to cover the Wellington's blind spots with 'beam' guns and 'dustbin' gun turrets rotating through 360 degrees. Hampdens suffered similar unsustainable losses.

Throughout the winter of 1939-40 the Whitleys of 4 Group struggled against bleak weather to drop millions of leaflets on German cities. Icing, frostbite, flak and nightfighters were constant, fearsome enemies, but losses were proportionately few compared to those of the Wellingtons and Hampdens on the December daylight attacks. The lesson could not be ignored. The Chief of Bomber Command, Air Chief Marshal Sir Edgar Ludlow-Hewitt, knew that the Air Ministry's plan to bomb the Ruhr in daylight would lead inevitably to terrible losses with negligible result. Night bombing it would have to be. New navigating methods and bombing techniques would need to be found and taught. The experience of the Whitley crews, gained on their leaflet and reconnaissance raids ('Nickel' in the jargon of the time), would be invaluable.

STRUNG UP

Although it was 27 March, spring had brought little warmth to rural Yorkshire. Snow lingered in sheltered hedgerows around RAF Driffield and ice crackled under the wheels of a Whitley V of 77 Squadron as it taxied, turned and roared along the flare-path on another 'Nickel' leaflet and reconnaissance raid to north-west Germany. Wireless operator/observer Sergeant W. 'Buck' Taylor was glad to be flying again. On operations since the war began, Taylor had recently been 'grounded' while recovering from an embarrassing bout of measles. He had now joined a new crew with just a few operations recorded in their log books.

The Whitley pilot, F/O J. 'Boardie' Boardman, and 'Second Dickey', P/O G. Norman, watched the port engine oil-pressure gauge intently. It was suspect. On their last operation the gauge had registered a pressure drop and they had been forced to turn back.

'It should be OK this time,' asserted Boardman hopefully but without conviction. 'That engine's been completely overhauled.'

17

Norman grunted in agreement, but both men continued to watch the needle on the dial.

All the crew members found themselves willing to disbelieve an indicated new drop in oil pressure. The port engine had been thoroughly checked; it *had* to be a faulty instrument. Another early return would mean probing questions from the Flight Commander and sly remarks from fellow aircrew. In any case, they wanted to complete the operation. The wish became a conviction – it *was* the pressure gauge that was 'up the creek'. Satisfied at having made a firm decision, each man settled down to routine. Over the dark North Sea the turret guns were briefly tested and fired, the tracer bullets curving brightly in the gloom. Loop bearings were obtained, the course checked and a sharp lookout maintained for enemy fighters. There was only a niggling doubt about that 'damned gauge'.

The outward flight was uneventful, just a little flak and a glimpse of the Rhine through a break in the otherwise impenetrable overcast. The cargo of leaflets fluttered down in thousands, but as Boardman set a course for home, the sudden rough running of the port engine was felt by the whole crew. At Boardman's call, Taylor climbed from the Whitley nose turret to help take the strain on the rudder cable in an effort to keep the aircraft steady. It was no use, the engine caught fire, the Whitley rapidly lost height and within seconds Boardman realised that the situation was hopeless. At 6,000 ft he ordered 'Abandon!'

Unable to grasp the ring of the escape hatch with frozen fingers, Taylor left it to P/O Norman and went back to guide wireless operator LAC Masters and rear gunner AC1 Cowie through the side door. Third to dive out, Taylor counted to four before pulling the 'D' ring – and prayed as the tailplane flashed past. Floating silently down, he thought he saw bushes below, but they were tall firs. His parachute canopy snagged on the tops, his descent slowed rapidly, there was a crackling and hissing of breaking branches and then he was suspended, dangling helplessly in the middle of four trees but unable to reach the trunks of any.

The ground was barely visible; it seemed a very long way down but Taylor knew he had no choice; he had to free himself from the harness and drop. He remembered with dismay that the harness was experimental, that there was no quick release as long as he hung suspended, with the harness taking his full weight.

Twisting and straining, Taylor reached for a small penknife in a pocket inside his Irvin suit. Swiftly sawing at the webbing, he was thrown to one side as the line parted. He was still hanging but was now askew. As he cut through the harness, Taylor felt that the webbing straps had already stopped the circulation to his legs and feet. Unless he freed himself quickly, he was going to die a lonely death in the forest.

He sawed desperately at the last strands of the webbing, but when it finally parted, the ground rushed up with a fierce suddenness. Taylor crashed heavily among the pine needles, painfully wrenching his back and ankle. But the relief of being alive flooded over him as he lay still, regained his breath and listened to the burning crackle of the crashed Whitley. In the opposite direction he could hear the distant clangour of a train.

As he tried to stand, agonising pain swept over him like a crimson wave. The hurt in his back was a twisting torment and his left ankle could take no weight. Early morning light shafted through the trees when Taylor, using a stake as a crutch, made his tortured way down the hill towards the sound of the train. Pain finally forced him to a halt. He knew he had parachuted close to the German-French border but, if he was on the wrong side, he had 'had it'. As daylight crept across the countryside, Taylor studied a signpost at a fork in a track. The arm pointed to somewhere named Prüy. With a sinking heart, Taylor saw the German *umlaut*. Reaching a seat overlooking a farmhouse, he sank down to ease the pain in his back and ankle. He was finished; he could not move another step. When a farmer walked out of the house, his accompanying dog immediately saw Taylor, its bark drawing the farmer's attention. The man's call of '*Komm hier*' to the dog was too much like English to be French. Taylor was definitely in Germany.

He remembered little of the journey to Hohemark Hospital. He had glimpses of Boardman, Masters and Cowie and he learned that P/O Norman was dead. The train journey to Frankfurt am Main and a rough, dark ride in a lorry over cobbles finally merged into the blessed relief of exhausted sleep.

Next morning he was visited by a *Luftwaffe* officer. Tall, slim, impeccably smart, *Major* Rumple, the *Kommandant* of Dulag Luft, told Taylor that Boardman had already been sent to an officers' camp and that the remainder of his crew, apart from P/O Norman, were in other rooms and unhurt.

With rest and treatment, Taylor strengthened and was transferred to Dulag Luft, the new interrogation and transit centre for captured airmen. He was immediately told to report for a second interrogation, this time by the Senior British Officer, Wing Commander Harry Day, known to all simply as 'Wings'.

Later Taylor was registered as a coder and wrote to, and soon received cards from, fictitious girlfriends.

Throughout the winter of 1939–40 and the spring of 1940, reconnaissance and training continued at full stretch, with the Whitleys still spreading their paper propaganda across Germany. There were losses, frequently due to icing, dense cloud and fog. Relative calm persisted until the bombshell of the German *Blitzkrieg* invasion of Denmark and Norway. The *Wehrmacht* entered Denmark almost unopposed. Norway was a harder nut to crack but, by 10 May, German forces had subdued both countries and were ready to invade Holland, Belgium, Luxembourg and France. Thereafter, poorly armed RAF Battles and Blenheims were thrown into the struggle to halt the German advance with low-level suicide attacks, particularly in the Laon area. The outcome was inevitable.

THE WIPING OUT OF 142

By 18 May 1940 the Allied armies were falling back rapidly before the German armour and infantry. The *Luftwaffe* blasted a way ahead for the *Wehrmacht*, covered by swarms of Messerschmitt 109s. The Dutch surrendered, Brussels and Antwerp fell and the BEF began its withdrawal to the west. It was in this situation of confused retreat that the last three Fairey Battles of 142 Squadron at Faux-Villecerf were thrown into the cauldron on the 19th.

142 Squadron was a sorry sight as Aircraftman Bert 'Rosie' Long studied the Battles. The squadron had, effectively, been wiped out. The three tired-looking aircraft were last-ditch replacements. Long's heart sank as, with pilot F/O H. Taylor and navigator Sgt S. Lang, he walked over to examine the battered and tattered aircraft. The machine-gun he was to use to break up a German column was of Great War vintage and rusty. Bert Long thought the outlook bleak as he climbed into the gunner's position. Like so many gunners then flying, he had not received any proper gunnery training. With grim irony he realised that, in this life and death struggle into which he was to be thrown, he was not qualified to wear the brass winged-bullet air-gunners' badge nor to receive the extra 6d. (2 $^1/_2$p) per day to which a trained gunner was entitled.

Throughout the flight towards the front-line German column, Long struggled to make the gun usable. To his misery but not his surprise, it jammed as the attack began. With flak bursting on all sides, Taylor flung the Battle around while Long sweated to clear the breech. Taylor lifted the aircraft over the brow of a hill and brought the relief of sudden comparative quiet as they drew away from the column. Still with his finger stuck in the jammed breech, Bert Long was suddenly jerked to one side as a loud report came from the engine and smoke poured back into the fuselage.

'We're on fire, bale out! Bale out!' yelled Taylor as he took the Battle upward. Long was momentarily jerked back by his still attached 'monkey chain', but Lang, behind him, released the dog clip and pushed Long over the side; he had to leave by the same exit.

The aircraft had been low, and within seconds of his parachute canopy snapping open, Bert Long was on the ground. He was captured by a medical unit and taken to a farmhouse crowded with German soldiers. The scene was watched with wide-eyed fear by a French farmer and his wife. A typical 'Fritz' soldier was seated at a table enjoying a plate of steak and kidney. Long, standing nearby, began to tremble; the effects of the violent action were beginning to show when the kitchen door crashed open and a 'band-box' smart *Wehrmacht* officer strode into the room.

'Ah! there you are,' he called to Long in impeccable English. 'We have been looking for you. We saw your aircraft crash – your crew must be dead.'

It was a crushing blow. Almost as an afterthought the officer remarked, 'By the way, you have killed eighty of my comrades.'

Long's heart sank still further but, instead of retribution, the officer turned to him and asked incongruously, 'Are you hungry?' Without waiting for an answer, he took the plate from 'Fritz', handed it to Long and ordered more steak from the farmer's wife. Bert Long sank down gratefully on to a chair. He needed to sit down. The effects of the action began to subside, he became calmer and started slowly to eat. It was the best meal he was to have for many a day.

Later, when Long and other prisoners were straggling their way across northern France, he met Sergeants Hopgood and Godsell, two of the crew of one of the other two Battles in the attack. Their wireless operator, LAC Boyle, had been killed and they had seen the third aircraft shot down.

'Three out of three,' groaned Long.

In another field in Belgium, he again met Sergeant Lang, who told him that their aircraft had crashed before he could bale out. The German officer had been wrong; his crew-mates were alive.

Of the nine crew members of the three Battles that had been shot down, six had been taken prisoner, all wounded to some degree, two had been killed and one, Sgt Ebert, incredibly, made his way back to his squadron.

For the RAF the attrition continued. They were fighting hard but were being overwhelmed. All the fierce daylight attacks by the Battles and Blenheims and the crippling losses of crews and aircraft had failed to blunt the spearheads of the German advance. The boy entrants, the apprentices and the regular airmen of RAF aircrew were being eliminated. 'Peanut' Parkin, a Cranwell 'boy', stopped reading the casualty lists, which were black with the names of fellow 'boys' whom he knew so well. Sgt Heslop, a survivor of the Battle of France and the Battle of Britain, was to say later, 'Never again did I encounter such opposition as we experienced in France.'

The situation was desperate for the Allies. Winston Churchill asked for four fighter squadrons to be sent to France, and then asked for six more. The War Cabinet agreed, but Air Chief Marshal Dowding did not. On 16 May he wrote to the Air Ministry stating his firm belief that any further reduction by sending more fighters to France would, with the fall of that country, involve the final, complete and irremediable defeat of Britain.

Just ten days later, Vice Admiral Ramsay began the evacuation of 338,000 Allied soldiers from the Dunkirk pocket in a motley collection of small ships and ferry boats.

As the last of the British Expeditionary Force that could be evacuated from Dunkirk was scrambling into the boats, the fighters of the ASSF in France were down to less than twenty aircraft. One hundred and six fighters had been lost.

THE MAP MAKER

Flight Sergeant Graham 'Knobby' Hall, although operationally a Whitley pilot, was experienced in many aircraft types. Chafing at the bombing restrictions, he continued to use the 'Nickel' flights to supplement his store of personal experience. Hall was keen to be competent when the time came to bomb military targets. Navigating at night over blacked-out enemy territory was still a hit-or-miss affair.

'Knobby' Hall was a 'character'. His luxuriantly spreading black moustache, beetling eyebrows and rosily healthy cheeks thrust him forward. In a crowd he would always be the first person one would notice. Yorkshire-born 'Knobby' had been in the Royal Air Force for nine years to the day when war was declared. 'Nickel' raids began for him five nights later.

Realising that in his dangerous trade there could be an occasion when he would be wandering, lost on the Continent, Hall 'acquired' sufficient parachute silk on which to trace an accurate map of Europe. He showed the map to his Station Commander, Group Captain Hunter, and that was the last he saw of it as it wended its way upward towards Air Ministry. Hall said 'goodbye' to the map and traced another, which his wife sewed into his uniform as a shoulder pad.

As he left the crew-room to fly on what was to be his last operation, an airman arrived with a message from the Group Captain. In an envelope was a beautifully coloured silk map of Europe with the message:

'You will be interested to know that this was invented by a chap at Air Ministry and you may have it with my compliments.'

THE CODERS

On the night of 19 May, when France was crumbling before the onslaught of the *Wehrmacht*, Flight Sergeant Hall's Whitley was shot down by anti-aircraft fire when attacking oil installations at Gelsenkirchen. As his parachute crumpled around him, Hall was met by a farmer with a menacing shotgun and quickly despatched to Dulag Luft.

The interrogators held him for ten days in the cells but achieved little. He had been warned by a party of orderlies carrying buckets past his shuttered window. Several were shouting and fooling about but one voice reached him loud and clear: 'Don't sign any Red Cross forms!' Hall got the message and common sense did the rest. In disgust the Germans sent him to the main camp and its Senior British Officer (SBO), 'Wings' Day.

To his surprise, Hall found that he was the senior NCO in the main camp. The permanent staff was run by a Sgt Slowey. 'All right, I am now the senior NCO and will take charge,' announced Graham Hall, but Slowey appeared to resent the flight sergeant's authority. Early next morning, without explanation, the German authorities removed Hall and sent him to Limburg, a transit camp, which at this time held 80 airmen, half of them English, the others French. Again Hall found himself senior NCO but was reluctant to interfere with the incumbent Tom May, who was coping well and had established contact with the Red Cross in Geneva. Previously a small number of prisoners had received mail and a few parcels, but German advances in the West now disrupted communications. The huge influx of army prisoners and the increase in RAF prisoners aggravated the situation. Red Cross parcels ceased and prisoners reverted to receiving what the Germans called rations suitable for non-workers and old age pensioners. But the prisoners lacked the facilities those Germans had to buy off-ration vegetables and restaurant meals.

Remnants of the British Expeditionary Force straggled into the camp, having been marched and cattle-trucked across Europe since the collapse at Dunkirk. With great forbearance, the RAF men, now 50 strong at Limburg, withstood the continual abuse from the soldiers and their cries of, 'Where was the RAF at Dunkirk?'

When Paris fell to the *Wehrmacht*, the prisoners were called out for the first *Sondermeldung*, a special announcement of a victory for the German Armed Forces. At Limburg Graham Hall studied the faces of the Frenchmen. Robert, their senior man, had already shown his disgust with surrendering *poilus*, ready with their suitcases of clothes and provisions. With tears of fury and shame pouring down his face, Robert now ripped the *Croix de Guerre* from his chest and threw it to the ground, crushing it beneath his heel. Many of the French airmen were crying. The British contingent at Limburg felt an overwhelming sympathy for them but it did not enter their heads that they could soon be in a similar situation.

There was another blow for the Kriegies. Due to difficulties created by the collapse of the Allies on the Continent, 'personal parcels' to prisoners of war were suspended.

With the advance of summer, the soldier prisoners were removed from Limburg to working camps in Germany and Poland.

Hall was glad when it was the turn of the RAF men to make the cattle-truck journey to Stalag 8B at Lamsdorf. A move to another camp was always seen as an opportunity by would-be escapers, and Hall's map, concealed in his shoulder pad, was copied several times. One airman who asked for help was Johnny Bowles. He, like W. O. Hancock, Alfie Fripp and Reg Winkler, was an old friend of Hall's. All were Halton Apprentices or 'Trenchard Brats'.

The 85 RAF men at Limburg were herded into one cattle truck. Graham Hall's protests at the crush drew only a sharp jab with a bayonet, but the squeeze meant that there would be no guards with them in the truck. Johnny Bowles amazingly produced a pick-axe head and went to work on a floor plank. There was soon a reasonably large hole and, as the train stopped for a few minutes after dark, Bowles dropped through to the track and was away.

At dawn the train stopped again, the doors were roughly thrown back and shouting guards rousted the Kriegies out.

'*Raus, raus, schnell, schnell!*' Rifle bolts were snapped back and bayonets pointed belligerently. The guards knew what they were looking for and it was clear that Johnny Bowles had been caught. When the hole in the truck floor was found, Hall, as senior man, was hustled off.

For the first time Hall was subjected to an exhibition of the hysterical screaming of a German officer. After being threatened with court martial for sabotage, the Kriegies were forced back into the truck and eventually arrived at Lamsdorf. Johnny Bowles was there to meet them, just a little the worse for wear.

Stalag 8B was a large camp which sprawled untidily and enclosed some 3,000 near-starving men. It was the task of Regimental Sergeant Majors Sherriff and Laws to see that the little soup and bread available was fairly distributed. Graham Hall joined the pair to act on behalf of the camp's RAF contingent. Discipline was maintained for the first round but when it came to doling out the few ladles of soup sometimes left over, there was near riot. No matter how carefully those serving tried to issue it to each block in turn, it became necessary to beat off the hordes with heavy metal ladles. Airman Len Ludlam was disgusted at guardsmen who, by fighting over a dixie of food, caused it to be upset into the sand.

Hall was not sorry when he was summoned to the *Kommandant*'s office and told that the airmen were to move to a *Luft Lager*.

'If you will give me your parole that you will not try to escape, *Herr* Hall, I shall see to it that you travel by passenger train, otherwise it will be in cattle trucks.' So, like cattle they journeyed north to the Baltic coast.

When, in mid-1940, Hall and his now 87-strong RAF contingent arrived at Stalag Luft 1, Barth, he found RAF officers already installed in their own compound. In the other compound thirteen NCOs under Sgt Ossy Lascelles were settling in, having arrived the previous day from Dulag. At last the flyers were on their own in a camp designated by the Germans solely for the RAF. When he was handed his first letter-card to write home, Hall carefully composed a letter to his wife, punctuating it so correctly that she was bound to notice. Mrs Hall had frequently complained that his punctuation was non-existent and Hall had told her, 'If ever I am a prisoner-of-war look carefully at letters from me. Any word after a full stop will be a code word.' His wife remembered and, with the cooperation of the Post Office and Air Ministry, Hall's letters were intercepted and decoded. It was a simple system and far from foolproof but Hall hoped for something better.

His letter bore fruit. Sgt Neil Prendergast had been in a German hospital suffering from burns. Now recovering, he was sent to Stalag Luft 1. Prendergast had been taught an approved and virtually unbreakable code and told that, should he be taken prisoner, he was to report to Hall. Graham Hall was elated; this was what he had been hoping for. Quickly learning the code, he and Prendergast then taught and registered suitable personnel as coders. Flt Lt Hyden, in the officers' compound, who had been taught the same code, duly instructed and registered 'Wings' Day and Sqdn Ldr Roger Bushell. At last, a coding system was working between London and the prisoners. With the contact they felt less isolated, less useless and not forgotten.

CHEATING COMPASS

Around the dispersal area at RAF Hemswell the Hampdens' 1,000hp Pegasus engines were being 'run up' as the bombers waited their turn for take-off. The *Blitzkrieg* in France was at a critical stage on 23 May 1940, and the bombers' task was to do anything possible to slow the German advance. Flight Sergeant 'Chiefy' Tom Ross and navigator 'Wimpy' Wooton made last-minute course checks while wireless operator Len 'Titch' Walker and gunner 'Paddy' Corrigan settled into their cramped positions facing the rear. The Hampden was a tight fit for the crew, but Walker, not known as 'Titch' without reason, squeezed into his seat in the narrow fuselage with comparative ease.

Flying towards the English Channel, Ross climbed the Hampden to avoid the balloon barrages. The coast of France was bright with searchlights and flak but, once over the border into Germany, all was quiet and deceptively peaceful. Ross brought the Hampden down to about 500 feet, but there were no trains to be found on the target railways, so the bombs were dropped on stations. The job done, Ross thankfully set course for home.

There was only the steady roar of the engines as the crew concentrated on watching for flak or nightfighters, until Ross called over the intercom: 'OK Titch – switch on the IFF – we're about 80 miles from the English coast – get a fix while you're about it.'

An inwardly warm feeling of nearing home cheered the crew. Within the hour their Hampden would land, they would walk, smoking and chatting to the interview with the Intelligence Officer and then stroll to the cosiness of the mess for breakfast, followed by the oblivion of sleep.

Walker, as asked, switched on the identification equipment but the radio signals from Britain for the fix, which should have been loud and clear, were weak and unreadable. Sudden bursts of anti-aircraft fire were strangely comforting as a kind of reception. The ack-ack batteries on the south coast of England must have picked them up.

'Give them the colours of the day Titch,' Ross called and, with the firing of the coloured recognition flares, the ack-ack fire ceased.

It was a comfort that at least they had been recognised, but Walker still could not raise home on his radio. Perhaps, he thought, the battery had lost its charge. Changing an accumulator in that confined space was a near impossibility, but slightly built Walker managed it. Against regulations, he carried a fully charged spare. An icy wind howled through the fuselage as the Hampden bucked and ploughed through turbulence, but Walker's struggle was in vain – the new battery made no difference; he still could not raise a home station.

Dark hours are few in late May and, with dawn breaking, Ross decided to descend through the cloud for a glimpse of the ground, to try to find a recognisable landmark.

Suddenly, the aircraft engines opened up with a full-boost roar and the Hampden shot upwards in a steep climb. The crew were pressed hard to the floor as the Hampden's nose lifted and its tail went down. Walker gasped in horror as the twin rudders flashed past the tops of pine trees a few feet below.

'We must have overshot and reached Scotland,' panted Ross as he strained back on the control column, 'but I don't know of any 6,500 foot peaks up there!'

The crew were catching their breath after the near pile-in when Ross's voice came through the intercom: 'We'll soon be out of fuel,' he said. 'I'll fly north-east for ten minutes and, if we don't hit the coast by then, we'll just have to get down.'

Gradually the cloud cleared and the ground below became distinct but still not recognisable. Ross brought the Hampden down slowly so that it was skimming the sunlit roofs of a small town at the end of a valley. Selecting a hedgeless, grassy field, Ross lowered the flaps and undercarriage and made a perfect landing. At the end of the run the grass gave way to soft, ploughed land and, as Ross cut the engines, the Hampden's wheels sank slowly to the axles.

Wearily the crew climbed out to stretch their cold, tired bodies. It was good to feel the earth beneath their feet. Bacon and eggs seemed nearer as Ross called to Wooton, 'Nip along to the village and ring for an RAF tender to come and collect us.'

The hours of tension were beginning to seep from them when Wooton came rushing back. There was something frightening in his manner. 'For Christ's sake set the kite on fire,' he gasped, 'we're in Germany!'

His companions laughed in disbelief, but a farm worker had followed Wooton back and, in response to the crew's frantic questioning, replied, '*Heil Hitler!*' Then, turning to point to the village, he continued, '*Das ist Horb.*'

Horb is in the Necke Valley. All doubts were dispelled. The shocked crew immediately started to burn code and log books, smashing equipment and firing Very cartridges into the almost empty fuel tanks. Ross leapt on to the already blazing starboard wing and detonated the charge to destroy the IFF radar equipment. The Germans would not get that.

As Ross dropped to the ground, a large black limousine lurched over the field towards the aircraft and crew. 'Run for it!' Walker yelled, but Corrigan restrained him. 'Don't be stupid,' he insisted firmly, 'the nearest cover is at least a mile away – it would be suicide.'

Within seconds the car disgorged several armed Brownshirts. 'Titch' Walker was a little slow at obeying the command '*Hände Hoch!*' but to Wooton the meaning was clear. 'Put your hands up, Titch,' he muttered.

Tom Ross was an expert pilot who had achieved his seniority in the days when promotion had to be earned by proficiency and time served. Then how did the crew come to be down in Germany when they thought themselves to be in Scotland? 'Chiefy' Ross and the others were far too experienced to have been misled by anything but a faulty gyro-compass. There had been rumours among pilots and navigators of the magnetic effect of the huge iron lode deep in German mountains which caused compasses to swing wildly. The Hampden had been flying low. Whatever the reason, there were now Brownshirts waving Lugers at them and shouting, 'For you the war is over!'

LAST OF THE FLYING 'ERKS'

War is an unnatural condition to any branch of the fighting forces, it disturbs the careers of time-serving men. — Geoff Parnell

May 27 1940 was an important day for the Royal Air Force, particularly for aircrew and prisoners of war. Air Ministry Order A416/40 authorised the making up to the rank of sergeant of all qualified aircrew. 'Chiefy' Ross's wireless operator, Acting Corporal Walker, was one of the last members of aircrew below sergeant rank to be taken prisoner. For ranker aircrew, wireless operators and gunners, it meant that all those doing the flying – the main activity of an Air Arm – would receive recognition and reward commensurate with the value and danger of the job.

For those fortunate to survive yet unfortunate enough to fall into the hands of the enemy, the promotion meant that, according to the Geneva Convention concerning prisoners of war, as senior NCOs they would not be required to work for the detaining power. The Germans, so punctilious in many ways, used or ignored the Geneva Convention in any manner that suited them. Ranker RAF men who had been shot down before the promotion of aircrew to senior NCO rank were made to work. When the first permanent camp for RAF prisoners was opened near Barth on the coast of the Baltic Sea in mid-1940, the 'Erks', as they were known, worked in a fish-canning factory or were put on other jobs such as shovelling coal in railway sidings. Many of the NCOs in the camp were envious; the 'Erks' were able to see the world outside, to receive a little extra rations and, above all, to 'acquire' on occasion other food such as fish. The movements of those forced to stay in the camp were limited to the circuit walked just inside the 'warning wire' a few yards inside the main fence.

STALAG LUFT 1 – BARTH

The fighting in Europe and the continuous attacks by the RAF had taken a toll of aircrews. Gradually, most of those captured were, from July 1940, assembled in the one permanent camp (the Luft Lager mentioned by the *Kommandant* of 8B).

Few Fighter Command men became prisoners at that time. If they survived being shot down, there was the chance that they would land in England, but many were lost in the Channel. The sea between Britain and mainland Europe became a monstrous mortuary for airmen. They came not only from Britain but from the Commonwealth, from occupied countries and from America. And, on the sea bed, too, were German aircraft and their crews.

By Christmas 1940 there were three single-storey huts in the NCOs' compound at Stalag Luft 1 where 200–300 prisoners lived. In that confined space they soon knew one another well. A single-strand barbed-wire fence with a small gate, usually open, separated the huts from the rest of the compound, which contained the cookhouse, the *Appell* or parade ground and the main gate to the *Vorlager*.

A feature of the NCOs' compound was the *Abort* or lavatory. David Young described the simple construction at Barth. It consisted of a long brick trench which extended two feet beyond the wooden-roofed enclosure. Over the trench was the 'throne', in which 24 circular holes had been cut in two parallel rows. There was a brief period in the spring and autumn when one could visit the building with impunity, but at other times it was necessary to be properly equipped. In summer a rolled-up paper swat was necessary to keep the swarming flies at bay, and in winter a stick was needed to knock off the top of the frozen pinnacle which grew like a stalagmite to seat level from the bottom of the pit several feet below.

The occasional emptying of the pit was done by simple yet effective thermo-dynamic means. A sad little man dressed in black would drive a horse-drawn cart into the camp. On the cart was a large, horizontal, cylindrical tank with the words NEPTUNE MOMENT SAUGER (literally 'The Neptune Instant Sucker') on its side. At the rear bottom of the tank was a valve connected to a four-inch diameter, flexible pipe. The free end of the pipe was lowered into the accumulated sewage under the trapdoor at the end of the hut and the valve opened. On the top of the tank was a two-foot-square flap-valve held closed by gravity. At the front of the tank, near the driver's seat, was a funnel and tap. The driver poured a little benzine into the funnel and then applied a lighted match. An internal explosion momentarily blew open the flap-valve, creating a partial vacuum. Soon the tank was half full and the sad little man left the camp to spread his cargo as fertiliser on nearby fields. None of the camps for NCOs was an improvement on Barth – many were considerably worse.

Len 'Titch' Walker was first into a room that he and five others were to occupy. Looking around, he saw the usual two-tier bunks and a wooden, typical service-issue wardrobe. Walker ran his hand along the top shelf and, feeling paper, drew it out and found he had a complete, coloured and detailed map of the whole of Germany. It was so improbable that the startled Walker could only guess how it came to be there. Polish workers who had lived in the room when building the camp must have left the map. From a friendly interpreter Walker obtained some cartridge paper and coloured pencils and during the long winter nights after 'lock-up', 'Titch' laboriously copied the map, square by square, in detail. Should the original be discovered, this treasure would not be lost to the Kriegies.

Visual contact between the less populous officers' compound and the NCOs' compound was difficult, but Chief Petty Officer Alec Brims could rapidly semaphore through a window to a Fleet Air Arm officer. Both compounds had been investigated for possibilities of escape. Even though the compounds were quite small and distances to the boundary wire comparatively short, it was not going to be easy; tunnelling into the sandy soil so close to the Baltic was made difficult by a high water table. Within six feet of digging, water would appear in the hole, necessitating continuous shoring of the tunnel roofs. The prisoners were new and inexperienced but desperately keen to escape from the frustrating confinement. They made mistakes.

Once sent to Barth, an airman was almost certain to know an inmate already there. Old friends were reunited, to their delight, and after the first excitement would walk around the 'circuit' to exchange news of home and 'gen' about the Germans and conditions. And conditions were grim. The misery of confinement within a few hundred yards of barbed wire fencing was made worse by the continual shortage of food. A few, personally addressed parcels were received via the International Red Cross, but there was little food in them, usually a small amount of chocolate among the underwear, scarves, socks and woollen gloves.

The distant church steeple and the high pennants on top of yacht masts represented freedom. Even life for the recruits at the Flak training school was seen as preferable to the curfewed and shuttered life behind the encompassing and detested barbed wire. Apart from the danger, hunger and humiliation of imprisonment, it was the close restraint and compulsion which was so distasteful to men who had volunteered to fly for freedom. They were used to unfettered travel, the wide open spaces of the English countryside around RAF aerodromes and the liberty of flight.

At Luft 1 bedboards began to disappear for use as tunnel shorers. The straw palliasses, supported by only four or so cross-members, soon became switchback-shape as the occupants' anatomies bulged through the widening intervals between the boards. If the remaining bedboards of the top bunk gave way, the occupant would find himself plunging four feet on to the lower bunk. The impact would take him and the lower bunk occupant through to the floor with a splintering crash. Tiny, spluttering fat-lamps would light the immediate area of the disturbance, while ribald comments about the cause of the crash sounded through the gloom as the participants cursed and rubbed their bruises.

For some prisoners of war Christmas 1940 was their second in captivity and by far the worse. As the prisoners at Barth contemplated their Christmas dinner of a sugar-cube-size of pork fat floating in greasy warm water, there was little to look forward to, and the meal on New Year's Day was no better. Vic Gammon removed the boiled slug from the small cone of stewed red cabbage with a hesitant reluctance, wondering whether its vitamin content would not be an asset to his general well-being. He had been suffering from a complication of athlete's foot which had been aggravated by poor diet and the continual wearing of flying boots. Suppurating ulcers bulged between and beneath each toe, making walking impossible. In the evenings room-mate George 'Wilbur' Wright would heat water on the upright tiled stove and bathe Gammon's feet with a gentleness worthy of a compassionate nurse.

Wright was variously known as 'Flak-Arse' or 'Pepper-Pot Bum' because of the craters left by an explosive shell burst which had punctured his buttocks and the back of his thighs in countless places. Pieces of shrapnel were frequently appearing beneath the surface of his skin in parts of his body remote from their entry point. Removing the little slivers and jagged pieces of metal was one of the interests and entertainments of Wright's colleagues.

There seemed little prospect of Red Cross parcels arriving in time to alleviate a food situation that was becoming desperate. Potatoes and swede had been poorly stored and exposed to frost; consequently they were rotten on arrival. The smell, even before boiling, was nauseous. The Kriegies looked at the resulting 'stew' with undisguised revulsion but forced the thin mess down their throats. It was a case of utter starvation or poison. Stomach-cramping dysentery was the usual result.

It was inevitable that the lack of hygienic arrangements would encourage lice. The Kriegies searched for eggs in clothing seams with a naked flame, a trick learned from their fathers' trench experiences in the Great War.

Unexpected skills were acquired through necessity, such as the ability to shave and then bathe from head to foot in a mug of water, or to divide a black-bread and sawdust loaf into fourteen equal parts and then divide one's own fourteenth piece into wafer thin slices in order to make it last throughout the day. Sauerkraut, so salty that the Germans could not eat it, was sometimes given to the prisoners. Soaked for hours, then drained, it became almost palatable to some. Perhaps once in a while a barrel of pickled beetroot was brought into the camp but it was so highly spiced with layers of caraway seeds as to be inedible.

A revolting and highly pungent spread known as '*Fisch Käse*' or fish cheese was occasionally handed out. Crusty on the outside with a milky liquid interior, the cheese was wrapped in triangular packets like Camembert, which it most certainly was not. Despite their desperate need, most Kriegies found it impossible to eat.

One wintry day small thin slices of dried meat were brought into Stalag Luft 1, slices similar to those that 'cat's meat men' used to sell on wooden skewers in British city streets before the war. Upon examination, the slices, one or two to a man, were found to be crawling with tiny white maggots, A quick wipe over with fingers and sleeve and they were eaten. Meat was too valuable to miss.

Pilot Officer Maurice Butt, with the officers at Thorn, described hunger and its effects during the winter of 1940-1. At that time any sport was found to be impossible, there was a complete lack of energy. Butt wrote:

> It was extraordinary to behold a man running with a ball and then suddenly to stop completely from lack of stamina - the result of the steady reduction of spare fat since capture, on a starvation diet. Injuries such as simple bleeding from scratches usually became septic and this was seen to be an avoidable hazard in order to survive. Hence sport was out.

There was little doubt that prisoners were given only those foods that the German population could not stomach. There was no real food shortage in Germany at that time. Shortages were felt only in the occupied lands which were being systematically looted. The 'guns before butter' slogan was forgotten now that guns had brought essentials and delicacies pouring in from occupied Europe, but in the concentration camps and prisoner-of-war camps hunger was a way of life - and death.

THE POSEN PARADE

George Booth was one of a dozen aircrew and 30 sailors taken in box-cars to Posen railyard. There they watched, with mounting horror, as thousands of starving, scarecrow-like British Army men, captured at the Channel coast, were disgorged from train after train. Shouting and pushing, the guards assembled a slow-moving column with Booth and the early prisoners in the lead. Behind them shuffled the thousands of lice-infested and dysentery-ridden remnants of the BEF, many barefoot and all in a haze of pain and misery as they were forced to parade, like hopeless drunks, around the streets of Posen. To humiliate the captives further, a car mounted loudspeaker blared out the lie: 'These are Churchill's soldiers, who have thrown down their arms and refused to fight.' The ragged procession was forced to double back over the same route, to reinforce the exhibition of the wretched prisoners to the Polish population.

When the grotesque propaganda show straggled into the Posen suburbs, women lined the streets, trying to pass bread to the famished men. They were roughly swept aside by rifle-butt-wielding guards, who kicked and punched whenever they could get close.

Many of the army prisoners were near the limit of endurance, dropping out of the column with stomachs pain-wracked through poor food, or lack of it altogether. The guards always forced them to stagger to their bleeding feet and pushed them stumbling onward.

Ahead were two large mounds of earth each side of a gate. Through the gate a bridge spanned a twenty-yard-wide dry moat. On top of the mounds machine-guns were manned by *Wehrmacht* soldiers. Booth shuddered, wondering if the prisoners were to be made to run a horrific kind of gauntlet. But the men reeled across the bridge into a dim tunnel the diameter of the London Underground. Lit only by a bare, small-wattage bulb, this was the entrance to their prison, a Napoleonic fort still being used to pen war prisoners after more than a hundred years.

FIGHT IN THE FIORD
Which way shall I fly ?
Which way I fly is hell.
— John Milton

Lieutenant Commander John Casson was boss of Blackburn Skua 803 Squadron, Fleet Air Arm. The Skua tried to be both a fighter and a dive bomber and its performance suffered as a consequence. Nevertheless, in the hands of a skilled pilot, the Skua was very manoeuvrable, as Casson was to prove.

33

On 13 June 1940, Casson's squadron was ordered to bomb the *Scharnhorst*. Flying from the rolling deck of the *Ark Royal*, Casson spotted the warship deep in Trondheim Fiord. Swiftly he led his squadron in a line-astern, 60-degree dive to the attack. The flak was accurate and concentrated as Casson dropped his 500lb bomb, missing the quarterdeck of the *Scharnhorst* 'by a whisker'. The Skua was thumped by the flak bursts and Casson felt it shudder, but there was no sound from Observer Peter Fanshawe in the turret, only the rattle of his Lewis gun. On full boost, Casson climbed to 2,000 feet and roared up the fiord, the sound echoing and buffeting back from the near vertical cliff walls, but there was an almost unsettling calm after the fierce action. Then he saw a Messerschmitt 109 manoeuvering to attack.

Casson, hoping that the enemy pilot might be a greenhorn, half-rolled, dived and levelled out ten feet above the water, leading the Messerschmitt a chase in and out of the fiord, trying to fly the German into a cliff. Discovering that he could just turn his plane inside the Messerschmitt, Casson roared towards the cliff face, slammed down the Skua's flaps and then turned hard to starboard. The Messerschmitt pilot just turned away. Hard flying had brought them both to the end of the mountains. Casson had held off the Messerschmitt for fifteen minutes but was now flying down a village street, below roof-top level, taking the tip off a fir tree with his propeller.

An accidental flick roll caused the Skua to do a high stall, bringing Casson down again to 50 feet above the water. They were in the open now, making it difficult to outwit the Messerschmitt pilot. Casson tried to guess the moment when the enemy pilot would fire and then swerved to starboard. Three times the Messerschmitt's tracers passed under his port wing. The fourth time the German took a good, long shot and Casson heard the rattle and crash as shells and bullets rammed home. A reek of petrol surrounded the plane as Fanshawe spoke for the first time on the intercom: 'There's a hole as big as your fist in the bottom of the tank and I've got a bullet in my shoulder.'

Casson calculated that he had four minutes flying left and no hope of reaching Sweden. Rather than be a sitting duck, he slammed the Skua down on to the water at 100 knots, skidding along the surface. Casson knew that he had not stalled enough but wanted to get the aircraft down before another attack. Thumping himself in the eye during the ditching, he looked back through a watery haze to see the Messerschmitt bearing down on them.

'Jesus!' he gasped. 'Now he is going to shoot us into the water.' But the German throttled back, did a slow circle, waved and flew off.

'It was a very interesting contest,' John Casson said thoughtfully when he and Fanshawe were on their way to Hohemark Hospital and Dulag Luft.

From the many actions in Norwegian waters, a few naval airmen filtered in among the RAF prisoners, bringing their own, very different taste of battle. Most had taken off in open-cockpit 'Stringbag' Swordfish from aircraft carriers such as the old HMS *Furious*. Low, straight and level torpedo attacks on German naval targets exposed the slow Swordfish to every gun.

The RAF prisoners welcomed the Fleet Air Arm men, who were to make a significant contribution in the years ahead. Among the NCOs, Alec Brims, in particular, apart from his useful semaphore, was an inspiration, a veritable rock of Gibraltar.

For all Allied prisoners the autumn and winter following the Dunkirk evacuation was a desperate period. The prospect ahead was one of impenetrable gloom. The French Army, the bastion of the West, had collapsed and the French nation lay crushed under harsh occupation. Mainland Western Europe was under Nazi domination from Norway's North Cape to the Spanish border with France. Italy, under the envious Mussolini, had declared war on France and England on 10 June, hoping to get a share of the spoils from the defeat of prostrate neighbours. Henceforth, 'Musso's lake', the Mediterranean, would be a dangerous place. Britain's communications with the Middle East, India, Africa, Australia and New Zealand were in jeopardy. It seemed, too, that there was every chance the Fascist Franco would join the Nazis, seize Gibraltar for Spain and plug the entrance to the Mediterranean.

A large part of Britain's army had been rescued from the beaches, but it was demoralised and had abandoned the bulk of its arms and equipment. The Royal Air Force had been weakened by enormous losses of valuable trained men and material and the *Luftwaffe* was beginning a bombing campaign against Britain. The U-boats were roaming the Atlantic, threatening to cut off supplies completely, and Germans with whom the Kriegies had any contact were still confident that there would soon be a comparatively easy invasion of the British Isles. The outlook could hardly have been more dispiriting for the hungry men shut away deep in enemy country. Yet those in Stalag Luft 1 never envisaged defeat. Victory, no matter how distant, was a certainty, but how it was to be achieved God only knew.

This, then, was the very time for the Kriegies to switch to the offensive, to start whittling away the overweening confidence of their captors. From the beginning, 'Goon baiting' had been practised and it was about to be stepped up. Every opportunity was taken to pare away their jailers' shell of confident superiority. The guards and interpreters were informed, with an air of sad and understanding pity, of the vast armies, huge air forces and powerful navies that even now were being lined up against Germany. Massive amounts of arms were pouring into Britain from the United States of America and it was only a matter of time before the Americans joined in the fight against the Third and Last Reich.

None of this was asserted in an aggressive manner; it was more subtle. The prisoners were certainly in no position to be arrogant and they knew that they would frequently need the 'friendly' *Posten*, if only to obtain the occasional extra portion of sawdust-bread. It was a gradual, and mostly subconscious, process which resulted in many of the German staff at Barth becoming more approachable and, in a few rare cases, corruptible.

The longer hours of darkness and increasing cold of approaching winter soon drove all thoughts but food from the prisoner's mind. Food became an obsession as the rations of rotten potatoes and watery soup diminished. Because of malnutrition, prisoners became prone to minor infections, which rapidly became major illnesses. They had little strength with which to fight; slight colds turned into pneumonia and pleurisy, small cuts quickly became pus-oozing sores. Weight and hair loss made many men resemble gaunt skeletons. By autumn all outdoor games were forbidden by the SBO. Had the prisoners even had the energy to play games, there was no possible way in which the slightest injuries could be treated; even water was difficult to heat, with fuel for the tall stoves being practically unobtainable.

COUNTING HIS CHICKENS

After lunch on 7 September, a fine Saturday afternoon, Hermann Göring, recently promoted to *Reichsmarschall*, settled himself with *Feldmarschall* (Smiling Albert) Kesselring and his staff near Cap Gris Nez to watch the vast air armada, his *Luftflotten*, fly across to bomb London. The *Luftwaffe* was to initiate the final phase of what Göring believed to be the lead-up to Operation Sea Lion. He planned that massive attacks against London should draw the remnants of Fighter Command into the air, where it would be effectively destroyed and unable to put up any resistance when the invasion was mounted. Instead, by his change of strategy, Göring had scuppered any prospect of successful invasion and Fighter Command was unbeaten.

36

It was just before 5 o'clock when the sirens wailed, followed by the first bombs dropping on London's dockland. Watchers throughout the south-east of England could see the steady formations of *Luftwaffe* bombers glistening in the blue sky, with their circling fighter planes weaving the air around them. Even so, the bombers could not be adequately protected, for Fighter Command had considerably weakened the *Luftwaffe* fighter force throughout August. But the formations came on, despite the Kent and Essex flight-paths being littered with swastika-decorated wrecks, and the dock area was ablaze.

The London Fire Brigade was overwhelmed by the fires around the Surrey Docks area alone. To cope with this massive conflagration it was calculated that at least 300 fully manned fire appliances would be needed. Moreover, if the *Luftwaffe* continued to bomb at night, the fires in the east would be a beacon which could be seen from the coast. It would be a simple matter to bomb to the west of the fires at night and wipe out huge areas of central and west London.

That evening, Pilot Officer 'Mac' Maclean lifted Wellington 'Q' for Queenie into the air off Marham's notorious 'hump' and set course for the French Channel ports. One after another, the Wellingtons of 38 and 115 Squadrons followed. To the observer on the ground each aircraft disappeared, while still on its take-off run, as it careered over the 'hump' and away down the hill, only to reappear with roaring engines as it clawed its way upward into the distant sky. As usual, the heavily laden bombers just cleared houses on the far side of the field, and then the crews breathed more easily. Once in the air, their task was simpler and the journey shorter and less taxing than the first RAF trip to Berlin a few nights earlier, when thick cloud had obscured the target for most of the flight. On that trip, full fuel tanks meant few bombs could be carried. This hop to Boulogne to bomb invasion craft was the reverse – a full bomb load and just enough fuel to get there and back. The flak was always heavy at the Channel ports but the barges were a tightly packed target.

Aircrews preferred these 'barges' operations to the cold, lengthy flights over enemy-held territory. The flak firework display could clearly be seen from Thames estuary towns or from the south coast. Provided all went well, they were quickly at the target, then it was a smooth dive on the aiming point, bombs away and, with fingers crossed, straight through the flak on to a course home. A snag was that some station commanders were reluctant to include a 'Channel port' trip as full operation counting towards the 'tour' needed before a break, and some bomber crews were reaching the end of their endurance.

'Q' Queenie had barely lifted off from Marham when gunner John 'Jock' Hamilton, in the front turret, first commented on the glow in the sky: 'There's one hell of a fire ahead,' he said, and his soft Lanarkshire accent over the intercom was almost a whisper of awe. As 'Queenie' climbed, leaving the glow to starboard, the crew looked on in shocked wonder. Far higher than they, a half circle of vivid orange incandescence lit the sky to the west and illuminated the inside of the aircraft. Near the deeper orange base of the fire, frequent bright flashes of light spurted within the glow. An orderly in the sergeants' mess had said that there were reports of heavy air raids on London, and here was the awful proof. The East End and dockland were burning. The huge conflagration had been visible from Marham in Norfolk, 70 miles away.

It was strange to think that the Wellington, heavy with bombs to be unloaded on German installations at Boulogne, was crossing the flight-paths of Heinkels and Dorniers with their high explosives and incendiaries destined for London. As 'Queenie' passed near the Thames estuary, the crew resolved to make every bomb count. It was just a pity that they were not going to Germany.

That afternoon, ex-BBC maintenance engineer Dave Young and three other airmen were on their way by train to a posting to RAF Abingdon. All four planned to spend a few hours in London on the way. Outside Watford the train was stopped by a wailing air-raid alert. With impatience they saw their stay in 'The Smoke' fading away with the delay. At last the train drew slowly into Euston station. As they climbed into a taxi to take them to Paddington station, the four were unable to tear their eyes from the scene to the east. The horizon was ablaze. The cab-driver had no difficulty in seeing his way; instead of the usual blackout gloom, the deserted streets were lit with an unearthly rosy glow. The 'Blitz' had started, London's East End was ablaze and code-word 'Cromwell' announced the imminence of invasion.

When David Young arrived at RAF Abingdon OTU on the evening of Sunday 8 September, he found the station in the throes of a massive invasion alert. The bombing of London on the previous evening, which Young and his friends had witnessed, had been a precursor to this. Every aircraft, including those normally non-operational, was armed and ready for action, and trainee crews had been briefed.

The 8th was a National Day of Prayer; it was also a 'stand down' evening for a few aircrew. At the 'Pilot' Cinema in King's Lynn, where *Broadway Melody of 1940* had been relaxing some of the 38 and 115 Squadrons' men from Marham, a slide with a hurriedly scrawled message was flashed on the screen. Superimposed on the still running film, its message was blunt, 'ALL SERVICE PERSONNEL ARE TO RETURN TO THEIR UNITS IMMEDIATELY.' There was a rustle of activity as soldiers, airmen and the occasional ATS, WAAF or WRNS girl left their seats as the house-lights rose to help them see their way to the exits.

Redcaps and Service Police raced round the blacked-out streets to every pub and hotel, shouting orders and chivvying laggards. The lounge of the Duke's Head Hotel (Officers Only) emptied rapidly and decorously; the public bar of The Rummer debouched noisily.

Airmen and soldiers poured into the town square where the single-decker buses assembled. Servicemen demanded to be taken to their camps immediately. Bus crews were noticeably reluctant, invasion or no invasion. The journey was unscheduled and the drivers had a sinking feeling that they were not going to be paid, especially when some airmen swore that, if the bus did not leave within minutes, it would be requisi-tioned, with or without the driver. There was much gesticulation and shouting at the Marham guardroom gate as the drivers tried, mostly unsuccessfully, to prevent men leaving the buses without paying. The officer of the guard smoothed ruffled feelings and arranged compensa-tion.

Throughout Britain, servicemen on pass or leave streamed back to their depots, aerodromes, docks and battle stations. There was a feeling that 'This is it!'

At RAF stations frantic preparations were made to use every avail-able weapon to repulse a landing. Fighter stations were already at a high state of readiness whilst on Bomber and Coastal Command stations and on every kind of training unit, any aircraft that could fly was 'bombed-up' and armed, many with 1914-vintage Lewis machine-guns. Aircrews in var-ious stages of training were warned that they might be needed to help repel an invasion by 'strafing' East coast beaches, and were then allocated positions on obsolete aircraft. Old Whitleys were taken off target-drogue towing and readied for the fight. The dulled perspex of old Wellington 1s was polished until the all-round, uninterrupted view from their 'roller blind' turrets was brilliantly clear. No breeches or mountings would hide an enemy fighter from the air gunners; the twin Brownings projected from the turret at the level of their knees. Hampdens of all ages were to bomb barges and lay mines, and Ansons, used for the training of wireless operators, were to be front-line bombers. Trainee Observer Ivan Kayes, on a bombing and gunnery course at Stormy Down, ruefully eyed the near-wreck of a Fairey Battle in which he was to confront the enemy and devoutly hoped that his particular enemy would not be flying a Messer-schmitt 109.

The British had finally realised that, with the fall of France in June, and the occupation of the Channel Islands, they really were in danger of invasion, occupation and subjugation by an alien power. An enemy had not succeeded in that since 1066, although the Spanish had tried and the French had made plans, all without success. Even though it had been necessary to consider the possibility of invasion during the Great War, no one seriously contemplated it on either side. This war was different: a victorious, powerful and capable mechanised army stood on the shores of France just 21 miles from Dover and it was backed-up by what seemed a strong and proven air force.

But experience was teaching the *Luftwaffe* the hard lesson that the RAF had learned in the first four months of the war – daylight bombing is suicidal without adequate fighter cover. The *Daily Mirror* cartoonist, Zec, sensed the mood of the moment. His drawing showed a huge poster, dated 15 August 1940, announcing A GREAT TRIUMPHAL ENTRY INTO LONDON BY ADOLF HITLER but at the top of a ladder an RAF man was pasting across it the words 'POSTPONED INDEFINITELY!'

"Tch-Tch! What big feet Corkwell's got!"

PART 2
1941

CASTLE AND FORT

The longer hours of darkness during the last months of 1940 and the first of 1941 meant that both air forces could operate further from their bases. In this the *Luftwaffe* had the advantage of flying from occupied airfields nearer to British targets. German bombers were able to spread their raids from London to Liverpool, Bristol, Southampton, Sheffield and other cities. In reply, the RAF had to do as much as possible to damage German industry. Now that western Europe was occupied, the Royal Air Force no longer had to pick its way around neutral borders to reach Germany, but the weather was an eternal enemy, always unpredictable and frequently at variance with what the crews were told to expect.

In response to the bombing of Coventry, a special raid had been made in mid-December 1940, with more than 130 bombers attacking Mannheim: a first and clear case of area bombing by the RAF. Losses throughout the period, although not great, were sufficient to bring a steady stream of new prisoners passing through Dulag and on to Stalag Luft 1.

The *Luftwaffe* prisoner-of-war authorities had consistently under-estimated the number of RAF aircrew likely to be taken and, in January 1941, they decided to ease the crowding by transferring some 'bad boy' officers from Barth to Spangenberg Castle. Those moving to Spangenberg were troublemakers who had previously attempted escape.

Later, in early March 1941, the Germans sent 400 Army and RAF officer prisoners from Spangenberg to the semi-underground fort at Thorn in Poland, but this time prisoners were told it was in reprisal for *Luftwaffe* prisoners in Canada being forced to live in tents. The German prisoners had deliberately burned their huts and were pleased with them-selves for having done their bit for Germany – until the full severity of the Canadian winter was upon them. They were forced to beg for alternative accommodation. The only space available was a disused penitentiary at Fort William on Lake Superior. It was accepted in desperation, but the *Luftwaffe* men nevertheless complained to the protecting power, and Hitler ordered similar treatment for British prisoners-of-war.

On arrival at Thorn, the officers were herded into the fort's main semicircular tunnelway and greeted by a *Hauptmann* reading a kind of

'Riot Act'. It was continually met with cat-calls and shouts of derision. The tension mounted until the *Hauptmann* angrily drew his Luger. This was greeted by the prisoners with a rousing cheer. Blustering and red-faced, the German struggled to hold his temper. He knew that bullets would have ricocheted in the tunnel, killing guards and prisoners alike; also that he had before him an unusual crowd, who refused to be cowed by bullying threats. The *Hauptmann* called the interpreter to march the prisoners to their rooms and lock them up for the night.

To ensure comparative treatment to that of the German prisoners in Canada, attention was paid to minute detail. Windows were partially blocked, limiting daylight to a fifteen-inch square for a room containing fourteen men; the rooms were locked at night, with just a jam tin left inside for sanitary use. The prisoners scrambled for a wash from a ten-minute trickle of water coming from a long pipe, which had one-eighth-inch holes pierced at two-foot intervals. With this primitive arrangement only one-third of the prisoners had any chance of washing themselves. The epitome of German plumbing ingenuity was in the lavatorial arrangements. Six holes were arranged in a circle so that the men sat with their backs to a central pipe into which emissions from the holes were funnelled. The pipe descended from six similar holes from the floor above.

The prisoners were limited to two one-hour exercise periods daily in a confined area between the earth embankments surrounding the semi-underground fortifications. This claustrophobic environment ensured there was no view of the outside world and little of the sky. It was a cloister-like atmosphere of underground rooms and corridors.

The Senior British Officer was General Fortune, a man singularly unperturbed and undaunted by German threats or their assumed air of aggressive superiority. The general had encountered that attitude while commanding the 51st Highland Division at St Valéry. Fortune drew up a list of complaints and demanded to see a representative of the neutral protecting power, the United States of America. In due course, no less a person than the American Ambassador arrived, escorted by a flurry of attentive German officers in their smartest uniforms and highly polished jackboots. The Germans agreed to all the demands for air, space and light, with a show of swaggering magnanimity, until General Fortune swung round and said:

'But Gentlemen, there is one other point – this camp is lousy, the bedding provided is creeping with fleas.'

The Kriegies watched with increasing amusement as a monocle dropped from one German's face and a deep hush descended on the group. General Fortune spun round again and barked, 'Lieutenant – fleas please!' Two junior officers leaped forward, each carrying a matchbox. Together they poked out the trays of the boxes so releasing scores of fleas which, with the sudden exposure to light, leapt in all directions. Also leaping away were the impeccably dressed and previously decorous group. The Kriegies collapsed in helpless laughter.

Maurice Butt expected to be on the move again. He was one of those taken in early March 1941 from Spangenberg to Thorn. At first, they had been quartered in the fort's dungeon-like atmosphere, but the camp was partly empty and rumours of evacuation abounded. Now, in mid-May, Butt and fellow officer Dickie Troward planned to hide in the empty part of the camp while six others talked their way out. They would then become 'sleepers' or 'ghosts', allowing the Germans to believe they had left with the escapers. They would remain in hiding until the camp was evacuated. When the guards had left, they too would leave – for Russia.

On the evening before the proposed escape, Butt went to the SBO's room to try to augment his escape rations. He stopped short with amazement when confronted with the extraordinary scene of the *Kommandant* and a short, strutty *Luftwaffe* officer in deep discussion with a roomful of senior RAF and British Army officers. It was unusual for Germans to enter the camp during the evening unless there was a crisis, but this yellow-lapelled, alert *Luftwaffe* man, very aware of his exaggerated importance and demanding full attention, was Franz von Werra, 'the one who got away'. He had escaped from a POW camp in Canada and made his way into the neutral United States, returning eventually to Germany. He had been promoted to *Hauptmann* and ordered by Göring to inspect RAF POW camps, with added instructions to inform camp *Kommandants* about the methods used by the British to prevent escapes. Von Werra was planning to buy an estate in occupied Poland and was combining duty with his own affairs. Maurice Butt, a bomber pilot, concluded that the posturing von Werra was a typical extrovert fighter boy. Butt tried the padre's room for a food supplement and accepted a tin of corned beef but politely refused, as added weight, a Bible which the padre and his room-mate thought suitable equipment for his journey.

Next morning the disguised six, three RAF and three Army officers, including Airey Neave, successfully talked their way past a recently changed gate-guard. One of the six spoke in fluent German, the others acknowledging in monosyllables. They had orders, they said, to report to the *Kommandantur*, about a mile away. A week previously, bars had been sawn through, then wedged and glued back. Now Butt and Troward saw the six go and immediately climbed out of the weakened window. Running to a bunker in which they planned to hide, they struggled with a skeleton key which failed to open the door. All they could do was try to hide in the shallow, shadowed entrance. The alarm was raised in the usual fashion, with whistles blowing and the customary frantic shouting, but the two in the bunker entrance had carefully combed and 'preened' the weeds and grass leading to the bunker so that there were no footprints or crushed plants to be seen. A fat *Hauptmann* stood for a time on the bunker, inches above their heads, the sun casting his shadow on the wall two metres from them. Dogs failed to find Butt and Troward huddled in the doorway that day but, as the six officers had been caught, the search now concentrated on the pair.

Next day the camp was thoroughly 'fine-toothcombed'. The *Feldwebel* known as 'Scarface' found them and fired two shots over their heads in satisfaction. Butt believed that the shooting was to scare them. It succeeded.

The small RAF contingent decided to tunnel through the clay subsoil from a hut just two metres from the warning wire. It was a cold and acutely uncomfortable task, as the winter rains ensured that the diggers lay working for hours in sodden long-john underwear, only to emerge uncontrollably shivering and utterly exhausted. Easter Sunday saw them burrowing with grim determination and reaching a phenomenal speed of five feet a day.

The disposal of the tunnel spoil was always a problem. The weight of the packed clay squeezed in the space between the hut ceiling and its pitched roof caused the ceiling to sag dangerously. It was a race between the outward progress of the tunnel and the downward sag of the ceiling. It was obvious, too, that the pendulously drooping ceiling would soon be seen – and there was more sodden clay to come.

At last it was decided that the tunnel was well beyond the wire; then Butt saw faces fall as the last digger described how he had pushed through the surface just half a metre from the footpath outside the main wire fence where the *Posten* plodded his beat. It was galling – the tunnel exit would be in the brilliantly floodlit perimeter area. The tunnellers debated the chances of scrambling from the hole and crawling to the trees while the sentry was walking away but decided it was too risky.

As the night wore on and the exit remained undiscovered, the urge to grab this chance grew. Butt and two other RAF officers finally spoke, almost simultaneously. 'I'm going to have a go,' announced Butt. 'Me too,' said another, and, 'I'm game,' said the third.

The long crawl through the dank tunnel led to a tense wait at the exit. They lay still until the sentry had passed and was out of earshot. A breathless scurry out of the hole and a silent, precipitous, head-long dive into the shadows of the trees beyond the wire. Panting silently, the trio waited, listened and watched. There were no shots, shouts, shrilling whistles or pounding feet.

Within two weeks all three were back in the 'cooler'. Much time was then given to working out where the careful application of Pythagoras by expert mathematicians had led to the tunnel being a few feet short. The inaccurate estimate of distances was a cause of many tunnel failures.

THE INTERROGATORS

As each new prisoner arrived in a camp, it was not only the Germans who interrogated him. Since the summer of 1940, at Dulag Luft, it was Squadron Leader Roger Bushell who questioned prisoners. A fighter pilot shot down and taken captive during the evacuation from Dunkirk, Bushell, a South African lawyer with a burning hatred of the Germans nursed an immediate desire to escape in order to continue the fight. As well as the latest news, Bushell and 'Wings' Day wanted to know what questions the Germans had asked and whether one could vouch for a particular person in the camp who could be a German 'plant'. Bushell had piercing eyes and Sgt Vic Gammon thought his staring intensity almost frightening. After probing questions, he would suddenly relax, shake hands genially and was all kindness and good wishes.

In the NCOs' compound at Barth, it was to Camp Leader 'Dixie' Deans that the 'new boy' was directed. Sgt Bill Baird, shot down on a Düsseldorf raid on 4 February 1941, told 'Dixie' and his committee that, just a week before his last trip, he had flown a civilian engineer to Boscombe Down, where he had taxied his Hampden close to a huge four-engined bomber called a Stirling. The committee members were frankly incredulous. The Hampden, Whitley and Wellington were the RAF's heavy bombers; a huge land aircraft such as Baird described seemed an impossibility.

'YOU LOOK LIKE A TRAMP!'

When it became obvious to a disgusted Hitler that the Italian Army would have to be rescued from the self-inflicted Albanian–Greek disaster, the *Wehrmacht* advanced down through the Balkans. A fierce defence by Greek, Australian, New Zealand and British troops could not hold the German legions, which included the crack *SS Leibstandarte Adolf Hitler* Division. On the morning of 18 March 1941, RAF 37 Squadron, which had been operating from Tatoi in Greece, was ordered to leave in great haste. The Germans were advancing with such rapidity that there was every possibility of the squadron being overrun. Rear gunnner Sgt John Howard was relieved when his Wellington took off. He had a feeling that the Germans were almost treading on their heels. After a long flight the aircraft landed at their base in Shallufa, Egypt. It had been touch-and-go; many servicemen were left behind in the turmoil of sudden evacuation.

The squadron was safe and the crews were promised leave in Cairo, but Howard's and two other crews of 37 Squadron were detailed at an hour's notice to leave for Shaibah in Iraq. The men were to take only blankets, small kit and a change of underclothing. In one of the many uprisings endemic to the area, the pro-British regent, Amir Abdul Illah, had been overthrown by Rashid Ali el-Gailani, a former premier of Iraq. Urged on by Ribbentrop, Rashid's troops were attacking RAF Habbaniya and laying siege to the British Embassy in Baghdad. Iraq, not for the first time, had changed sides.

Before a daylight raid on Al Rashid aerodrome near Baghdad, the Wellington crews were told that, among a mixed bag of aircraft, the Iraqis were using Gloster Gladiators. 'Be careful,' they were warned, 'do not confuse these with similar RAF planes operating from Habbaniya.'

This was a very different kind of land to that in which the crews had previously operated, green only between and around the Tigris and Euphrates rivers and the marshes, with almost endless desert sand and rock elsewhere. There was also this problem of aircraft recognition. The RAF and the Iraqis were using similar planes, but there was no doubt it was an Iraqi Hawker Audax that swung up under the Wellingtons as they turned on to the run-up to bomb Al Rashid aerodrome. Howard took careful aim, fired a burst from his rear turret guns and watched, fascinated, as the Audax turned slowly on to its back and dived straight into the ground.

The Wellingtons flew across the aerodrome, their bombs creating eruptions of huge fountains of earth. They had not been diverted from their target but, as they turned away, diving low and racing for home, three Iraqi Gladiators intercepted, firing as they passed.

Two of the Gladiators went on to attack the first two Wellingtons. The third turned, diving down to dead astern, for a second try at destroying John Howard's aircraft. Through his gunsight Howard watched the Gladiator. He had given the Iraqi a couple of short bursts but the pilot was cautious, realising that the Wellington had a sting in its tail. He stayed at maximum range, content to play a cat-and-mouse game from behind, just firing an occasional burst towards the Wellington.

Puffs of smoke from each side of the Gladiator's fuselage showed each time the Iraqi fired. Howard held his fire, hoping the Iraqi would think the Wellington's rear gunner had been hit and so be tempted to close in. It worked. As the Gladiator closed in, filling the gunsight, Howard squeezed the triggers, firing a long burst. The Gladiator turned to port immediately, climbed some 100 feet, turned over and dived to earth. The Wellington's crew whooped with approval. John Howard had shot down two attacking aircraft.

Next day another visit was ordered to Al Rashid aerodrome. As they neared the airfield, the Wellington crews were alert, knowing the defences would be expecting them. Two runs were necessary but the bombs made their mark and the captains turned their aircraft to make a low run, allowing the air gunners a chance to shoot up anything seen as a worthwhile target. The Wellingtons were met by intense ground fire. Howard felt a heavy impact just behind his turret and another missile passed through the perspex close to his head. The aircraft shuddered and the pilot immediately turned for home, flying at about 500 feet, the crew on the lookout for fighters.

Howard, listening to the urgent intercom talk, heard that the starboard engine had been hit, oil pressure was dropping and the Wellington losing height.

The aircraft bounced as it grazed the ground, then flew another quarter of a mile before skidding along on its belly, finally jolting to a halt in a cloud of dust. The 'retracted undercarriage' warning horn blared loudly in the sudden silence. Howard, still sitting in his turret, suddenly realised that they had actually crashed in hostile territory. Releasing the turret doors, he heaved himself out into the fuselage and started to make his way forward. He was walking on the ground; the whole of the bottom of the centre and aft fuselage had been torn away. He found the crew shaken but uninjured.

The captain had pinpointed their crash as near to Al Falluja and close to the Euphrates. They had to act quickly if they were to escape capture. Feluccas had been seen on the river, so the crew decided to try to capture one and sail it as far as possible down the Euphrates towards the Persian Gulf. An attempt was made to burn the Wellington but the 'port fire', issued for just these circumstances, failed to ignite and the Very pistol had to be hacked free with the emergency axe. It was a bad start. Trudging across the rough ground, through shoulder-length grass, the crew set off towards the river. They carried two Vickers machine-guns from the aircraft in case of need. The navigator took the Very pistol whilst Howard pushed several cartridges under his pullover. It had been cool in the air, but now on the ground the heat was searing. The sight and sound of one of the squadron Wellingtons distantly winging its way to Habbaniya brought that instant feeling of envy that every airman down in enemy territory knows. They hoped they had been seen and their plight would be reported at base.

Their surrounding by Arab horsemen was sudden and unexpected. The Arabs seemed to have come from nowhere. They did not appear hostile and indicated to the airmen that they should accompany them to a small hutted village. A further crowd came to meet the party and ominously formed a circle around the airmen, hemming them in. Tension rose immediately. Howard felt the crowd move around him, deliberately separating him from the rest of the crew. Then two heavy blows on his head knocked him down. The Vickers gun clattered to the ground. He passed out.

As Howard's head gradually cleared, he saw Arabs still grouped around him. Convinced that he would be killed, and determined to sell his life dearly, he rose groggily to his feet, feeling for his revolver. Through clouds of pain he realised that he should have known the holster would be empty. The revolver had been taken from him while he was insensible. Knocked to the ground again, beaten on the head and body, Howard was dragged half-conscious to the river bank and unceremoniously dumped there with the rest of his now-battered crew. All had been severely beaten. Dazed with pain, they were certain they were to be killed and dumped in the river, or suffer the worse fate of prior mutilation, for which these people were notorious. A chosen method was to hack off a captive's genitals, sew them into the victim's mouth and leave him to die in hopeless agony. To avoid this, the captain offered the Arabs a paper printed in Arabic and known to airmen as a 'Goulie Chit'. The paper guaranteed a reward for the airmen's safe return. Doubting they could even read, Howard saw the chit thrown away.

Jock, the navigator, certain now of the Arabs' intentions, began another brave but fruitless struggle. The Arabs rained blow after blow on him, wielding the long-handled shovels and implements used for tilling the fields. Jock fell to the ground screaming as they hit him again and again. The rest of the crew watched in impotent agony; there was nothing they could do to aid their brave friend who was being murdered before them.

Later, soldiers of the Iraqi Army arrived and searched the prisoners. Howard was threatened with a knife, forced to hand over his wristwatch and wallet, and was punched in the mouth when he asked if he could keep the photograph of his wife. Spitting out a tooth, Howard decided to keep a still tongue.

Taken down river on one of the feluccas they had hoped to steal, the crew were flung into an office in a brick building in another small village. John Howard cradled Jock's head on his chest, trying to support and comfort him, but Jock was very badly hurt, suffering from internal injuries. He began to vomit, blood soaking Howard's pullover. A guard brought a bucket.

Jock was taken away, to hospital, the crew were told. After an abortive interrogation from an Iraqi officer, who strongly disapproved of their name, rank and number answers, they were led blindfold to cars and taken to Baghdad where they were driven on a slow tour, on display, through the crowded streets. It was a terrifying experience. Unable to see, and feeling the effects of his wounds, Howard feared the worst as people climbed on to the side of the car, hammering it with their fists and rocking it from side to side, at times almost tipping it over, and continuously shouting 'Bloody, f------ Churchill,' their sum knowledge of English. The Iraqi officer accompanying the crew became apprehensive, saying that he hoped the mob would not try to take them from the car. They were so hostile, he said, they would most probably kill him as well, if he tried to protect the crew.

Eventually, their blindfolds were removed and they were obviously in the hands of some higher authority. An officer, trying to put them at ease, said:

'We are now friends, and the war is now over for you.'

Their wounds were cleaned and dressed and an anti-tetanus injection given. John Howard realised that his paybook had not been discovered and he managed to conceal it once more. During individual interrogations the conducting officer attempted to intimidate them, repeatedly insisting that they had attacked a hospital clearly displaying the Red Crescent insignia. He achieved nothing.

For the next few days the prisoners saw and heard RAF aircraft and the sound of explosions in the distance; occasionally, if an aircraft was low, the guards would fire their rifles, hoping for a lucky hit.

Iraqi officers were curious to see the first prisoners. Most spoke English and, although guarded, were fairly cordial. One claimed that it was he who had shot them down. As he seemed so pleased with himself, none of the Wellington crew attempted to disillusion him. The same pilot went on to say that the previous day his friend had been shot down during a raid on Al Rashid aerodrome and, when they recovered his body from the wreckage, they discovered he had been shot through the stomach. He had been flying an Audax, Howard remained silent. He felt awkward, for the officer had just given them some Camel cigarettes. The same man had been to inspect the crashed Wellington and seemed to think it amusing when he mentioned that he had noticed the bullet holes in the rear turret and that he, John Howard, had nearly 'bought it'.

One evening shortly afterwards, when they had settled down to sleep, the guards aroused the crew and ordered them to dress. The local population, they were told, was not well disposed towards them. It was too dangerous for them to remain in Baghdad, and for their own safety they were to be moved. For some days Sgt Howard had been trying to dispose of his paybook by chewing a bit each day and washing it down with lots of water. It had become an obsession. Now, as he dressed, he hastily stuffed the remains of the paybook inside his shirt.

At Baghdad railway station the five prisoners were ushered into a carriage, with three armed guards seated opposite. Howard, sitting nearest the window, puzzled about a way to dispose of the indigestible outer cover of his paybook. With luck, he thought, the guards might become tired and lax in the early hours. As the train rattled on, Howard forced himself awake, watching each of the guards in turn, until their heads drooped and all were asleep or dozing. Taking the remains of his paybook from inside his shirt, he slipped it slowly into the opening between the wooden window slats and the side of the carriage. It dropped out of sight.

Hours later, the train stopped at Kirkuk, some 200 miles north of Baghdad. The prisoners were jeered by a threatening crowd as they left the train. A car took them to Kirkuk Hospital, an army truck armed with a Lewis gun following close behind. Their wounds were treated in a more professional manner there and Howard's head was shaved.

Later they were taken by car to a bungalow, which had been occupied earlier by a family working for the Iraqi Petroleum Company and abandoned at the outbreak of hostilities. The RAF men were astonished to find the bungalow fully furnished and intact; apparently the Iraqis had not bothered to make a search. Several cupboards were locked and these the prisoners opened, causing as little damage as possible. They still felt obliged to respect the owner's property. In a larder they found several tins of food and some jellies. In another cupboard they discovered a small radio set, which was hastily concealed for future use.

The Iraqi officer in charge made no objection to the prisoners using the gramophone, and during the day they enjoyed the music, but in the evening, records by Elizabeth Welch and Adelaide Hall were played as a cover for the radio news while two of the crew acted as lookouts.

For John Howard and the crew in Kirkuk, this was a week of luxury, but then they were moved to the fort of an oil pumping station which had also been hurriedly evacuated. Food was not scarce but was always monotonous, usually a mystery stew and chappatis. After six weeks, they were joined by six men from a British Army force who had been landed at night at a nearby airfield. Their attack had failed and they had been taken prisoner.

Spirits rose when the prisoners were told they would receive pay sufficient to purchase razors, blades, toothbrushes, etc., which a Syrian cook would buy them in Kirkuk. The cook also brought back some powdered milk, tea and sugar. In a cupboard the prisoners had discovered an electric iron. This they supported upside-down between two large stones, placed a quart tin of water on its base and switched on. The water never boiled but, after a considerable time, it was hot enough to make a brew.

In the morning and late afternoon, they were able to exercise below the wall surrounding the fort, or play a game with a ball made from pieces of rag. They had many discussions among themselves and it was suggested that, if the opportunity to escape arose, they might try to reach the Persian border, about 100 miles to the east. The chance never came.

Every other day the monotony was relieved for Howard by a doctor's visit. His wounds had turned septic and were oozing pus which every day dried into a hard crust. The bandages were soaked in ether and then ripped off, leaving the wounds raw and bleeding. The doctor cleaned and freshly dressed them but they continued to suppurate until the next visit. *Luftwaffe* officers also came to the fort, but they strutted around without comment, giving the prisoners a disinterested glance.

For Howard, his crew and the six British soldiers, it was a great day when an Iraqi officer announced that Indian troops of the British Army, commanded by Major General 'Bill' Slim, had made a rapid advance from Basra and had accepted the surrender of the Iraqi troops. The rebellion was over, but part of the Iraqi Army would not surrender and was fleeing north towards Kirkuk. The officer feared the rebels would reach Kirkuk before the prisoners could be evacuated. Telling them to pack, he said he would put them on a train that evening for Baghdad, and try to get a message to the British Embassy so that they could be met on arrival at Baghdad West station.

That evening they were driven to Kirkuk station and ushered into a carriage with windows closed and shutters drawn. For the first time, they were without guards. During the tense night journey, they peeped through the shutters and could see groups of rebel forces sitting around fires, with rifles stacked nearby.

Shortly after dawn the train drew into a station. The men, cold and hungry, assumed they had arrived at their destination, opened the carriage door and climbed down to the platform. They instantly realised that something was wrong. The platform was crowded with fierce-looking natives, most carrying weapons. Then an airman saw the station name, it was Baghdad East; they wanted Baghdad West. Hurriedly climbing back in the train, they slammed the door behind them, only breathing more easily as the train pulled out. At Baghdad West the British group began to feel uneasy again. Crowds of inquisitive natives were gathering on the platform, muttering and pointing. The tension was broken when transport from the British Embassy eventually arrived and they were driven rapidly through the teeming streets of Baghdad. Burning, shooting and looting was still in progress.

At the British Embassy a signal was sent to Habbaniya and a Vickers Valentia aircraft arrived at the bombed and deserted airport. The men scrambled on board and, within fifteen minutes, were passing over the RAF camp. The whole area was strewn with wrecked transport. As the aircraft was making an approach, Howard was startled by a loud explosion. For a moment he thought that the aircraft had been fired upon and hit, but one of the crew had fired a Very pistol recognition signal close behind him.

The men were taken for a check in the camp hospital. Howard was in poor health but had two very good reasons for being jubilant – he was free and it was his twenty-first birthday.

When his wounds healed, Howard made his way back to Shallufa near Suez. Arriving late in the evening, with the orderly room closed and nowhere to sleep, Howard made for the sergeants' mess. His reception there by the Station Warrant Officer was explosive. 'You look like a tramp,' roared the SWO. 'How dare you enter the mess in that condition?'

Howard's indignant explanation that he had been an unwilling guest of the Iraqis, that the dirty shirt, shorts and dilapidated flying boots were all the clothing he possessed, immediately mollified the SWO, who apologised and took him straight to the bar for a drink.

Next morning at an interview with the Squadron Commanding Officer, he recounted his exploits. The CO remarked, 'You will have an interesting story to tell your grandchildren,' adding with a chuckle, 'I am glad that you are still capable of having them, your voice has not changed its pitch.'

John Howard was not sorry when told he would be posted back to England.

CAPTAIN COURAGEOUS

On the night of 27 March 1941, four Manchesters were among 39 aircraft detailed to bomb targets in the city of Düsseldorf. Australian Flight Lieutenant 'Johnnie' Siebert DFC was the captain of 'P' Peter, a Manchester of 207 Squadron. Siebert was a veteran of 40 operations, as were three other members of his crew. Most of their operations had been carried out in the draughty, confined space of Hampdens. The Manchester was different. Wireless operator Jim Taylor found it roomy. The Manchester also had a more effective defensive armament and more than double the bomb-carrying capacity of the Hampden. Generally, the crews liked the Manchester, but there were always doubts about the reliability of the Rolls-Royce Vulture engines and their capacity to deliver the power necessary for a large airframe. Operational now for a month, none of the Manchesters had been lost over enemy territory.

Siebert successfully made two runs over the target. The orders were that the high explosive bombs and the incendiaries were to be dropped separately. Turning for home and crossing Holland, the crew saw an aircraft go down in flames to the south of their track. Extra precautions were necessary as they entered the *Himmellbett* system of the Kammhuber Line.

Near Bakel in Holland, a Messerschmitt 110 slid unobtrusively beneath the Manchester and sprayed it with cannon and machine-gun fire. As fire roared through the aircraft, the five NCO members of the crew escaped by parachute. Siebert jumped too late from the blazing plane, as did so many captains who fought to keep their aircraft flying so that the crews could escape.

The victory for *Oberfeldwebel* Gerhard Herzog, pilot of the Messerschmitt, was the 84th of the *Luftwaffe*'s nightfighter system since it was instituted in the autumn of 1940, and Herzog's personal 24th. But Herzog had a more important 'kill' than he suspected. The Manchester was the first to be shot down over enemy territory – Herzog claimed a Wellington.

SPRING CROP

By April 1941, David Young, still with the London Blitz fire-glow in his mind's eye, was a seasoned observer of ten operations with 77 Squadron based at RAF Topcliffe. He had seen constant changes in the crew-room population. Missing crews were replaced by fresh faces from operational training units. Sometimes crews were killed on air tests or spent a few days in a dinghy. Occasionally one heard that an airman, previously reported missing, was now posted as a prisoner-of-war. Young knew all the dangers but was content because, despite a 'heavy involvement' with an accounts section WAAF called Pat, if he 'went for a Burton' there would be no widow.

On 9 April, 77 Squadron was asked for a 'maximum effort'; their Whitleys were to be part of a 90-aircraft raid on Berlin with the aiming point the General Post Office. Using his own 'safer' route to Berlin, Young navigated the Whitley to arrive on time. A few fires were visible as he lowered himself into a prone position over the bombsight. On the run-up to the target, Young lined up what he thought was the GPO between the illuminated bombsight lines and pressed the button. When the 'bombs gone' light flashed, it was as if a simultaneous effect was produced below. A dozen searchlights snapped on, the Whitley was coned and the interior was dazzlingly bright. Black smoke-puffs from shell-bursts floated past and, as Young reached his seat behind the pilot, the Whitley lurched, metal rattled around the fuselage and shrapnel stung his right leg. The port engine note changed to a wounded whine while the reading on the temperature gauge fell back to zero. A stream of white vapour trailed from the engine and the rear-gunner, Sgt Budd, reported smoke and sparks from the port-side. Use of the fire extinguishers just produced another puff of smoke.

The Whitley was rapidly losing height, so pilot Sgt Lee requested a course for Sweden. But time had run out, the fire increased and white-hot magnesium could be seen through the gaps in the cowling. As the airscrew stopped, Lee ordered 'Abandon'. Young jumped, had a fleeting glimpse of the tail wheel as it swept overhead, and then felt motionless as his parachute took his weight. He could see a parachute above in the moonlight and another below. Quite suddenly, a house swept by, then a tree and, with a final crumple into a pile of straw around the tree roots, Young found himself in the back garden of a house.

Within moments a door opened. A shadowy raincoated figure emerged, stood looking at him but did not speak. Breaking the strange silence, Young wished him an incongruous, 'Good morning'. There was no reply but, before long, a car arrived with two *Luftwaffe* men, who dashed in, spoke to the silent figure and then to Young. Their English was limited to six words: 'For you the war is over.'

TEATIME AT ROTTERDAM

As a crew member, Pilot Officer John Brewster had carried out several operations from RAF Dishforth on 51 Squadron Whitleys, but now he was to be captain of his own aircraft. Why then was he told that he was to go on a 'nursery' trip? He was aggrieved; it was as if he had never flown on operations before, but orders were orders.

'Your aircraft alone is going to Rotterdam,' he was told in the operations room. He had just reached the door when Ops called out, 'and you will drop your tea in a residential area.'

Brewster hesitated, was about to ask about 'tea' but decided not to show his ignorance. 'I am either daft or "tea" must be some sort of code that I don't know about. Perhaps it's another name for "Razzle",' he thought, and decided to ask a corporal fitter about this 'tea' stuff.

'It's tea all right,' said the corporal, 'three barrels of little bags with tickets on them saying "a present from the East Indies".'

Brewster was glad they also carried bombs to drop on Rotterdam docks. Bombs gone, he banked the Whitley to fly over the residential area while the crew went back to tip the teabags out through the flare chute. The inevitable happened; the teabags blew back and they were flying everywhere, inside the fuselage as well as outside. At that moment, flak burst all around the aircraft and Brewster threw the Whitley through its normal jinking routine as the crew members staggered about trying to gather up the flying teabags. When the crew decided to call it a day, two and a half barrels of teabags had been poured into Rotterdam's night sky.

The homeward flight was uneventful until the moment the Whitley touched down at Dishforth. The lights went out, the flare-path was doused and impenetrable darkness surrounded the still-rolling aircraft.

'The miserable B's,' Brewster swore beneath his breath. 'Why did they do that?'

Calling the second pilot to fetch the Aldis lamp, and opening the top hatch so that they could alert dispersal, Brewster had his answer. An aircraft passed over the Whitley 'going like hell'. Later, the group captain told him that everyone had been on tenterhooks for the half-hour the German had been following him in over the North Sea.

Another Whitley was sent on a similar lone 'nursery' flight a few nights later. Next morning, Brewster saw the ragged pieces of a Sidcot flying suit in the locker room and, outside in the field, the wreck of a Whitley. A cannon shell had passed over the head of the tail-gunner, shot past the navigator and wireless operator, and then between the second pilot, who was sitting on the step, and the captain. At that moment the captain had put his arm out over the throttle; the shell neatly took it off. The Whitley 'piled in'.

'Great God!' Brewster thought grimly, as he looked at the wreckage 'all for a packet of tea'.

Two months later, shot down on a raid on Düsseldorf, Brewster walked through the main gate into Dulag Luft.

A NOISY, DAZZLING ERUPTION

The Empire Air Training Scheme not only produced flyers, it gave young men from many countries a chance to see more of the world. Ron Damman, an Australian from Victoria, had been imbued with enthusiasm for flying by the exploits of a pioneering aviator, 'Hustling' Bert Hinkler. Having finished training on No. 1 course in Canada, Damman landed from a troopship in Glasgow as a member of a group of 40 on their way to RAF Uxbridge. They were to have ten days' leave before being sent to the Operational Training Unit at Bassingbourn.

Australian squadrons had not then been formed as part of Bomber Command, so Sgt Ron Damman and fellow Aussie, Joe McCullough, were sent after training to form a Wellington crew with 9 Squadron at RAF Honington.

The fifth operation the crew carried out was an attack on the industrial city of Emden. Defences there were always 'hot'; the Wellington was severely battered by flak and both engines failed. Damman gave the order to 'bale out'. Rear Gunner Sgt Channing jettisoned the turret doors and threw himself out backwards, but front gunner 'Jake' Jacobs became wedged with his parachute in the escape hatch. By the time he was extricated, only a crash-landing was possible. Holding off at 500 feet, with 'wheels up', Damman brought the Wellington down in the darkness, praying for luck, not knowing what lay beneath. As the aircraft slithered along the ground, he had a glimpse of trees ahead and to the right, and houses on the left – but the plane slewed round and stopped.

The crew scrambled out, with hardly a scratch between them. The Wellington was notorious for 'brewing-up' or 'doing a flamer' when attacked, or during a crash-landing, but this one did not want to die that way. The crew knew they were in occupied Holland, so they fired Very cartridges into the inflammable parts of the wounded aircraft, but it was an hour before it suddenly exploded into a spectacular, bullet-spraying firework display that lit the sky for miles.

'How exciting,' said the laconic Jacobs with massive understatement as he stepped back from the flaming heap. During the whole of this noisy and dazzling eruption no one approached to help or apprehend the crew.

It was time to split up and take what chances there were to get away. Of rear gunner Channing, who had baled out, they had no knowledge, so P/O Reid and Sgt Jacobs went south and Sgts 'Mac' Graham and Damman went north-east, towards the Dutch coast.

It was twelve months to the day since Damman had joined the Royal Australian Air Force.

'It's too risky to cross by the bridges Mac, there are so many bicycles and pedestrians,' said Damman. 'Let's borrow one of those dinghies and row across the canal.'

It seemed the safest way. A boat was purloined and Damman pushed it into the water. Immediately it began to sink, giving Mackenzie Graham a chance to make light of their desperate plight by jibing, 'You were never much good at pushing the boat out.'

Eventually, feeling desperately hungry, the two decided they had to knock on doors and ask for food. Their reception was mixed. When it became known who they were, they were sometimes helped; other doors were slammed in their faces. The airmen could hardly blame the Dutch. The harsh penalty for helping escapees, enforced by the German occupiers, was to face a firing squad. Remembering advice given in escape lectures, the pair decided to follow a padre from a church to the presbytery. In the small town of Hoonhorst they saw the priest enter the presbytery across the road. Following his footsteps somewhat timidly, they knocked at the side door. A voice spoke in English with a strong foreign accent: 'Come in gentlemen.'

Warily they walked into the house and were immediately greeted with a handshake, food, cigars, a map and compass. The warmth of their welcome was overwhelming. Their new friend telephoned the local GP, a Doctor Reysen, who advised them to make for the north of Holland because the east coast was well patrolled. The doctor passed them to a farmer, who hid them in a loft above his milking shed. Damman remembered with a pang that he should have met his WAAF girlfriend Mary that evening, outside the cinema at Royston.

Flying boots are uncomfortable for walking if worn for any time. The couple were glad of a rest in the middle of the following day. There were few Germans about, but it was a busy Sunday morning. They had been receiving curious glances from some Dutch people. At Deventer, it seemed that the only way to cross the River IJssel was by the bridge. Mixing with the crowds, they managed it without being challenged. By now they had finished their food, so they knocked at the door of a cobbler's house, only to have it hurriedly closed in their faces.

They ran for cover but the alarm was up. That evening, they were arrested by a local policeman and taken to the *Bürgermeister*'s at Heine. Onlookers were amazed to hear them singing 'Rule Britannia', 'God Save the King', 'Land of Hope and Glory' and other patriotic songs just to raise their spirits.

The *Bürgermeister* was kind, fed the fugitives and talked for some time before informing the Germans of their presence, but soon they were on their way to Dulag Luft, cheered by Dutch people. At Utrecht station, Dutch travellers handed them cigarettes and food and sang English songs until threatened by the German guards. At Dulag Luft interrogation centre, much interest was created by Damman's 'Blue Orchid' uniform. He claimed the dubious honour of being the first Royal Australian Air Force man to be captured.

SPRING IN POMERANIA

The prisoners at Barth welcomed the spring sunshine. It was possible to lay a blanket on the dusty soil, close one's eyes and drift away in fancy to another world. But the reality upon looking round again was all the harder to endure. The intrusion of bitter truth would strike like a hammer blow. The caging barbed wire was just feet away and ubiquitous dark firs limited the view to 100 yards in any direction. The watchful guards, with rifles slung over their shoulders, patrolled the paths outside the barbed wire, and *Posten* in the high boxes gazed down over the barrels of their machine-guns.

Then there was hunger. The lack of sufficient food had caused stomachs to contract and the pangs to become less agonising, but they were replaced by a dull, hollow feeling deep in the bowels. A man was no less ravenous but was controlled by the certain knowledge that no more food would come his way that day and very little on the morrow. And worse, no end to this gradually debilitating wastage of life could be seen.

There were few consolations; occasionally, interpreters and guards brought copies of the *Deutsche Allgemeine Zeitung* or the *Völkischer Beobachter* into the compound; it was fine propaganda from their view, the reports were always good for Germany. But Kriegies were quick to notice the steady increase in the number of obituaries of individual German servicemen who had 'lost his young life for his *Führer und Vaterland*'. Soon the black bands and black crosses bordering the obituaries spread over the back pages of the daily newspapers.

The bleak misery of near starvation and the biting cold of winter gave way to milder spring weather and the Kriegies suddenly came alive when, in May, Barth had the first delivery of Red Cross parcels. The invasion of the western nations and the collapse of France had faced the International Red Cross with complex difficulties in establishing a route for food parcels to reach the camps. Now arrangements through Switzerland and Sweden were working and it became possible for the prisoners to think of matters other than food and survival. The luxury of a full belly and warmth was like an injection of energy and creative ideas.

For most prisoners escape was a 'non starter', unless an opportunity presented itself during a move or outside on a working party. Such chances were rare and the camps were so deep in enemy territory that only a dedicated few worked ceaselessly at escape plans. There was a certain feeling of safety in numbers, even in confinement, and it needed a powerful streak of inner courage to take on the hostile world outside the camp, alone and hunted. But everyone was willing to help, in any way, the man who wanted to have a try at a 'home run'. There were always those in the very worst of times who lived, thought and planned escape, to whom confinement was a far greater punishment than being without food, and to whom the outside world was where they needed to be – no matter what the odds.

Many escapes were attempted at Barth but the Kriegies were raw and their first efforts were frequently unsophisticated and uncoordinated. Sgts Peter Tebbutt and Freddie Phillips had bad luck when they attempted an escape from a working party and were making for a ship in which to stow away to Sweden. They were passing an airfield when a tractor emerged from a perimeter gate, driven by a *Luftwaffe* man who had once been a guard at Stalag Luft 1. Despite Tebbutt's impassioned plea that they were foreign workers, the ex-guard had recognised Phillips. They attempted to run while the *Luftwaffe* man called for help, but the game was up.

With the warmer weather, clothes could be washed without their being frozen solid. Accumulated lice and their eggs were destroyed and blankets were hung out to air. Now that food was more or less adequate, exercise could be taken within the limited area of the compounds; nets were made from the string tied around Red Cross parcels for use in a form of volleyball, and the compound surfaces were reduced to a fine, all-permeating dust by the pounding of hundreds of feet as a continuous line of men walked 'the circuit', just inside the warning wire. Like zoo animals, they walked the longest distance possible within their cage.

All had escaped death by seconds and, for many, religious services were a consolation and a comfort. The close confines of the wire and the dark, deadening monotony of the surrounding conifers beyond, meant that one's vision had to be extended by imagination or focused on the near distance in card games or chess.

When the wooden shutters were clamped across the outside of the windows and the men locked in for the night, a blanket would be placed on a table, wooden forms drawn up and a pack of cards produced. Cigarettes were the currency and the gambling stakes. Quick-fire and noisy games of brag, pontoon or poker would be taking place on one table, while on another there would be sober, quiet rubbers of contract bridge, with a reasoned post-mortem after each hand. At nine o'clock, when the room lights were switched off from outside by the Germans, the small, fat-fed lamps would provide light for those who wanted to carry on playing, sometimes into the early hours; after all, they were not going anywhere the next day. The harsh and hungry winter was becoming a haunting memory.

BLENHEIM CARTWHEEL

A 139 Squadron Blenheim 4 took off from RAF Horsham St Faith near Norwich on the fine night of 7 May, 1941.

Navigator Sergeant Bob Coles, known as 'Smudge' to avoid confusion with wireless operator Sergeant Bob Hale, gave the captain a course for the Hook of Holland. There was little cloud, a brilliant moon and a slight breeze. This was the crew's first night operation and they were to bomb any enemy shipping, or failing that, fly into the mouth of the Ems and attack ships and landing craft in the harbour of the Dutch port of Delfzyl. As they were accustomed to daylight raids, the crew decided, because of the bright moon, to use the same low-level tactics. There was an advantage in flying low; the approach was less obvious to the enemy and the bombing more accurate.

Once beyond the Norfolk coast, and with moonlight shining on the North Sea, Sgt Pilot Bill Middleton brought the Blenheim down to 50 feet above the waves. Sighting a convoy target, he dropped to 10 feet, then made a fast climb up and over the stern, with Coles dropping half the bomb load. Bob Hale yelled confirmation of a good hit as he fired his twin Brownings at the ship. Flak was heavy all around the Blenheim; a lone attack on a convoy means every gun is concentrated on the attacker.

Middleton turned the Blenheim away, deciding to leave the convoy to someone else and make for Delfzyl. Distracted for a second by 'Smudge' trying to identify a landmark, Middleton allowed the aircraft to sink, saw his mistake and immediately pulled the stick back. At that low level the move spelt disaster. As Middleton pulled the nose up, the tail dropped and hit the water with a startling crash. The aircraft took off again, the engines running smoothly and relief surged over the crew, but within moments there was a terrifying impact. The Blenheim somersaulted three times, during which 'Smudge' Coles was dazzled by blinding lights, deafened by noise and twisted with pain until knocked unconscious.

Cold water brought Coles back to hazy realisation that he was submerged, with his feet stuck firmly in deep mud. Kicking his way out of his flying boots, he surfaced and found the water to be shallow. Winded, and groaning to force air into his bursting lungs, Coles stared around. The Blenheim was blazing furiously and Bill Middleton was trying, reeling like a drunkard, to pull himself upright. Where was Bob Hale? With hardly a word the two released their parachute harnesses and dragged themselves as near to the burning, mangled mess as the heat would allow, always shouting for Hale. They decided that, if he was in there, there was no hope. Reluctantly, they staggered away. As they did so, Coles kicked the dinghy floating in its pack. He grabbed it; it was going to be useful for the coast of Holland was about two miles distant and the water seemed to becoming deeper. When they were about 50 yards from the wreck, the bomb load detonated and hot shrapnel hissed into the water all around. In the wake of the explosion they heard a call. Bob Hale was standing near the Blenheim's tail, illuminated by the distant flames. With the crash, the Blenheim's tail had broken off, throwing Hale into the sea. His 'Mae West' life jacket had supported him and the explosion had restored him to consciousness.

Adding to his own predicament, 'Smudge' Coles found that he now had two injured men for whom he must care. Middleton was bleeding from head injuries and Hale was seriously battered and delirious. After cutting off his harness, Coles bundled Middleton into the dinghy and lifted Hale in alongside him. Near to exhaustion, but determinedly kicking with his feet, Coles began the long swim pushing the dinghy to the coast of Holland.

The progress of the dinghy was so slow and difficult that eventually Middleton, despite his injuries and weak condition, climbed out of the dinghy to help. Hale, in his delirium, asked continuously, 'Where am I – what has happened?' He was racked by uncontrollable shivering from shock and cold.

Nearing the shore, they saw the outlines of houses and shouted for help. It seemed inconceivable that they could not be heard, or that the fire and explosions had gone unnoticed. Yet there was no reply. The last few yards were some of the worst, as they heaved their feet from deep, sucking mud. Then they were on the shore.

An officer and six German soldiers, armed with automatic weapons, appeared out of the gloom. They searched the three with reluctance; their head-to-foot coating of slime did not make it an easy job. It was not until they were taken to a local officers' mess and seated in front of a blazing fire, that their involuntary shivering calmed. Hale removed his sodden clothes and fell into a deep, shock-induced sleep. They had been through much but, even in their direful situation, Coles could find humour. When a leopard skin rug was thrown over the sleeping man, his tousled wet hair covering his face, 'Smudge' Coles, with an inward smile, could not help comparing Bob Hale to a sort of vanquished Tarzan.

Middleton and Coles were questioned about life in England. Their captors were sure that the U-boats had reduced the British to a diet of potatoes and would not be convinced otherwise.

After a day of X-rays, sutures and sleep at Leeuwarden Hospital, the three were taken in a rickety ambulance on a bumpy journey to the Wilhelmina Hospital in Amsterdam, and put in a ward with a dozen soldiers. Despite the pain and bruises, their journey had been interesting. They were seeing at close range what they had previously seen only from the air. The beautiful, clean appearance of everything was striking. So too were the cyclists – cyclists everywhere and in enormous numbers. Whenever traffic halted, people would come to the open windows of the ambulance, asking the guard what had happened. When told who the wounded men were, kindly smiles of encouragement wreathed their faces. 'Smudge' thought the smiles very heartening – especially from the ladies.

Like others before him, Coles had difficulty in eating the strange hospital food. Raw bacon, spinach, barley and the sour, rough brown bread was plentiful but unpalatable to British tastes. He was to get used to it and often be thankful for the smallest portion.

Coles looked around the ward. Two more English airmen had moved in: Johnny Mason, suffering from a broken neck, and Barry Fleury, who was being fitted with a false eye. Others in the ward were German servicemen, some fanatically worshipping Hitler as a god. Passing a large laurel-leafed portrait of Hitler, they shot out their right arms in Nazi salutes.

The two weeks in hospital allowed Coles time to think, and it dawned on him that they were destined to stay in Germany for a long time. Weeks, months and even – he would not allow himself to think of it – years; escape would surely come sooner.

His and Middleton's legs were now much stronger but Hale still staggered painfully in splints. It was certain that Coles and Middleton would be moved to a prison camp before Hale. Escape would be easier from the hospital, so Coles, appearing casual, made a few trips to the windows to spy out the land. At the hospital gates sentries paced back and forth beneath the swastika flags. Dressed only in their nightshirts, with the name of the hospital blazoned across the chest, there was little chance of the airmen getting past the guards.

Plans were made between the prisoners, who used slang, catchphrases and scraps of Scottish and other dialects unlikely to be understood by the Germans in the ward. Other methods of communication were tapping in morse code against a book or lightly pricking relevant words in a novel and asking for it to be passed to one another.

Although Coles winced when his legs were examined, the German doctor was obviously unconvinced by his evident malingering. Escape was becoming urgent.

Coles and Middleton planned to get away by 3 a.m. and to be clear of the hospital grounds by the lifting of curfew at 4 a.m. That night they slept fitfully, feeling sure that they were suspected by two German wounded who whispered incessantly.

At zero hour, Middleton peered round the partition and raised a questioning thumb. Coles looked about him, then raised his thumb in reply. Even though the German in the next bed had his eyes open, Coles was reasonably sure he was asleep. Bob Hale knew that he would be a hindrance. His legs were still painful, so he declined to go. Quickly Coles stripped a sheet from his bed, padding out a bolster and pillow in the form of a sleeper.

Coles was sorry for the guard, who had supplied him with cigars and was now probably playing cards with the night nurse. He was sure to be in trouble after their escape, but Coles decided this was not the time to go 'soft' about a German.

A search of the lockers had yielded two pairs of *Luftwaffe* uniform trousers, a pair of socks, a pair of jackboots, a pair of slippers and some scissors.

With silent handshakes and whispers of good luck to Hale, the pair crawled under beds to the door. As footsteps passed, they slipped quickly back until all was quiet, then crept into the corridor to the balcony door. It was unlocked. They stole out into the cold, cutting night air. Swiftly knotting the sheets together, they tied them to the balcony rail and slid to the ground. Coles cut a strip from a sheet and tied it round his waist to keep up the uniform trousers, then, with his boots under his arm, he and Middleton set off to find a way out of the hospital grounds. Looking back, Coles saw the white streamer of sheet hanging from the balcony and wondered how long it would be before it was discovered.

It was late May, but the mornings were still very cold, so when Coles and Middleton found that one side of the hospital was bordered by a canal, they decided they had no desire for an early morning swim. In another direction, near the maternity wing, they found a road running parallel to the building, but they were barred by high railings with spear-like spikes. Three attempts were made before they managed to clear the spikes, Coles having to jump down from twelve feet to hide in the bushes as someone passed. Now, it was a matter of moving rapidly to put as much distance as possible between them and the hospital.

They stopped briefly in the dark streets of Amsterdam and Coles reluctantly cut off his luxuriant 'heavy bomber' moustache with his stolen scissors.

Milkmen and newspaper men were now beginning to people the streets, but little attention was paid to the strangely attired pair as they crossed the city in as near an easterly direction as possible. As it grew lighter, passers-by began to follow them with their eyes. Coles had to steel himself to avoid looking round; he could feel their eyes boring into his back. Both men held their bare arms across their chests when anyone approached, hiding the hospital name printed across their nightshirts.

Their erratic progress was a nightmare of dodging down side-streets, to avoid policemen, and detours caused by the dozens of canals. Every cycle they attempted to steal was firmly chained, and walkers in this city of cyclists were conspicuous.

By 6 a.m. they had reached the Amsterdam suburbs. The houses were a different type from those in the city and beyond them were fields. Barring their way ahead was the River Amster. Turning right along the banks, they now had sailing barges to their left, with the crews calling out, '*Guten morgen*'. Cyclists on their way to work greeted them in the same manner and stared. Outside a house a German soldier stood on sentry duty. It was the first German they had seen and Middleton, with amazing cheek and elaborate carelessness, stopped in front of the soldier and lit a cigarette. They passed on unchallenged.

Within another mile, Coles's feet were blistering and painful in the jackboots, and Middleton, his heels bleeding, was walking barefoot. There seemed no turning from the road, no hedges in which to hide and every depression was filled with water. 'Water, water, bloody water everywhere,' Coles groaned.

As the nurse leaned over a bed to rouse the occupant with a cup of coffee, she found only a bolster and pillow. Within moments the hospital was in an uproar. It was 6 a.m. and the runaways had not been missed until then. It was normal for German officers to rage, jump up and down and shout when angry or frustrated. Bob Hale said that this one exceeded the usual frantic display. The guard was led away under escort and the German patients berated for not reporting the escape. Hale, his legs still in splints, Mason, with his broken neck, and the other British airmen were immediately taken to the local barracks and locked in the cells.

Coles and Middleton were desperate, in agony with every step. A farmer refused when they asked to spend a day in his barn. He was sorry, but his life and those of his family would be put at immense risk. The fugitives did not blame him.

It now seemed hopeless, but they carried on over a bridge. The bridge-keeper appeared to note every detail. It seemed certain that they would be reported as suspicious. Women leaning from windows stopped their gossiping as the strangely garbed couple passed. Dogs barked and children ran behind shouting and laughing. The dishevelled pair smiled and went on.

On a bank, just below road level, they sat down to rest and discussed plans for the next move. They were at least out of sight from the road, but not from some farm buildings.

A signpost for Utrecht now meant nothing; exhaustion, hunger and pain had made the need for rest and shelter urgent. Coles examined his cut and bleeding feet and rubbed his knotted leg muscles. Both men were in the same condition and knew that further progress in their present state was hopeless. They watched an approaching farm hand with a mixture of relief and apprehension. He stood before them, asking unintelligible questions. Suddenly his faced wreathed in smiles as their identity dawned on him. The RAF men trusted him instantly. His sabots did not prevent him from making an agile leap over the farm fence and a fast run back to the house. Within seconds, after a quick look around, he signalled them to come over to his barn. There the farmer's wife waited with a jug of milk and plates of bread and cheese.

They found it easy to communicate and Middleton explained what had happened. The farmer thought it a huge joke, but Coles was concerned for the Dutch family's safety. The direction of their flight was known and the death penalty was punishment for hiding or helping them. But the farmer was adamant. They must rest. German troops and police were actively searching for the escapers, so they had to leave the barn and hide with pigs in their sty. But they had food and, that evening, two other friends of the farmer supplied them with civilian clothes, a large-scale map of Amsterdam and, especially welcome, a pair of shoes for Middleton. Coles cut the tops from his jackboots and drilled holes with their scissors for string laces. Now they were better equipped for their journey. Their hosts asked the pair to wait until they could find proper contacts for an escape route but, mindful of the grave danger to the Dutch farmer, and anxious to be off, they decided to get on the road again.

Coles and Middleton wrote down their home addresses, shook hands with the farmer and his wife, then crept from the farmhouse. With hat brims turned down, they walked off in the evening twilight. This time, perhaps they would not stand out so prominently. Only a few courting couples and cyclists were passed and, just before midnight, they climbed into some straw to rest. Even in late May, a chilling wind flows from the North Sea and to the RAF men the cold seemed intense. Late the next morning, they circled round the farm and made their way in the direction of Schiphol. People stared. 'Perhaps they might take us for tramps,' Middleton said hopefully, but Coles was sure that a Dutch tramp would be on a bicycle.

They realised they had made a mistake immediately they started out. They could hardly walk; every step was an excruciating, limping agony. Their slow progress was suddenly halted by a man who had overtaken them on a bicycle. He asked them if they had travelled far, and if they were German; without waiting for a reply, he said, 'You are the airmen who escaped from the hospital.'

Telling them to wait while he brought a friend who spoke good English, and who would help them, he pedalled away. Coles did not trust him. The man looked cunning and, as far as Coles was concerned, was condemned by his Hitler moustache. But they were unable to run, so they waited – and hoped.

'You are the English airmen, aren't you?' A young labourer stood before them, holding out his hand. 'My work-mates over there have had a "whip round" for you,' he continued, at the same time handing them money and offering to take them to his home.

Coles was amazed at the nerve of these Dutchmen. Here they were, in public, in the street, and the labourer didn't give a damn! Coles and Middleton told him of their doubts about the first man who had come along and their new friend shook his head. He did not like the man either – he could be all right, but many people were 'playing up' to the Nazis these days. The labourer was persuaded to leave, just in case.

When the first man reappeared, he handed them a rough map and a note with directions to the American Embassy. He said that he would try to borrow a car to take them. Within half an hour, he was back with some sponge rolls and an apology for not being able to get a car. As they crossed a field, hoping to hide in some sewage pipes, they heard shouting. Their helper cycled near, muttered that they had been seen by a policeman and tore off at high speed. Quickly they were rounded up, searched and taken to the police station. Middleton managed to drop the note they had been given on the police station step, where it was undoubtedly seen and dealt with by Dutch people outside.

A clerk in the station told them that they were unfortunate to be seen by that pro-Nazi policeman. Others would have walked away. Soon the German *Feldgendarmerie* arrived and took them to the headquarters, where the runaways waited with some apprehension for what was to come.

'Smudge' Coles and his companions were escorted to Dulag Luft. The Oberursel camp seemed almost luxurious, particularly by comparison with their next stay at Stalag 18A at Wolfsberg, deep in the Austrian Tyrol. Wolfsberg must have had the most splendidly spectacular surroundings of any prison camp, but its location in this setting of natural beauty, where the local people wore traditional Tyrolean costume and the mountain cattle-bells tinkled prettily, gainsaid its purpose and regime. Wolfsberg was a grim camp, an *Arbeitskommando* for Austrian coal mines, where the inmates were British soldier-miners, who were always near starvation, and the guards had been selected from the most vicious and bullying *Wehrmacht* men.

Although they were to travel in a train of dirty, uncomfortable and dark cattle trucks, the RAF Kriegies were pleased to leave the Wolfsberg camp on 18 June. Coles had the impression that the *Wehrmacht* was also glad to see them go.

Before the *Wehrmacht* guards had climbed into their section of the railway truck, the Kriegies had loosened three planks. They noted that none of the guards had pistols, all had rifles and bayonets, which are not so easy to use in a confined space. The journey to their unknown destination was calculated to take three and a half days, according to the minimal rations of bread and tinned meat they were given.

Throughout the journey, requests for water and a chance to defecate were refused. Despite a guard being posted on either side of the open door, the heat was stifling. Twice a day, exercise consisted of walking round in circles on a station platform, while civilians looked on in undisguised amusement.

Conditions grew steadily worse, until ten of the Kriegies decided enough was enough; they would leave at the first opportunity. It was reckoned that they would leap from the train while those left would knock aside the guards' rifles. Chances did not come that day; the train was either travelling too fast or passing through houses or open fields devoid of cover.

The next morning, after an uncomfortably cramped night on the bare boards, the tousled and bedraggled men felt the jolting train slowing to a halt. It was Munich and they were to be allowed outside the trucks for a break. A railwayman was persuaded to allow the Kriegies to 'shower' beneath one of the 'fountains' used to fill the locomotives. He turned on the full pressure and the stripped Kriegies gasped as the icy water poured over them, but after the foul and foetid atmosphere of the closed truck, it was refreshing to feel clean, if only for a short time. Again, an amused crowd of both sexes gathered to watch; women in passing trains and nearby houses leaned from windows to enjoy the spectacle. The Kriegies were past caring, they were being transported and treated like animals anyway.

The train journey was resumed and, at last, Coles saw the opportunity for which he had been watching. It was dusk and the Kriegies had been singing lustily around the open door. The guards were amused and further convinced that the English were crazy, but Coles had been looking ahead. He had seen that forest trees reached almost to the railway line. There was ample cover and the train was slowing.

Coles and Middleton raised their thumbs in question and reply just as they had in the hospital. Middleton prised open the catch on the other door and, within seconds, there was pandemonium. A guard had heard the click and jumped up, bringing his rifle round to the ready. There was no time to think, no time to wonder whether the train had slowed enough. Kriegies jumped from the train more swiftly than Coles had expected, so he quickly followed. A shouting guard raised his rifle, aiming at Coles's back as he leapt, but Dave Fraser charged the guard at the vital moment.

Coles was bouncing alongside the track like a cork. The train had been steaming too fast for the jump, and he had pitched forward on to his face and crashed among the granite chips. Grazed, bleeding and bruised, he dragged himself up and ran through a waist-high stream, making for the woods, just as shots rang out. Five Kriegies found one another in the woods. Bill Middleton was very shaken, Bob Hale had swollen eyes, Coles was cut from the temple to chin and everyone had bad grazes of the knees, elbows and face. Together they dashed into the wood, passing within a few feet of a gamekeeper with a shotgun. The gamekeeper shouted to the Kriegies to stop, but one gave him a classic rugby hand-off, which thumped the man down into the undergrowth. They must have appeared very desperate and the gamekeeper made no subsequent attempt to stop them.

Five hundred metres further on, they stopped. They were making too much noise tearing through the brush, so they lay prone in a thicket, waiting for darkness to hide them from the guards who would certainly be sent to hunt them down. With the first shots, the train's speed had begun to decrease but, Coles calculated, it would probably take a mile to halt. All was quiet for a considerable time and then, with much shrieking from its whistle, the train started again, the noise slowly fading into the distance.

For three gruelling and dangerous weeks Coles and his companions were on the run, through forests and towns, through drenching rain and swift-flowing rivers. Soon they had been soaked and dried several times. After an abortive plan to steal an aircraft and make for Switzerland, they were caught by a German who was struck by their unkempt and exhausted appearance. A short while in a prisoner-of-war camp at Lodz was followed by a year in Stalag 8B at Lamsdorf. Then they were sent on, to their joy, to Stalag Luft 3 and to the comparative order of a camp of Kriegies run by Sgt James 'Dixie' Deans.

'BAD' BAD SULZA

It was 13 May 1941, and the 217 Squadron Beaufort had been searching for the U-boat Pens at St Nazaire for hours. Wireless operator Sergeant Bill Bennett knew that fuel must be near exhaustion so it was a relief when the skipper decided to turn for home. They might not have enough petrol to reach base at St Eval in Cornwall, but at least they could land somewhere in England.

As they set course for home, colourful light flak curled up from the airfield at Carpiquet. It looked harmless, but a sudden jolt, as the Beaufort was hit, jerked the crew from any complacency. The Beaufort was suddenly in a steep dive and Bennett thought immediately of their bomb on board. He was certain this was the end.

The aircraft crash-landed, did not explode or catch fire but the skipper and observer were killed. Bennett regained consciousness, a full two weeks later, in a hospital near Caen, only to feel the agonising pain of his dislocated legs, broken jaw, multiple cuts and shrapnel wounds. The crew's air gunner was lying in a bed alongside him. He had also survived the crash but his forehead was lined with deep cuts and his thigh was broken. The two were a painful and sorry sight, owing their lives to *Luftwaffe* men who had dragged them from the wreckage and to the devoted care and watchfulness of two nursing nuns. One nun had stayed with Bennett night and day, sleeping in a chair beside his bed throughout the two weeks of his coma.

Caen Hospital had been commandeered by the Germans, who renamed it *Marine Lazarett* and filled it with wounded *Wehrmacht* soldiers recuperating from the Battle of France. The German doctor in charge of the patients was kindly, and grateful that a *Luftwaffe* friend was being treated well in England. The person in overall charge of the hospital, however, was a very different character, a Nazi Brownshirt, who claimed to have been in hiding with Hitler in their early days. Bennett soon realised that it was best to talk as little as possible to this man. Any disagreement between them caused the menacing and bullying behaviour of the street thug to appear.

At the end of July, while he was still having difficulty in walking, Bennett was sent, without warning, to Dulag Luft and then, because Luft 1 was full, to Stalag 9C at Bad Sulza.

Humiliation was the routine at 9C. Bennett was among arriving prisoners assembled on the village green, where they were told to strip to be searched in full view of grinning villagers. A jeering party of *Hitler Jugend* enjoyed throwing anything that came to hand at those naked and helpless before them. The Kriegies were pleased to be led away to be locked in for the night.

CRETAN SPRING

It was difficult to see from where Germany was to draw the troops necessary to occupy her conquered lands. The *Wehrmacht* was spread from the Arctic north of Norway to the warm lands beside the Aegean; from the coast of France, just 21 miles from Britain, to the demarcation line bisecting Poland. Yet Rommel was demanding, and getting, a large, well-equipped *Afrika Korps*. Britain, even with soldiers from Australia, Canada, New Zealand, South Africa, India and elsewhere in the Commonwealth, seemed hopelessly extended. Rapidly withdrawing their forces to Crete from their last toehold in continental Europe, the British forces drew panting breath and waited.

It was cool, yet the early morning Mediterranean sun brought a promise of warmth as it rose, casting long shadows among the olive and almond groves, the barley fields and vineyards of Crete. The long, shining days of late May seemed to make Crete ideally restful and sleepily quiet, but the expectant tension among the ANZAC, British, Greek and Cretan troops could be felt.

Along the northern coast of the long, narrow island, men watched and waited. All knew that some kind of German attack from the Greek mainland was certain. Some Allied troops were demoralised by their hasty and disorganised retreat from Greece and much of their materiel had been abandoned in the face of the rapid advance of the *Wehrmacht*. Now they steadied and steeled themselves for a further blow as the Germans prepared an all-out attack on the strategic island.

Maleme airfield in the north-west of Crete had briefly housed the tattered Blenheims of RAF 30 and 33 Squadrons remaining after hard battles in Greece; then some of the ground crews were flown to Egypt. Those remaining, with a few of the officers, joined various army units in the defence of the island. Attached to a New Zealand Army unit, 30 Squadron man Ken Stone was digging trenches and carrying out duties for which airmen had received little training, but he quickly got used to handling a rifle.

To the east, at the airfield of Heraklion, Aircraftman Neville Northover was a member of the airfield defence squad. The defenders boasted a modest arsenal of a few rifles and machine-guns. There had been concentrated bombing and strafing of Heraklion's key points in previous weeks but the night of 19 May 1941 had been comparatively quiet. Northover was struck again by the majestic splendour of the eastern Mediterranean sunrise but, accompanying the brilliance, was an ominous, distant, almost half-heard, throbbing hum.

The hum became a roar as, low across the sea, came the bomber aircraft and fighters, followed by the troop-carrying and glider-towing Junkers 52s. Passing over Heraklion, they flew west towards Maleme. Northover heard the continuous roll of gunfire and the deep crump of bombs to the west. This was not the usual 'Morning Hate' to which the men had now become accustomed; the invasion of Crete had begun.

As the Junkers crossed the shore near Maleme, the defenders watched in amazement, fear and wonder as hundreds of coloured parachutes poured from the doors of the Junkers, and gliders slid, almost silently, towards the ground. Other gliders were torn apart as the shells from the British Bofors guns ripped into them, spilling airborne troops tumbling helplessly into the sky.

The troops soon discovered that the parachutists were at their mercy during their slow descent. Ken Stone, attached to the New Zealanders' 22nd Battalion at Maleme, saw most of the attacking troops riddled before they touched the ground. So great was the slaughter that the German attack on Maleme faltered, and the surviving airborne troops formed themselves into small defensive positions to await reinforcement.

Later that day, it was the turn of the forces elsewhere on the north coast to be attacked, including the airfield at Heraklion. There the German parachutists met with vigorous resistance from the Australians, members of the Black Watch, the Leicesters, the Yorks and Lancs plus the RAF airfield defenders. By nightfall, the parachutists had gained neither the airfield nor the town.

Generaloberst Student looked at his battle plan and found that nowhere had the Germans succeeded in grasping enough land to enable more troops and supplies to be put down, except, possibly, at Maleme. He decided to risk everything on a bold effort to capture the airfield. Losses among the élite *Fallschirmjäger* were crippling and, if this last thrust failed, the invasion of Crete would have to be called off.

The next morning the position was much the same at Maleme, but the lack of an immediate counter-attack by the defending forces gave the Germans time in which to consolidate from the air. Once Maleme was firmly in German hands, twenty Ju 52 transports, loaded with men and materiel, were landing every hour, and the end was in sight for Crete's defenders. German reinforcements poured in and more troops and supplies made their way behind the defending forces. Among the inevitably large numbers of New Zealand and British forces captured at Maleme were 57 members of 30 Squadron RAF, 17 of them wounded. They left 28 of their men dead around the airfield and in the trenches. The men of 33 Squadron suffered similarly.

The collapse of the forces at Maleme placed those elsewhere on the island in an untenable position. At Heraklion, the small force of Australians and British was treated as a major defence point, and the weight of a whole bomber group was used to pound them. Then the parachutists fell from the skies like confetti at a wedding. They were met with a withering hail of crossfire, every gunner picking his target, trying to make sure that his particular parachutist did not reach the ground alive. Some fell, writhing and screaming in the agony of their death throes, others were silent, just thumping to the ground and lying still. Still more of the lumbering Jus crashed in flames with their full load of dead and dying men.

In the days that followed, the diminishing band of defenders of Heraklion were gradually overwhelmed by sheer weight of numbers. It became obvious that they were not to be relieved. Gunner Neville Northover took time to dispose of secret and private papers before being suddenly confronted by a large *Feldwebel* who looked like an alien from space in his parachutist's smock and his skull-round helmet. His Schmeisser machine-pistol was pointed straight at Northover's stomach.

Crete fell, but such was the slaughter of their troops, that never again were the Germans to attempt such an airborne landing. In eight days' fighting in Crete the Germans had lost more men, killed, wounded and missing, than in the whole of the Balkan campaign. However, the way was now clear for an advance on Egypt from land, sea and air.

Admiral Cunningham averred that three squadrons of fighters would have saved Crete. The Royal Navy saved some 16,000 Australian, New Zealand and British troops, but after 1 June no ships could approach the Cretan shore. The *Luftwaffe* had complete mastery of the air. For the

13,000 soldiers and airmen left behind and captured, it meant a sojourn in the primitive and notoriously grim camp at Salonika and a journey through the Balkans to Germany.

German troops were in no mood to be gentle with those who had caused such havoc among their parachute and airborne troops. Prisoners were roughly handled, beaten and starved in the hell camp of Salonika. POW Peter Mason watched with horror as a Yugoslav, attempting to escape, was shot and left hanging on the barbed wire for all to see. Later, a dog was shot at during a parade and the prisoners were forced to stand and watch it die.

The sick, with a minimum of care, were laid in rows on to the marble floor of the Greek building used as a temporary hospital. The hospital had a few paper bandages and no drugs at all. All beds and bedding had been removed by the Germans but there were plenty of bugs and fleas and a sickening smell. Neville Northover, racked with malaria and dysentery, was surrounded by wounded, sick and dying, their gasps and groans occasionally punctuated by screams of some in their final agonies.

In a lucid moment, Northover raised his head and saw that, while unconscious, he had been moved across a chalk line which divided the sick lying on the floor. Those on the right side of the line would still be allotted a small portion of bread, but the nearer a patient was to the line, the nearer to death he was considered to be. Those placed on the left of the line were thought certain to die, so they would not be fed. Bread was too scarce to be wasted on them. Northover was on the left of the line. The discovery that he had been placed on the 'dying' side and was to be denied his small bread ration spurred him to action. Raising himself unsteadily on to an elbow, he loudly demanded to be moved to the other side of the line and to be fed. It was the beginning of his slow recovery.

A MINOR VICTORY

During 1941, Stalag Luft 1 at Barth filled, so captured RAF airmen were shipped to other camps throughout Germany and Poland. On his way to Stalag 3A at Luckenwalde, Neville Northover passed through the notorious and brutally run Salonika camp. Orders to prisoners at Salonika were always accompanied by a kick or a blow from a rifle butt. The follow-up troops who ran the camp were callous torturers and killers. All the prisoners suffered from dysentery, many had jaundice and, like Northover, many had malaria, but they were treated no differently. The same boot-and-butt, harsh and heartless treatment was applied to the women who attempted to give bread to the prisoners as they straggled through the streets to the camp. The Greek populace was suffering severely under German occupation. There was no pity or compassion here, only merciless, ferocious and sadistic grinding under the Nazi jackboot. Even in his sorry state, Northover felt an agony of commiseration for the Greek people.

A nightmare journey in a crammed-full cattle truck brought Northover and other prisoners from Crete to the camp at Luckenwalde, south of Berlin. Winter found him working in the company of two other RAF men and some Scottish soldiers in the sawmill section of a large Berlin factory. Here the Britishers were able to carry on their own war. It was a task of the prisoners to knock out bolts from old railway sleepers so that the huge circular saw blades would not be damaged as the sleepers were reduced to firewood. The bolts were knocked out but were then halved and a piece put back into the hole, which was then plugged with oily dirt and sawdust. As each wooden sleeper went through the mill, a few teeth were visibly torn from the saw blades. Such an insignificant and fairly useless action probably did little to harm the German war effort, but to the prisoners it was uplifting. They felt they were at least hindering rather than contributing.

This small act of sabotage was akin to the burying of broken razor blades in the pig swill, which would ensure, the Kriegies at Barth said, 'that the bacon was already sliced on the hoof'.

This practice was voluntarily stopped, not merely because of a German threat, but because it was not a humane way to treat pigs. It was noticeable, however, that the Germans more frequently disposed of pig swill as rubbish. It was another minor victory.

PULLING RANK

At an *Appell* at Barth in mid-1941, Flight Sergeant Graham Hall and nineteen others were suddenly and brusquely separated and told they were being 'purged' to Lamsdorf. They were watched while they collected their few possessions and then taken to the *Vorlager*. The nineteen were held in a guarded room but Hall was locked in a cell in the 'cooler'. When a *Gestapo* man entered his cell, accompanied by a nervous *Hauptmann* Buchwig as interpreter, Hall knew he was to be interrogated. He was irritated by the attitude of the *Gestapo* man and, perhaps not appreciating what could result from his truculence, gave impertinent or 'no comment' replies for what seemed hours of questioning. Buchwig increasingly quivered with fright.

'Please, Mr Hall,' he pleaded, 'do not make this man angry.' Finally Buchwig asked, 'Where does your wife live, Mr Hall?' Hall was puzzled; he had sent and received his full quota of mail which was obviously censored – so he remained silent. Several times the question was asked until

Buchwig said with emphasis, 'He knows her address in Cambridge and says that if you do not cooperate he will bomb her.' It was all Hall could do not to burst into scornful laughter; he doubted if *Luftwaffe* bombing was any more accurate than that of the RAF.

To Hall's surprise, the interview ended inconclusively and he was not grilled again; instead, he spent the night lifting himself to the window to see if Sgt Fancy's 'mole' tunnel had succeeded. Fancy had started the 'mole' that evening but had seen the extra guards and sensibly 'scrubbed' the idea. Next day the selected twenty were on their way to Lamsdorf.

Back at Lamsdorf, Hall found the camp much improved. Red Cross food parcels had transformed the health of the men, and self-discipline had restored their confidence. The RSMs had regained proper control and the camp was running smoothly. The soldiers had to go out to work as allowed by the Geneva Convention, but the havoc they created was probably greater than the value of any work. Some break in routine was made by airmen swapping identities so that they could get outside the wire and plan their escape.

A band playing dance music had been formed under the baton of ex-band boy Corporal Jimmy Howe. The band, a Maori choir and various singing groups helped to alleviate the monotony of camp life.

A friendly interpreter told Hall that there was a camp leader of the RAF men whose father was a South African millionaire. The German authorities were greatly impressed but, when Hall reported to Alan Morris, he laughed aloud. Hall was never quite certain whether the story had any substance, but he was impressed by Morris's personality and his command of German. Morris wanted to hand over the job of senior man but Hall was keen to carry on with his coding work and escape plans. Besides, he wanted a rest from what he considered a thankless task.

During his absence there had been several attempted escapes, Flt Sgt Tom Ross and Sgt 'Pip' Wright had both been in Prague, where Czechs had sheltered them until the Germans had flushed them out. Canadian Reid 'Red' Gordon had been through the wire in a snowstorm but soon recaptured.

Escape was in the air at Lamsdorf. Only airmen had their photographs on the German identification cards, so swaps with soldiers were easy once an airman had memorised the details of his new identity. Swapovers were arranged during inter-compound activities such as football matches and concerts.

But the chances were slipping away as the Germans were constructing a new camp for flyers, Stalag Luft 3, at Sagan in Silesia. Once at Sagan, there would be no soldiers in adjoining compounds who were able to work outside the wire. There would be no one with whom to swap identities but there had to be a journey from one camp to another. Given the chance, Graham Hall and his friend planned the unplannable.

Hall's co-conspirator was Sgt Stan 'Cherub' Lang. Lang had acquired his nickname when a fresh-faced youngster on the North-West Frontier. Now, with his adult features and his keenness to escape, Hall thought it difficult to imagine anyone less cherubic. For the journey to Sagan, the Germans misguidedly put all the 'bad boys' together in one cattle truck in order to keep a close eye on them. In fact, they had brought together dedicated escapers who would help one another and who knew how to provide a convincing diversion to cover an escape.

This box-car was luxurious compared to most. Long benches had been placed across the truck and no aisle space had been reserved for the six submachine-gun armed guards. Even more surprising was that the small shuttered opening high in each corner had been left open and did not have its usual lacing of barbed wire. It looked hopeful.

Hall decided to 'pull rank'. He and Lang would be the first to make the attempt. Taking up positions near the corner, they waited for an opportune moment. At a signal several Kriegies stood up to put on their coats. Few bodies were needed to obscure the guards' view. Lang went first, finding a previously noted hand-hold, while Hall pushed his legs out. Lang swung on to the box-car buffers. Hall sat down and, as their move had so far gone unnoticed, he passed out food and clothing to Lang. Hall went through the hole next, his feet pushed out by Maurice Stretton. Together, Hall and Lang rode the buffers until the train slowed sufficiently for them to drop safely to the trackside. Picking themselves up and dashing into the trees beside the track, they exulted in their sudden liberty. Visions of reaching the Baltic coast and quietly boarding a Swedish vessel to freedom filled their racing thoughts.

As the clanging clatter of the train faded, it was replaced by the joyous sound of a nightingale in full song. Hall and Lang were transfixed; never had freedom seemed more desirable or more attainable than at that moment when the free spirit in the trees called.

For three nights they made good progress but then became careless. At dawn on the fourth morning, they rashly decided to sneak through the main street of a village but froze as an officer on horseback, heading a contingent of the local garrison, marched into the street ahead of them. Quickly the Kriegies threw up a 'Hitler' salute and strode on. Looking ahead for cover, Hall saw with dismay that the nearest woodland was miles distant. They pretended not to notice the policeman on a motor-cycle, but his fierce cry of 'Hände Hoch!' could not be ignored.

In the village jail Hall and Lang quickly wolfed down the food they had held in reserve before the Germans had the chance to take it away.

A few days later, they were being escorted past the Stalag Luft 3 Guardroom and into the camp, when a *Luftwaffe Unteroffizier* passed them, escorting two other Kriegies on the way out.

'That's Harry Ligget,' Lang whispered as the three passed. Hall heard a guard call out a jocular remark to the bogus *Unteroffizier.* The accented reply immediately aroused suspicion that this was another Kriegie attempt at escape. The three joined Hall and Lang in the 'cooler', which was so crowded that the camp authorities were forced to abandon the usual sentence of solitary confinement. The Kriegies were three or four to a cell.

Despite careful checking by the guards, several soldiers had made the journey to Sagan and an equal number of airmen joined the army working parties outside Lamsdorf. Jimmy Howe complained with a smile, 'RAF men are unreliable as members of the Stalag 8B dance band. Whenever I need them they have either escaped or are doing "solitary" in the cooler.'

At the age of nineteen, Sgt Harry Wink had completed a remarkable 41 operations when he was shot down in the early evening of 9 June 1941. He was the wireless operator in a Wellington from 9 Squadron sent to attack a convoy which had been sighted off the Dutch coast. The Wellington carried a 1,000lb armour-piercing bomb as well as a mine. Perhaps the convoy had already made port, or perhaps the information concerning its whereabouts was wrong; certainly the crew of the Wellington could not find it. Instead, the crew decided to attack German shipping off Zeebrugge, a dangerous venture for a summer evening. Heavy flak quickly found its target and fire ripped through the fuselage of the Wellington. All but the pilot baled out over the sea and were picked up by a German patrol boat within the hour.

For three days they were held in prison in Zeebrugge, then they were transferred to Dulag Luft and then to Stalag 8B, Lamsdorf.

THE TERRIBLE TWINS
Ever since the battle-cruiser *Scharnhorst* had sunk the armed merchant cruiser HMS *Rawalpindi* and then, during the Norwegian campaign, despatched the aircraft carrier HMS *Glorious* and a couple of British destroyers to the bottom of the sea, the Royal Navy had developed a healthy respect for her and her sister ship, the *Gneisenau.* In their last Atlantic foray the two battle-cruisers had between them destroyed 22

merchant ships. Now, in July 1941, the battle-cruisers were bottled up in Brest harbour undergoing repairs. It was a chance for Bomber Command to put them out of commission altogether.

Command knew well the terrible losses it had incurred in previous daylight raids, but it was felt that on this occasion the crews *had* to see their target, so a powerful attack by some 150 bombers was planned. At the last moment, as if to frustrate Bomber Command's plans, *Scharnhorst* was moved to La Pallice, so the attacking force had to be split. Fifteen unescorted Halifaxes were to attack the *Scharnhorst* at La Pallice; the remainder, including eighteen Hampdens, were to draw up the fighters over Brest. Seventeen aircraft were lost that day.

Hampden wireless operator/air gunner Sgt Allen Clarke was a wiry, compact man who could fit easily into the close confines of the 'Flying Suitcase'. Messerschmitt fighters attacked his aircraft as it flew from the target. Within seconds, the port engine was blazing and the life of the Hampden was numbered in seconds. Baling out, three of the crew went into the sea. The navigator died in the aircraft.

With other airmen taken that day, Clarke was soon to find himself imprisoned in Stalag 3E at Kirchain, just south of Berlin. There Clarke and his companions learned what it was to be hungry. One loaf of the dry, sawdust bread was issued for each group of five men, and a knife with which to divide the loaves into portions was lent by the Germans to each room of 50 men. In an unforgettable routine the loaves were cut with great care and accuracy and distributed to the tables. There a rota was maintained to ensure that each man took his turn to have the end of a loaf. One sharp-eyed Kriegie saw that the man who had cut the loaves scooped up and ate the crumbs left on the table. Thereafter, a rota had to be kept for each man in turn to have the crumbs. Some men kept their crusts of bread, pulped them into a mash with water, laid them in a tray in the sun and had some sort of caked material when it dried.

As a punishment, after an abortive escape attempt through a tunnel lined throughout with bedboards, the men had their boots and shoes removed by the Germans and exchanged for agonisingly pain-inducing wooden clogs or sabots. They were forced at machine-gun point to walk without rest or relief round a field of long grass. To keep the clogs on their feet it was necessary to slide or slouch along in increasing pain. Some Kriegies collapsed but were forced to their feet and made to stagger onward. Their footwear was never returned and the Kriegies found it easier to walk around barefoot.

How could they get their revenge for the ill-treatment they received from the Germans? One day the prisoners were ordered to transfer a large number of oil-fired hurricane lamps from a store just outside the camp to a waiting lorry. A chain of Kriegies was formed and the lamps were passed down the chain but, by the time they reached the lorry, all the lamps were useless. Every wick had been removed and a hole was punched into the bottom of each oil chamber.

HARVEST MOON

The Hampden was virtually obsolete but brave crews still took the inadequate machine into perilous skies. The night of 7 September 1941 was a lovely night for flying, with a full harvest moon, a cloudless sky and the flickering lights of the aurora borealis as 'J' for Johnny of 50 Squadron took off from Swinderby. The main force was bound for Berlin; 'J' for Johnny, captained by Sgt Dennis Good, with Sgt Douglas Endsor as second pilot and navigator, was part of a diversionary group whose target was Kiel. The other members of the crew were wireless operator Sgt 'Willie' Williamson and air gunner Sgt Iain MacDonald.

As they approached Kiel from the north, the crew could see plenty of activity in the target area. Good attacked from about 18,000 feet, the bomb load was released and, within seconds, flak was bursting around the Hampden. A second salvo shattered the nose and both engines were hit. 'J' for Johnny headed for Sweden. Over the Baltic, with both engines ablaze, the crew realised that their only chance was to turn back and, once over land, to bale out.

They baled out, in the vicinity of Oldenburg, just after midnight. The Hampden was then flying at 12,000 feet. Moments after he left the aircraft, Doug Endsor heard the Hampden explode and was 'amazed how quiet everything then seemed'. Landing in a field near a hayrick, he scrabbled his parachute into the hay and dropped off to sleep, 'very thankful to be alive but envying the chaps flying above on their way back home to eggs and bacon'.

With the breaking of dawn, Endsor decided to knock on the door of a farmhouse, but there was no response. He had not walked far before he discovered Williamson, who had landed safely on a farm and breakfasted well. Almost immediately, an *SS* policeman arrived on a motor-cycle and their days of freedom were over. At a nearby station they joined MacDonald and Good. All were taken by train to Dulag Luft and later to Stalag 8B Lamsdorf.

GEE

Adolf Hitler was so confident that Russian resistance would soon collapse that, on 14 August 1941, he issued a directive about an imminent reduction in *Wehrmacht* strength, urging greater concentration on the production of ships and planes for the destruction of Britain. RAF men in the prisoner-of-war camps, although confident of victory against all odds, could almost understand his reasoning.

Up to the autumn of 1941 the advance of the *Wehrmacht* into Russia was rapid and effective. Hundreds of thousands of prisoners trekked into Germany to become slave labourers until their deaths by shooting, overwork or starvation. The cities of Kiev and Odessa were under relentless attack and Leningrad was besieged. To relieve the weight bearing on the hard-pressed Red Army, Stalin demanded the immediate launching of a Second Front, but Britain was in no position to attempt a landing on the Continent alone. There was just one way to help – a bomber offensive. But here, too, there were difficulties.

It was at this time that the first service trials of GEE, a navigational aid, took place. Three widely separated radio stations transmitted a train of synchronised pulses, in a set order, from which a decoder in the aircraft could calculate the time differences between the two outer beams and the central master. From these time differences was calculated the distances of the aircraft from each slave and the master. A point where each constantly moving line crossed the other gave the position of the aircraft. The navigator, by reference to a GEE map, could obtain a reasonably accurate fix while at a maximum distance of 400 miles. The accuracy of the system improved at a shorter range. The great Ruhr industrial complex of vital factories and mines was well within the operational range of GEE, as 115 Squadron Wellingtons proved in a test.

The navigational aid was just in time to improve on the damning results of the Butt report. The report showed that of those crews who claimed they had attacked their target, only one in three got within five miles. Inaccuracy increased the deeper the bomber penetrated into Germany. Accuracy also declined when opposition and industrial haze was at its most intense – as in the Ruhr – and as the moon waned. A final indictment summed up by apparently proving that only one in five aircraft got within five miles of its target. GEE was more than just opportune – if the whole bomber offensive was not to be a complete waste of life, time, effort and money, GEE was vital – yet, on 18 August, Bomber Command was told that GEE would not be used again until sufficient aircraft were equipped and the crews trained. An aircraft fitted with GEE had been lost on a raid on Hanover and although demolition charges had been fitted, there was no way of knowing whether the demolition had been successful. Even had the charges worked, the Germans would have known that something special had been destroyed.

ORDEAL AT SEA

One aircraft flying to Berlin on the icy night of 7 November 1941 was a Whitley V. The cloud base looked solid enough 'to get out and take a stroll' and the air was bitterly cold. Over Kiel a flak burst set the port engine on fire. The pilot, Squadron Leader Peter Dickenson, feathered the propeller and the fire extinguishers worked successfully, but despite jettisoning the bombs and anything else movable, height could not be maintained on one engine. With 200 miles to go against a 90mph headwind, the rapid loss of height and the overheating starboard engine, the end was inevitable. As the engine faltered and the mountainous, curling waves snatched at the aircraft, the crew braced themselves as Dickenson cut the throttle.

The Whitley planed down the side of a huge wave and ploughed through the next with a bone-shattering crash. Second pilot Brian Walley was up to his chest in the water before he could struggle free from the tangled wreckage, leaving his left boot behind. He clambered, and half swam, through the open top hatch to see Sqdn Ldr Dickenson, navigator F/O David Simpson, wireless operator Sgt Chambers and air gunner Sgt Carpenter already sitting in the rubber dinghy. One moment the dinghy was ten feet below in the trough of a wave, and the next ten feet above on the crest. Jumping when he judged the moment right, Walley was dragged aboard. and lay there gasping.

But their immediate danger had not passed; the umbilical cord, necessary to prevent the dinghy being prematurely swept away, was still firmly attached to the rapidly sinking Whitley. Dickenson did not hesitate; he dived overboard and swam to the submerging fuselage. Just as the dinghy was on the point of being dragged under as the Whitley sank, the cord was freed, the dinghy righted and Peter Dickenson's head surfaced a yard away. With a couple of strokes he reached out and grasped the thwarts of the dinghy, gripping hard while the others in the dinghy grabbed hold of him.

'Don't let go lads,' he gasped, 'or I'm a goner.'

Walley, Chambers, Carpenter and Simpson held tightly to Dickenson's arms and, when he had recovered sufficiently, hauled their skipper into the dinghy. Looking over the side, Walley could see the landing lights of their aircraft twenty feet below the waves. Another wave rolled by and the lights disappeared. Walley realised then that there was just a few thousandths of an inch of rubberised fabric between the crew and a watery grave.

There would be no hope of rescue before daylight, so the airmen searched among the floating wreckage and items in the dinghy to check their supplies. There was an air pump, fresh water, a repair kit, a knife, two distress signals and a pack of emergency rations. It was a good start. The duffle bag, with the flasks and sandwiches, had been left in the fuselage in the flurry of action.

Dickenson, 'who must have had a bellyful of sea water', was the first to be sick. The rest of the crew followed suit but eventually settled down while the dinghy rolled from one wave to the next, turning and tossing like a cork in a pan of boiling water. Walley's leg was now just one dull ache. He was sure that the thighbone was fractured and his kneecap broken across. His right thigh was severely lacerated and bruised. The other crewmen were unscratched.

As dawn broke on the desolate scene, Walley studied his companions. Stubbled, wan faces stared back at him. Huddled together for warmth, soaked to the skin and chilled to the bone, they lay inert with little flecks of ice peppering their clothing. Walley's estimation of his skipper rose even higher when Dickenson suggested in a humble voice that they should turn their thoughts to God and pray for succour.

To their alarm, they found the edge of the rubber dinghy felt softer. A seam was leaking. They had to pump and bale out with a tin. Walley used his other boot as an extra bailer. Then, when they were on the crest of a wave, a powerful gust of wind picked them up bodily, overturned the dinghy and threw them all into the sea.

Chambers and Carpenter disappeared among the huge breakers. They were not seen again. The remaining three could not muster enough strength to right the dinghy and climb back. Weighed down with waterlogged flying kit, they spent an hour trying, until Walley decided that he had had enough. Swimming away from the dinghy, he felt that drowning was preferable to this unequal and hopeless struggle. It is said that a drowning person's life passes before him at such a moment, but Walley had a vision. Quite clearly he saw his mother sitting in her favourite chair, her Bible in her hands, talking to him.

'Go back son,' she said, 'you're in God's hands.'

He turned in the water to see Canadian Simpson roll over the edge into the dinghy and then help Dickenson on board. Brian Walley was next. They were out of the water but had lost everything in the capsizing, and the edges of the dinghy were softening. Taking it in turns, the weak men blew into the inlet valve and held their fingers against the leaking seam. Throughout the day the storm showed no signs of abating and night came again all too soon.

Then Simpson cracked. Staggering to his feet, he told the others that he was going to climb out of the dinghy and walk home. There was a horrifying risk that he would capsize the dinghy but the others managed to restrain him. As he quietened down he seemed to sleep fitfully until midnight when, with hardly a murmur, he died. The two survivors looked at each other with compassion and dismay. Had David Simpson not climbed back into the dinghy and helped them scramble aboard, neither of them would be there now. Could that have been only this morning?

The second day dawned. Only Walley now had the ability to blow occasionally into the inlet valve, but his strength was waning. He believed that the storm was blowing itself out and they were shipping less water. About midday he thought he saw land but his eyes were so encrusted and lacerated with salt spray that opening them at all was difficult. When, on the next wave-crest, he could see nothing, he fell into the deepest despair, but an hour later hope revived; there *was* land ahead. He shook Sqdn Ldr Dickenson to tell him, but Dickenson just lifted his head, barely opened his eyes and lapsed back into unconsciousness. Walley watched in mute anguish as his skipper drew a last rattling breath. Then Brian Walley was alone in a leaking rubber dinghy in the rough, cold waves of the North Sea with the bodies of his comrades.

It could not be long to nightfall. His bruised, battered and numbed body no longer ached. He felt quite comfortable, was sure that he was settling down for his last sleep and was too tired to care.

The noise of the seaplane seemed to fill the sky as it swooped above him. He raised a weary arm and tried to wave. There were black crosses on the wings but that did not matter, the seaplane was his last hope. As the Heinkel turned and taxied towards Walley, the front gunner swung his machine-gun round towards him. Walley found himself looking straight down the gun barrel. Half expecting a burst of fire, he found himself saying, 'Oh God, not after all this.'

The German airmen lifted Walley and the bodies of his comrades on board, stripped him, wrapped him in warm towels and blankets and, when he asked for a drink, he was given a bottle of cognac. Then followed a haze of stretchers, ambulances, interminable corridors and five doctors who worked to keep him alive. He remembers one of them saying, 'For you the war is over, no?' He couldn't have cared less.

'WHO'S TAKING YOU HOME TONIGHT?'
(popular song title of the 1940s)

The highs and lows of Kriegie hopes were mentally exhausting and, for young and active men, close confinement was debilitating, unless an absorbing interest filled the mind. Even when there was adequate food and a chance to achieve and retain physical fitness, the mind had to be occupied. The obvious preoccupation was escape but there, too, the discovery by the Germans of plans and the loss of the gruelling, secret work of months or years was to plunge some men into unplumbable depths of black despair. A Kriegie who was 'wire happy' needed at least one other man to keep a constant eye on him. Attempted suicides were rare but they happened. Hanging oneself was difficult because a Kriegie was rarely alone, but the lethal slash by a razor-blade across the wrists or throat was achieved in seconds. So, too, was the step across the warning wire in full view of the *Posten* in the 'Goon Boxes', or those patrolling outside. The *Posten* had orders to shoot and, in most cases, they did not hesitate. Over the years several men, who could wait no longer, were dragged off the tangled wire, their bodies riddled with machine-gun bullets, their minds at peace at last, but leaving their friends sorrowing, mentally exhausted and blaming themselves.

Books began to arrive from the YMCA and the International Red Cross, and a library service was initiated. Organising and running a library gave some men a feeling of doing a necessary and welcome job. To the readers it was a matchless boon. Discussion groups sprang up on every subject under the sun and talks by those who had previously worked in interesting occupations were popular. Other groups were formed by people native to particular areas, such as White and Red Rose clubs, Burns Clubs and national groups.

For married men, the pangs of realising that their children were growing up without them, and never knowing when or if ever they would see them again, was particularly hard to bear. Unmarried men were aware that Britain was full of servicemen and foreign troops and that wartime had led to a laxity in manners and a friendliness among people that had broken down pre-war reserve. Suspicions about fiancées and young wives festered in circumstances where men were helplessly confined, hundreds of miles from their loved ones and out of touch for long periods.

The apparently unstoppable advance of the *Wehrmacht* into Russia was a further cause for depression and the 'home for Christmas' hope had to be revised. If there was any compensation, it was that the Germans were almost fully occupied with the 'Eastern Front' and unable to devote their undivided attention to Britain. Obviously too, the forces in Britain were being enlarged, armed and trained. Yet, freedom seemed a very distant prospect. Help from the United States had achieved massive proportions but it was certain that unless America joined Britain in the armed conflict against Germany, there was no foreseeable chance of the Kriegies' release.

Russian prisoners brought with them something the Germans feared almost as much as the Asiatic hordes: the lice-carried disease, typhus. Panic-stricken that typhus would run rife among their troops, the *Oberkommando der Wehrmacht* ordered that all German servicemen and Allied prisoners were to be inoculated. The Kriegies at Barth flatly refused, having heard rumours of the killing of concentration camp prisoners by injection. Some were convinced that the injections were to induce impotence as part of a programme to ensure only the survival of the *Herrenvolk*. These theories were not so fanciful, but the Kriegies eventually submitted when the Germans, surprisingly, agreed to a suggestion from 'Dixie' Deans, that they should inoculate one man from the nearby flak school for every prisoner, the procedure to be overseen by British senior men. The jab was applied to the fleshy part of the left breast and the Kriegies were gratified to see that trainees from the *Luftwaffe* flak school had as many men keel over as they.

The RAF Kriegies were entering a period of the war when life was measurably easier. The early prisoners had suffered hunger, cold, disease and acute discomfort, particularly during the winter of 1940-1. Now it was changing; some parcels of food were delivered to the camp, which made life more tolerable. Red Cross food should have been a supplement to the rations supplied by the German authorities, but it became a replacement. The Germans still only supplied such items as a small portion of brown sawdust bread, rotten potatoes, occasional weak millet soup, uneatable fish cheese or occasional highly brined sauerkraut. New prisoners still found hunger the main cause of their misery but to those who had experienced the rigours of the previous winter and had adjusted to the shortages, such conditions seemed almost luxurious.

But the extreme cold sapped energy. Washed clothes, hung out to dry, immediately froze. The watery, so-called milk soup, collected hot from the cookhouse across the *Appell* ground, carried a layer of surface ice by the time a Kriegie had returned to his hut. Should he run a comb dipped in water through his hair, then carelessly leave his head uncovered when outside, the wet hair would freeze. The rooms, crowded and insanitary, dripped condensation continually so that men sleeping in the upper bunks would wake from a troubled sleep to find their clothing soaked. At Lamsdorf the condensation collected on the concrete floor, making it an ice-rink by morning, and the inside walls carried a thick layer of ice from condensed frozen breath.

When typhus attacked the Russians in their compound at Lamsdorf, the Kriegies were worried that the disease would thrive among men confined in a cramped space and insanitary conditions. 'Smudge' Coles noted the tarpaulin-covered bodies in a cart that left the Russian compound daily. The Kriegies took every precaution possible in the conditions, shaved every hair from their bodies, scrubbed their clothing and shivered until they were dry. The Germans regularly took palliasses and clothing to the camp 'de-louser', where the lice were gassed. This heat and gas treatment did not seem to kill the lice eggs in the seams. The grey crawlers soon reappeared.

In most prison camps throughout Germany and Poland, a similar delousing procedure was taking place. The method was to place the clothing and bedding in a sealed room, where it was steam-heated and disinfected. The strong fumes of the disinfectant gases persisted for more than twelve hours but the Kriegies did not mind too much. Apart from temporarily getting rid of the lice, they had the chance of a communal hot shower, perhaps the only opportunity of a good wash in a year.

As Christmas 1941 neared, hopes of being at home were abandoned and most camps organised a concert, play or pantomime. Materials were scrounged in the same way as escape items.

At Barth, on 1 December 1941, photographs were taken of groups of Kriegies with old-fashioned magnesium flashes. Suspicious about their use for propaganda, the Kriegies were at first reluctant to be photographed, but the assurance of the 'tame' interpreter that each man would receive copies and that it might be possible to send some home, was irresistible.

News of the Japanese attack on Pearl Harbor on 7 December stunned Kriegies throughout Germany. Incredulity gave way to joy. At last, hope glittered on the horizon. The aggression of the Japanese seemed foolhardy in the extreme and only a few sagacious pundits had any inkling of the shocks and the tragedies that were to come.

In New York at the time of Pearl Harbor was Air Marshal Sir Arthur Harris, whose efforts to obtain munitions came to a halt with an embargo on all exports, due to America's own sudden and serious situation.

Would America be preoccupied with the Pacific or would she help in the West? Churchill set to work to persuade the United States Government that the European war should be settled first. Happily for Britain, President Franklin D. Roosevelt, his special adviser Harry Hopkins, US Army General George Marshall and US Air Force General Henry 'Hap' Arnold agreed. Only US Navy Admiral Ernest King felt that the navy alone could win the war in the Pacific if given a greater share of the resources.

NO OTHER MEDICINE
The miserable have no other medicine
But only hope... — Shakespeare

On the afternoon of Christmas Eve 1941, snow began to fall again at Stalag 3E Kirchain. To Alex Kerr it was like a gentle white mantle which softened outlines and made even the surrounding barbed wire look like sparkling silver garlands. So very different to his native Australia. To give the huts a festive appearance there were decorations made from tinfoil and cardboard from the Red Cross parcels. In the evening, Kerr went to a crude pantomime (heroine Miss Putten Take) on an equally crude stage. The sing-song that followed the show was too much for him and he stole out into the night. Even the constellations in the brilliant starry spectacle overhead were different from those above his home in Australia. He had to be alone – he had to hide his tears of overwhelming homesickness.

Sergeant Don Boutle, observer on a 115 Squadron Wellington, found Christmas 1941 quite a pleasant occasion, despite his being a prisoner. Boutle had been injured when his plane crash-landed near Louvain in Belgium on 6 August. Now he was comfortably settled in a ward of the Institut Bordet in Brussels, where the treatment and Red Cross food made life happier.

The Red Cross sister in charge of the ward spoke excellent English and was in the unusual position of having relatives fighting on both sides. The lady, who had spent many years living in Colchester, had a brother in the *Afrika Korps* and a cousin in the Brigade of Guards, also serving in North Africa.

During the warmer weather Boutle and the other prisoners at the Institut had been able to sunbathe on the roof; now, in midwinter, their time was spent in the ward, but it was far from unpleasant. Belgian friends sent in packages containing, among other welcome gifts, apples, sweets and Belgian cigarettes. Novels in English and card games helped to pass the time and the walking patients found keeping the ward clean and making the beds an easy task.

The hospital was overcrowded, with German wounded in beds lining the corridors. At Christmas the hospital was decorated throughout with fir trees, garlands and holly. Belgians had sent in bottles of wine, fruit and jellies for the prisoners. With the addition of Red Cross food, the table was loaded with cakes, chocolate biscuits and trifles. For dinner there was pork, peas, asparagus and potatoes and presents from the officer-prisoners. Small wonder that Boutle described Christmas as very enjoyable in spite of the confined circumstances.

Ron Damman, however, at Lamsdorf, saw Russians so hungry that they resorted to swatting flies and eating them. A piled-high cartload of bodies left their compound daily.

Reverses in the war, the dark depth of the winter bringing the interminable nights when they were locked inside, the shuttered windows, the thick claustrophobic atmosphere of too many men in a confined and closed room, could have spawned fractious quarrels; yet arguments were few and were rarely about food, which was strictly and accurately divided, although it was generally assumed that those in the 'Rackets' – the men working in the cook-house – had a larger portion of what bellyfilling and nutritious food entered the compounds.

The shortage of food varied, much depending on the ease or difficulty with which the International Red Cross could find a route to the camps in Germany and her occupied territories. The Germans naturally gave preference to the transport of war material and troops; supplies for enemy prisoners had the lowest priority. The bombing by the RAF of railway marshalling yards and junctions worsened the situation.

A poignant and abiding memory of those low days of Christmas 1941 is of the men lying silently on their bunks (there was nowhere else to go), listening intently while Frank Hunt played 'Silent Night' on his violin. From the *Vorlager* German voices could be heard singing the same tune, '*Stille Nacht, Heilige Nacht*'.

The year ended in an atmosphere of melancholy for RAF men at Lamsdorf. Their compound was surrounded by other compounds, making the outside world seem even further away and heightening their feeling of dependence on the Germans who controlled what came in. The Silesian winter was one of the coldest for many years; snow was constantly falling and lay deep. Christmas had passed and the chief thoughts of the Kriegies were centred on how to keep warm. Fuel for heating was scarce. Sgt Jeffrey Reid decided to try to reach a piece of rough wooden cladding that the Germans had erected against part of the barbed wire between the compounds. The Germans said it was there to control drifting snow, but the constant rocking of the wind had caused part of the wood to loosen, and this Reid endeavoured to pull away for firewood. That he went over the warning wire to reach the wood, there is no doubt, though some said that the wire was obscured by deep snow. The noise of the splintering wood brought a few of the Kriegies to the window. Jeffrey Reid was seen by guards and two shots echoed and re-echoed across the camp. Although it was dark, in the bright snow and against the wood, he must have been a clear target. Sgt Bill Lamberton was in the latrine block when he heard a shot and was hustled to Block 16 by a furious rifle-wielding guard. As he ran, he saw a dark shape lying in the snow beside the fence. *Another shot was then fired.*

There was an immediate surge of anger among the RAF men in the *Straflager.* It was obvious that Reid was not about to make an escape attempt, the shooting was cold-blooded murder. Sgt Tom Mutton, who bunked next to Reid, said the first shot was from a *Posten* tower and the second from a guard patrolling the wire. Some claimed it was the grim work of the *Unteroffizier* 'Ukrainian Joe' Küssel, that he challenged Reid and shot him as he turned with his arms raised.

The sound of the shots brought shouting guards running into the compound, rifles unslung. Their job was to keep the Kriegies away from the windows. Tempers continued to rise as Reid's body lay in the snow for 30 minutes before medical staff were allowed to approach. Sgt Ray Scruton-Evans remembers that the situation nearly erupted into a riot and Sgt David Denchfield felt that a 'hair trigger' atmosphere existed for days. Block Leader Flt Sgt Taylor-Gill contacted British medical officers in the camp and an enquiry began. The guard and his officer swore that only one shot had been fired.

Sgt Desmond Dunphy, another member of Hut 16A, heard from Lamsdorf Hospital that British Army doctors were not allowed to examine Reid's body, but Lamberton says that one British MO sneaked into the mortuary and found the body had two bullet holes.

Rumours persisted after the shooting that a guard, rejoicing in the Kriegie-donated name of 'Wanker's Doom', had been posted to the dreaded *Ostfront* and that the guards themselves had been upset that this individual had opened fire so unnecessarily.

Two days after the shooting, Jeffrey Reid was buried in the local cemetery at Lamsdorf, Army Padre Capt A. G. Robinson officiating at the funeral.

As official codes at Lamsdorf were still unsure, Sgt Roy Kilminster was asked to send the details of Reid's shooting to the Air Ministry via a code operating between him and his brother.

With 1942 approaching, the thoughts of the prisoners in all the camps turned to hopes of being home before the end of the new year. The possibility of future release was almost always measured by Christmas, and now that the United States and Soviet Russia were fighting on the Allied side, there was at least a chance that this time it might come true.

But Jeffrey Reid, one of three survivors of a blazing Wellington, would not be at home with his family next Christmas. He had spent his last Christmas cold and hungry and then he had died a cruel and needless death in the snow beside the barbed wire of a German prison camp.

PART 3

1942

THE NEW BOSS

When Sir Arthur Harris returned from his American mission in January 1942, Air Chief Marshal Sir Charles Portal quickly promoted him to Commander-in-Chief of Bomber Command. When he assumed command Harris had just over 300 medium and heavy bombers with crews, plus 50 light bombers which were unsuitable for night operations. Harris, like his boss Portal, had a vision of a 4,000-strong heavy bomber force with which to attack Germany. There was a very long way to go.

In Britain posters were now appearing carrying a picture of a surprisingly benevolent-looking Stalin with the legend 'HELP UNCLE JOE – SECOND FRONT NOW!' Russia was at her lowest ebb, the winter counter-offensive had petered out but this stage was really the last in which Germany could win the war. The *Wehrmacht* was no longer the great fighting force of the previous summer. Nominally there were more German Army divisions in the field but the actual numbers in each division were severely reduced. Harris believed that, given enough bombers and crews, a Second Front would not be necessary and, even with the small present force, a crushing bomber campaign was a very good substitute.

There was rarely a night now that Bomber and Coastal Command were not operating somewhere in Europe, if only on 'Gardening' or 'Nickel' raids. The bombs of the Royal Air Force were the only proof of opposition to the Nazi regime that the oppressed people of Europe could see, and every bomb that fell on the hated, tyrannical occupiers was greeted with concealed rejoicing. But the losses that Bomber Command was suffering could not possibly be sustained. It was hoped by the commanders that improving spring weather and the new navigation aids would reduce losses and that the increased capacity of the coming four-engined bombers would enable Bomber Command to attack targets with greater power and precision. There was an urgency for Harris to prove that Bomber Command was an effective force with war-winning potential.

When the news of Sir Stafford Cripps's speech criticising Bomber Command seeped through to the thousands of prisoners in German hands, they were horrified at the thought that this man could be condemning them to more years behind wire while the European theatre was put on hold until the Allies had attended to the Pacific conflict. The dismay of the Kriegies was even greater than that of Harris.

The Lancaster changed Bomber Command; its bomb-carrying capacity, its speed, climbing power, resilience and the affection in which it was held by its crews, ensured its high position in the annals of the command. The Lancaster made its first operational flight on the night of 3–4 March 1942, when 44 Squadron dropped mines off the coast of Germany.

Sir Arthur Harris nevertheless considered the outlook for crews as desperate. Other units were continually poaching personnel, even from the Operational Training Units. Other men were posted for duties all over the world. Harris called it a heedless and fantastic extravagance.

The loss of two trained pilots on each downed aircraft was also leading to a serious deficiency. At the end of March 1942 Portal and the Air Council decided to drop the carrying of a second pilot in heavy and medium bombers. The new flight engineers were to become 'pilots' mates' in the heavies. Front gunners were to be trained as bomb aimers, thus relieving over-burdened navigators of that responsibility. In twin-engined bombers, such as the Wellington, bomb aimers would function as second pilots except when a 'sprog' pilot was being blooded.

Harris wanted his aircrews to carry out two operational tours and two Operational Training Unit tours and not to take leave in good flying weather. In long periods of good weather they were to be recalled from leave and stood down during bad periods. The plan for intensive use of aircrews took little account of equally intensifying *Luftwaffe* nightfighter and flak opposition.

If Sir Arthur had a weakness, it was that he had small patience with the other services; he frequently accused them of indecision and even incompetence. Every criticism of the Royal Air Force by them was, in his opinion, unjustified and merely a cover-up for their own inefficiency and ineptness.

It was about this time that Group Captain Bufton, the Deputy Director of Bomber Operations, suggested in a minute to Harris that he should designate six squadrons for the job of marking targets. Harris would have none of it, perhaps because the idea came from Bufton.

'I am strongly opposed,' he said, 'to creating any sort of élite force.' In a reply to Bufton at Air Ministry he wrote: 'I am not prepared to accept all the very serious disadvantages of a Corps d'Elite in order to secure possibly some improvement of methods which are already proving reasonably sure and certainly very costly to the enemy.' Harris was concerned that there might be 'a serious loss of morale and efficiency to the other squadrons'.

DISAPPOINTMENT AT MÜHLBERG

At Stalag 4B Mühlberg the German issue of food was at an all-time low during the harsh weather of early 1942. The Red Cross parcels dwindled, then stopped, and the Kriegies' faces acquired the haunted, lacklustre look which comes with near-starvation. One bleak Saturday morning a solitary lorry arrived with parcels. Hopes rose and were immediately dashed when it was found that the severely limited supplies consisted of 'invalid' parcels containing just the odd tin of Bemax, Benger's Food, small tins of sardines and so on: little to fill hundreds of empty bellies.

When the parcels were opened it was plain that the most anyone could expect was one item per person. Lots were drawn and soon the room buzzed with excited comments on the relative merits of prunes, Marmite and so on. Only Sgt Bob Anderson was quiet, supine on a bottom bunk and staring blankly at his prize in the draw. The tin of kaolin he held was no doubt an excellent plaster for boils.

'OSTFRONT FÜR SIE'

On the morning of a barrack search at Barth the Kriegies were forced outdoors in the compound as the 'ferrets' ransacked every room in the huts. Guards stood over boxes of confiscated personal property outside. The airmen were standing in groups, talking or sitting on the only remaining grass in the compound, near the warning wire.

One man rolled over, his foot inches from the prohibited space. Without hesitation, a patrolling guard outside the wire raised his rifle and fired at the Kriegie, the bullet entering and smashing bones in the man's ankle. Others ran to his aid and quickly applied a tourniquet to the leg of the shocked, ashen-faced man. At the main gate, Kriegies were shouting for medical aid. It was then that a small crowd turned their full, furious attention to the guard, still patrolling surlily outside the wire and trying to ignore the shouting Kriegies. Fists were shaken at him and cries of 'murdering bastard' echoed round the compound until the German unslung his rifle again and clicked back the bolt. The fine judgement of how far to push a guard had been exceeded. He was obviously prepared to fire again. Luckily, the sound of the shot had brought *Oberfeldwebel* Glemnitz at a run, and the guard was quickly replaced and hustled away to the now threatening Kriegie cry of '*Ostfront für sie!*'

'Dixie' Deans protested to the *Kommandant* about the shooting. Such was the anger among the prisoners, said Deans, that he could not be held responsible for the trigger-happy guard's safety should he enter the compound. It was bravado; there was nothing the Kriegies could do that would not entail severe reprisals. Nevertheless, the guilty guard was posted away – it was hoped to the Russian front.

In this 'posting' threat the Kriegies found that they had an effective blackmail lever with which to prise contraband and information from those of the camp staff who feared that the Kriegies might actually have this power to influence events. The prospect of immense distances from home, the crushing cold, the stealthily vicious partisan raids and the Russian treatment of prisoners, sent stark terror through the men with comparatively safe jobs at home in the Fatherland. Even the deadly monotony of patrolling outside the barbed wire of a prison camp, in all weathers, was infinitely preferable to fighting the 'barbarian' on the steppes, with its deprivations and eternal, paralysing fear. The sequence of *Wehrmacht* victories and the procession of Russian prisoners from the east could not disguise the fact that winter on the Russian front was hell. The words, '*Ostfront für sie!*' may not have been correct German, but the meaning was clear enough to strike fear into the hearts of home-based *Posten*.

Major Burchardt, *Kommandant* at Barth, had been a prisoner in South Africa during the Great War, spoke fluent colloquial English and hated his job. 'I do not like to see men in cages,' he once said to Sgt Gammon. 'I am a soldier not a jailer.'

During the previous spring he had allowed a few parties of some twenty Kriegies to give their parole and, under guard, go to swim in a nearby tree-screened Baltic creek. Swimming trunks were made up from anything available. Now, with spring once more in the air, the *Kommandant* would come to watch the football games and chat with the spectators, on one occasion sending his immaculately uniformed, *Luftwaffe* cadet son climbing into the tangled wire to retrieve a football. It was an astonishing display of friendliness.

THE AMERICAN 'MARKED MAN'

Pilot Officer William 'Tex' Ash from Dallas had been flying in Fighter Command since early 1941. He had listened to Hitler's speeches with loathing, hated Fascism and was determined to volunteer in any way he could to fight against the Nazis. Abruptly uprooting himself from his studies at Texas University, he made his way to Windsor, Ontario, where he joined the Royal Canadian Air Force. Now, in March 1942, 'Tex' was flying 411 Squadron Spitfires from the soggy surface of Southend Airport.

Escorting bombers on daylight raids was not a fighter pilot's favourite job, but the twelve escorted Bostons successfully attacked Commines power station and turned for home without loss, the Spitfires still in attendance. Then *Luftwaffe* fighters roared into the attack and fierce dogfights developed. The first attack was beaten off but 411 Squadron fell behind the rest of the wing and were finally engaged single-handed with the enemy. 'Tex' Ash was in the thick of the fight when his aircraft was hit. With a 'dead' engine, Ash successfully brought his Spitfire down for a crash-landing in a field near Calais.

To be suddenly alone in an occupied country was daunting but 'Tex' Ash was helped by an eighteen-year-old girl, Marthe, who passed him on to the Resistance. He was moved to Paris where he lived with a young couple in a flat in a block near the *Bois de Vincennes*. For ten weeks he waited for forged papers to be completed for an escape through Spain, but the wait was too long. Ash says: 'I was within an ace of making it when someone must have seen me, wondered what I was doing there and tipped off the *Gestapo*.'

He was arrested and sent to Dulag Luft. Thereafter he took part in an astonishing series of escape attempts. He was despatched to Stalag Luft 3 at Sagan and later in the year to Schubin. There he swapped identities with an army private, escaped from a working party and was recaptured. Then he was concerned in a tunnel escape and with a companion tried to reach Warsaw. Caught after four days, Ash managed to exchange identities once more, this time with a New Zealand sergeant pilot. Sent by the Germans to the NCOs' camp at Heydekrug, he became one of the prime movers of the tunnel that astounded the Germans when they discovered it after a dozen men had crawled out. Again Ash was recaptured but now he was a marked man. He was sent back to Stalag Luft 3 where he was kept under close surveillance. Nevertheless, he remained throughout an active member of the escape committee, always searching for a way out.

Marthe, the young girl who had initially helped Ash, subsequently joined the Resistance herself, was eventually caught and sent to a concentration camp. She survived and was awarded the *Légion d'Honneur*. Ash found her again after the war and they remained in contact until her death.

The young couple who had sheltered Ash in Paris were sent to a concentration camp. He learned after the war, to his great relief, that they survived but he was never able to find them again.

GALLIC HERO

The majority of aircrew on 150 Squadron or, indeed, any bomber squadron, were aged between 19 and 21; any flyer aged 25 was thought to be 'getting on a bit'. An airman aged 30 or more was inevitably called

'Pop'. Chris Maltby, 33 and the father of two children, was considered positively ancient.

On the night of 1 April 1942, 40 bombers attacked the Ford Motor Factory at Poissy near Paris. Crews claimed accurate bombing but photographs failed to confirm this; so 50 aircraft, including the Wellingtons of 150 Squadron, were detailed to attack the factory again. Chris Maltby was 'spare' that night, and was asked to replace a sick Canadian as rear gunner. The crew had carried out 23 operations together, apart from their second pilot who, on this occasion, was to be no less than Group Captain Webb, Commanding Officer of the station.

The previous night's attack had forewarned the flak crews. They were waiting. Maltby's Wellington was quickly hit and burst into flames. The aircraft's screaming, fiery descent ended with an explosion in a wood which fuelled a raging inferno. It seemed impossible that anyone could have survived.

A young French boy, Albert Guerbet, raced towards the scene of the crash. As he neared the roaring mass, he saw that the trees around the plane were burning, ammunition and petrol were exploding and the flames were too fierce even to look at. Yet he heard a voice calling for help. The Wellington's rear turret, broken away from the fuselage, was intact but about to burn with the rest of the aircraft. Guerbet ran to the turret. Maltby was seriously wounded but conscious and vainly trying to extricate himself from the tangle of metal and perspex. Guerbet, seared with heat, found the strength and tenacity to force open the turret doors and drag Maltby to a safe distance from the explosions and flames.

He turned again to the blaze to look for more survivors, but there were none. Others from the village began to arrive and constructed a stretcher from branches. Maltby was carried uphill for half a mile to a large house. The aircraft had crashed in the extensive grounds of 'La Banbannerie'. Although in agonising pain from a broken thigh, Maltby remained conscious throughout. To his astonishment, he found an English lady of about his own age tending his wounds. Madame Jeanne Schweisguth was the wife of a Frenchman.

The *Feldgendarmerie*, attracted by the flames, soon arrived. Maltby's wounds were too serious for any thought of escape, so he was passed to the Germans, who took him to a hospital in St Germain. It seemed a deliberate act that Maltby was placed in a ward with casualties from previous air raids, among whom there were several children. If the intention was to cause friction, it failed dismally. The children, instead, saved their chocolate ration to give to the British airman. This touching gesture so discomfited the Germans that they had Maltby transferred the next day to a Paris hospital.

The rest of the crew had perished; all that was left for the local people to find were a few charred bones on a bed of glowing cinders. The Germans collected what they could find and took them to the cemetery near Versailles. The Protestant pastor arranged a funeral service but, as the number of people likely to attend appeared to be large, the Germans forced a last-minute change of time and place. Nevertheless, when the service was held, it was in the presence of a huge crowd.

At the site of the crash, unknown hands set up a cross and flowers were placed at its foot every day. The Germans were angry and threatened the population with reprisals if the cross was not removed, so it was hidden in a thicket, later to reappear.

'THE *LUFTWAFFE* PLAYED CLEVER'

Squadron Leader Ken Campbell, commander of 403 Canadian Squadron, led the North Weald Fighter Wing into the air at 6.30 p.m. on 27 April 1942. The wing was to meet Spitfires and Hurricanes from Hornchurch and Biggin Hill for a fighter sweep through France. 403 Squadron were top cover but, having gained their height and position over the Channel, they discovered, on arrival at the French coast, 10/10ths cloud from 21,000 feet upwards. The top squadrons had to lose height to get below the cloud, and Campbell's squadron found itself just beneath the cloud base, with other squadrons in front, on either side and below, all weaving from side to side. The *Luftwaffe* fighters had, in Campbell's words, 'played clever'. Before the RAF planes had reached the cloud base, the Messerschmitts and Focke-Wulfes had split up into the cover above, periodically dropping their noses through the cloud-base, firing a burst at any aircraft in front and then rapidly zooming up into hiding. Because of this, Campbell had to concentrate upon the weave of the squadron and also watch behind for enemy aircraft popping out from the clouds.

While on a left weave, Campbell glimpsed an enemy aircraft dropping from the cloud behind his Blue One Flight Commander. Shouting a warning on the R/T, Campbell immediately had to weave to the right. Returning on a left-hand weave, he was startled to see a Spitfire turning straight into him. Instinctively he put his aircraft into a hard climb but it was too late – the flight commander's Spitfire smashed into his tail. As his Spitfire flipped over into a rapid right-hand spin, Campbell knew he had lost all control of the aircraft. The rubber ball of the hood jettison release came completely away but, suddenly, the hood fell off and Campbell released his R/T wires, oxygen fittings and Sutton harness. Striving to climb out of the cockpit, he was continually forced back by the aircraft's centripetal spin. With the fruitless struggle and lack of oxygen, he lost consciousness.

As his senses returned, Campbell felt comfortable and in a sitting position. It was with an abrupt shock that he realised that he was free-falling. Quickly pulling his 'D' ring, he was relieved to feel his fall checked as the canopy snapped open. Only then did he dare to look down. France was some 8,000 feet below.

Campbell found that he was unable to lower his chin to his chest, his right leg hung limply and, even worse, an offshore wind was blowing him out to sea. He quickly forgot his injuries and tried to side-slip his parachute to lose height quickly so that he would come down on land, but he had been weakened and, having the use of only one arm, had to resign himself to dropping into the Channel. He inflated his Mae West and struck his harness quick release as his feet touched the water. Spluttering to the surface, he hauled in his pilot dinghy lanyard but to his dismay there was only a frayed end.

Campbell's efforts to swim towards the French shore were useless, but he was eventually picked up by a French fishing vessel. The crew were kind and gentle; they took Campbell below decks, helped him out of his wet uniform and lent him a large white seafaring pullover. With his little French he asked the captain if he could hide, but the latter replied ruefully:

'The Germans will also have seen your parachute and will be here for you immediately.'

It seemed only seconds before Campbell felt a bump at the side of the vessel and a gabble of guttural voices. Quickly handing the captain his escape tin, Campbell asked him to hide it and use the money, just as a *Luftwaffe Obergefreiter* came clattering down the gangway. Campbell, painfully hopping on one leg, climbed the forecastle gangway to the deck, then hopped to the bulwarks, where a small boat was held against the side. He was too slow for the *Obergefreiter*, who pushed him over the side into the boat. Showing the cussedness with which he would approach prisoner-of-war life, Campbell flatly refused to allow one of the German crew to photograph him full-face.

The *Obergefreiter* called six *Soldaten* to carry Campbell the quarter of a mile to a boarding house, on the front at Le Touquet, which was being used as an officers' mess. Lying on a table in the front room, Campbell was irritated by the continual inspection by all the occupants of the mess. Annoyed with the manner in which they were staring, he complained, 'If there is anyone who understands English and considers himself a gentleman, perhaps he will have the decency to bring me a blanket?'

Nothing was said but a blanket was suddenly produced. Then Campbell was briefly examined by a German military doctor and ordered into an ambulance. After a period of silence the orderly travelling with him spoke to Campbell in English. 'I am an Austrian,' he said, 'I was conscripted without option. I wish the war was over.'

At St Omer Hospital a tubby, jolly little German surgeon straightened Campbell's dislocated shoulder and bandaged his brightly coloured, contused and swollen right leg.

Two days later, Campbell and eleven other RAF wounded were sent to Dulag Luft. The rapid move was due to new orders. Since Wing Commander Bader had made an escape attempt from St Omer Hospital earlier, it was decreed that any wounded prisoner who could stand on his feet was to be moved immediately from the hospital to Oberursel.

A month later, Campbell left Hohemark Hospital and joined 300 other officers from Dulag Luft for the train journey to Sagan. Stalag Luft 3 came as a revelation. He had never seen a prison camp before and was staggered by the double barbed wire, the *Posten* boxes, the armed guards, the raw-wood hutments, the bleak grey sandy soil and the brooding pines which surrounded this new supposedly escape-proof prison camp.

As new prisoners entered the main gate, those inside gathered round, hungry for news, 'Is London still standing? When is the invasion coming?' Campbell was startled by the motley collection of strange attire. Full uniform, half uniform plus a weird assortment of clothing, but mostly, in the fine summer weather, practically nothing. Handlebar moustaches and beards proliferated. It was easy to distinguish 'new boys' by their comparative pallor against the sun-tanned longer residents.

Sqdn Ldr Campbell was soon meeting and greeting friends, particularly among the Fighter Command men with whom he had trained or flown. Wing Commanders Ayre, Stanford-Tuck and Bader were quick to shake hands. Campbell was among old friends.

His leg and shoulder were painful, increasingly stiff and swollen due to lack of attention. Although he had received mail and was relieved that his parents knew him to be safe, Campbell felt 'like a collapsed balloon'. The relief that he had no longer to get up for 'Dawn Readiness' or fly over France on sweeps and circuses, overcame him. He felt tired and listless, his mind emptied and blank. He would only recover his interest in life as the pain in his leg eased and he was able to occupy his time in work for the prisoner community.

TAKING ON THE *TIRPITZ*

Running the gauntlet of U-boats and *Luftwaffe* bombers, the Arctic convoys had one of the most hazardous tasks of the war. Losses were heavy but it was vital to get supplies through to the hard-pressed Soviet Union. In the spring of 1942 the Admiralty was apprehensive; lying in a Norwegian fiord near Trondheim, well placed to deliver a killer blow to the brave convoys, was Germany's latest battleship, the formidable *Tirpitz*. Somehow she had to be kept out of action and the job was given to Bomber Command. Harris resented the distraction from his bombing campaign against Germany but the Navy's arguments over-persuaded the War Cabinet.

The first assault took place on the night of 30–31 March when 34 Halifaxes took off from Lossiemouth which was as near to Norway as was practicable. The raid was not a success and six bombers were lost without a single survivor. Two more sorties on consecutive nights at the end of April had doubtful results. Seven more aircraft were lost but loss of life was incredibly light. Twenty men were taken prisoner, seven evaded capture and reached Sweden. One of those was Wing Commander Donald Bennett, a former Imperial Airways pilot, author of a book on air navigation and soon to become Commanding Officer of the Pathfnder Force. Bennett's navigator on the night of 27–28 April was Sergeant T. H. A. 'Phil' Eyles.

Bennett's 10 Squadron Halifax was in the second wave, their mission to drop mines from low level. Pinpoint accuracy was essential if the mines were to hurt *Tirpitz*. The aim was to drop the mines between ship and shore, a matter of 50 feet or so. The problem was that Faetten Fiord had such steep cliffs that to fly over the battleship at low level was virtually to commit suicide since the aircraft could never be lifted over the cliffs in time. The ship was in any case covered by a heavy smoke-screen – which was a surprise to the aircrews. So the mines had to be dropped a calculated distance from a landmark, Salt Island, and from several hundred feet higher than the 150 feet suggested to crews.

The first wave of bombers were to bomb, from 6,000 feet, first the target battleship and then the gun emplacements which protected her. They had to be well clear before the low-level attack began.

Each Halifax in the second wave carried five 1,000lb spherical mines, which protruded beneath partially closed bomb-doors. As Bennett reached the moonlit coast, the defences opened up and the Halifax was hit. The rear gunner, F/L H. G. How, was wounded. A fire in a port engine was brought under control but menacing flames streamed from one of the starboard motors. Their bombing run was aborted because of the smoke-screen and Bennett turned to go in again. There was no time and on Bennett's orders Eyles released the mines, vaguely in the direction of the *Tirpitz*. Bennett strove desperately to gain more height to enable the crew to bale out. They all carried out the drill perfectly. Eyles went out first. The flight engineer, F/Sgt J. Colgan, helped the wounded rear gunner out of the aircraft and clipped Bennett's parachute on to his harness, so saving a few seconds and probably the life of his commanding officer whose parachute only just broke his fall into snow.

Bennett quickly hid his parachute in the snow and set off to attempt to reach Sweden. After an hour, as he made his way through trees in the dark, he encountered his wireless operator, Sgt C. R. S. Forbes, to the surprise of them both. The pair floundered through the snow, waded through icy streams and slid down mountainsides at night. After two days, exhausted and suffering from frostbite, they reached a house where they found sympathy and friendship. When they had rested and dried their clothes, they were escorted to the border, in two stages, by young Norwegians. When they reached a brightly lit building, they knew they were safe. They intruded on a dance, were welcomed to Sweden, then arrested and taken to an internment camp. There they were reunited with Colgan and Bennett's second pilot, Sgt Walmsley. It was not easy to persuade the Swedes to release them but Bennett exerted every kind of pressure and they were back in England within a month. The wounded How, Canadian Sgt J. D. Murray, the mid-upper gunner, and Sgt Phil Eyles were taken prisoner.

Eyles, too, had hoped to make his way to Sweden. Paw marks in the snow alarmed him. He thought they could belong to wolves and, to throw them off the scent, made his way down a cold stream until it joined a river. There were a few houses and he knocked at them. An elderly couple took him in and dried his boots and trousers. The old lady cooked a large pancake for him, but Eyles was not hungry and, when she left the room, he rolled up the pancake and put it in his pocket. On her return, believing he had scoffed the pancake, she made him another. That also went into his pocket when she was not looking.

Eyles managed to convey to his hosts, their daughter and another villager who had arrived, that he wanted to depart at moonrise. Meanwhile he slept. But someone in the small settlement evidently informed the Germans and he was awakened as soldiers rowed across the river to collect him. When they searched him, he insisted that the Norwegians leave the room before he allowed his trouser pocket to be emptied. When they found the pancakes, the Germans saw the funny side and allowed him to return the food to his pocket so that the kindly old lady was not embarrassed.

Taken by car to Trondheim, Eyles was given a guided tour of the town by his German escorts until finally he was taken to a fortress prison. A day or so later, he was taken by train to Oslo and thence to Dulag Luft.

BRISTOW AND THE FIRE POOL

In the NCOs' compound, separated by a high wooden fence from the officers, John Bristow, David Young and Peter Stubbs were working out how to get the radio working again. Some of the parts brought from Barth had been disguised as theatrical equipment and were supposed to remain in German custody until the Kriegies themselves converted one of the barracks into a theatre. The irrepressible Bristow was able, by distinctly questionable means, to recover vital parts, and by pirating electricity the trio got the all-important radio to function. Not a man to remain inactive, Bristow installed the steam-engine he had made at Barth in a steamboat which he launched in the static water tank, usually referred to as the fire pool since it was intended to be the source of water for a fire emergency. As the steamboat travelled in fine style across the water, the Germans watched with amusement and some took photographs.

Excavation for the tank had created piles of sand at the sides which gave the appearance of small dunes. With half-closed eyes and a great stretch of imagination, Kriegies lying there under the summer sun could believe, for just a moment, that they were on a sun-drenched Mediterranean beach, especially when a dip in the fire pool followed. The water changed rapidly from clear to translucent to opaque. As there was no drain, it was necessary to empty the pool with a bucket chain of sweating Kriegies and to refill it with water from the ablutions block. Most thought it was worth the effort.

Half a century later, the ruins of the fire pool and the theatre are all that remain identifiable of Stalag Luft 3.

'MEIN GOTT! – WHERE ARE THEY?'

There was a lift in morale at Stalag 3E, a small camp, when the Kriegies were allowed to march to Kirchain town, on Christmas Day 1941, to attend a service conducted by Norman Hennessy in one of the town's fine churches. By the early months of 1942, however, life had reached a depressing low for Alex Kerr. A New Year's Eve camp lottery settled on June 1942 as the optimistic date for the end of the war. Even the most pessimistic prisoner could not see it lasting longer than 1943. But Kerr was still suffering from an open and discharging stomach wound necessitating several painful visits to hospital. The fall of Singapore had been disheartening news and, even worse, there was a rumour that the Japanese had already invaded his home country, Australia. The news of the RAF raid in March on the Renault factory in Paris upset the French prisoners in the camp, some of whom violently attacked RAF men. The Germans conducted a camp search and confiscated unopened tins of food and, from then on, doors were locked and the prisoners' comparative freedom within the compound was denied. The one consolation was the tunnel, which was well under way from the room where Alex Kerr, Deryck Polley and others lived. There had been some swaps, so all occupants of the room wanted to try a break.

A sudden announcement by the Germans that they were about to concentrate all RAF men in a new camp at Sagan spurred working parties on the tunnel and their numbers increased. On 5 May, as they neared the end of their digging, a *Feldwebel* told the Kriegies that the first batch of 100 men would leave in two days; all of them continued working at the tunnel until they left. Although the work force was severely diminished, the three-month job was finished with six hours to spare before the deadline, the day on which their party was scheduled to move to Sagan, albeit without shoring the last twenty feet of the tunnel. It was 11 May 1942. Kerr had been a prisoner exactly a year and Polley nine months.

There were two ventilation shafts, but the air in the tunnel was very poor, allowing a maximum working time of half an hour per person. Work down there was confined and claustrophobic, the height and width of the tunnel being governed by the length of a bedboard, about 30 inches. There had been the usual troubles; a face collapse caused a wild panic, a front man passed out and, on another occasion, a wasp strayed into the tunnel, causing the workers a nasty half-hour in complete darkness. When a German officer kicked a rock covering an air-hole, watchers held their breath, and when two face workers could not climb out in time for a snap *Appell*, their absence had to be covered swiftly.

Alex Kerr looked at his watch and the breakout began shortly before midnight. The exit hole was just outside the perimeter wire and dangerously close. But the risk had to be taken – it was now or never. Unusually, a guard patrolled this area on the inside of the wire, which gave the escapers a chance. If they could creep from the tunnel exit and get away unseen, it could be some time before the broken earth was discovered. Deryck Polley, Alex Kerr and 50 other Kriegies emerged in twos and threes, their hands and faces blackened to camouflage them on the 100-yard crawl across the open field to the woods beyond. Kerr felt that he could only look forward in the moonlit silence. Not daring to look around, aware that at any moment a guard in a *Posten* tower might be taking a bead on the back of his head. His tongue and mouth were so dry that he could not swallow until he reached the edge of the woods and sped off to put as much distance between himself and the inevitable discovery of the exit hole. The only residents to remain in the hut were two medical orderlies who occupied a small room of their own. They replaced the trapdoor, pushed the bunk back to cover it, and waited.

The absence of 52 Kriegies was not discovered until the early morning, when they were due to depart for Sagan. A nice-mannered, elderly *Oberfeldwebel* habitually opened each hut in turn and called out: 'Good morning boys.' On this day his cry altered in mid-sentence: 'Good morning – *Mein Gott!* where are they?' In the remaining rooms frantic guards rushed the Kriegies on parade. Then they too began shouting: 'Where are they?'

The Germans were baffled. They could not see how the prisoners had been able to leave the hut, but they had made the mistake of cramming as many three-tier bunks as possible into the room. Although the bottom bunk above the trapdoor was unoccupied, it was always made-up with a palliasse, bedboards and blankets when the trapdoor was not in use. Much later, a 'ferret' found a hole in the field outside the camp, but the Germans still had no idea of the location of the entrance. The 'ferrets' hated this situation because it was then necessary for a nervous member to crawl down the exit hole and make his frightening progress along the tunnel to find the entrance in the deserted room. At least he had a torch.

For the next few nights Alex Kerr and two companions travelled through the German countryside, finding vegetables wherever possible; but it was May and few were mature or edible. They did, however, strip a small rhubarb plot, carefully cutting off the leaves and replacing them on the stumps so that in the early morning light the plot might look untouched. It was hilarious at the time but not so funny later when they had to endure stomach pains. On another night they were constantly disturbed by aircraft and explosions. During the morning a car full of *Luftwaffe* officers arrived to plot bomb positions. The Kriegies had unwittingly squatted for the night on a *Luftwaffe* practice bombing range.

For several following nights they jumped freight trains, leaping on the wagons when the train slowed at the top of a slow drag up a hill, then climbing from truck to truck, converging on the man in the centre. Roughly an hour before dawn, they would wait for a suitable slope, giving themselves enough time to find a hiding place before daybreak. But on the ninth night they made an over-hasty decision and jumped from the train in a treeless area. Whilst congratulating themselves at having jumped unseen into a large hole in a ploughed field, they were astonished to see a burly forester emerge from the gloom, pointing a shotgun at Kerr's stomach.

The Kriegies immediately claimed that they were French and spoke only French between themselves. They had heard that Allied aircrew were being maltreated by German civilians in the bombed cities and had agreed not to reveal their identities until they were in the hands of the *Wehrmacht* or the *Luftwaffe*.

The ploy failed. They were taken back to 3E where they learned that 52 Kriegies had made the break and that so far 48 had been recaptured and returned to the camp. The next day three more were brought into the room. Don Sugden and another Canadian, named Calvert, were being questioned by police near Dresden when Calvert pointed to his socks and asked if he could keep them. His action frightened the nervous young guard, who shot him through the heart, killing him instantly and leaving an unbelieving Sugden in a state of shock.

Calvert was the one casualty in a mass escape that had provided a lot of experience, sent shock waves to Berlin, severely shaken the German camp administration and engaged the attention of the *Gestapo*. Deryck Polley realised in retrospect that the escape was ill-equipped and not very professional compared with later escapes, but it was a fine effort, using the longest tunnel, 175 feet, through which a successful exit from a camp had been made.

The interrogation that followed was carried out both by the *Luftwaffe* and the *Gestapo* from Berlin. They were pleasant, offering the Kriegies cigarettes and drinks despite a lack of cooperation. Many of the escapees had been caught with forbidden possessions – clear evidence that guards had been trading. The *Gestapo* were anxious to catch them but, although the interrogations lasted several days, the identities of the guilty guards were not revealed. The Kriegies now had a life or death hold over the guards. The punishment for trading was execution. As long as the names of the guilty were withheld, the Kriegies could blackmail almost anything from the guards. Kerr and his friends lived for the moment and enjoyed unusually good food from the German cookhouse.

Before they left for Sagan, the *Gestapo* indicated to Jock Alexander, the Kriegies' senior man, that should the escapers from 3E change their minds about providing information about the commerce with the German guards, they would arrange for a representative to go to Berlin to talk with them. Now safely settled in Luft 3, the 3E escapers held a meeting and elected two representatives to take a list of the German traders to

Berlin. The representatives spent two pleasant days in Berlin being wined and dined as guests of the *Gestapo*. Several weeks later, the plotters in Sagan heard the results of their Berlin jaunt. The *Kommandant* had been shot, the Camp Administration Officer had been sentenced to ten years in jail and other guards on the list to one year.

Looking back, most of those involved felt a little guilty, although only they knew that the names on the list were not the names of the Germans who had traded with them but the names of guards who had ill-treated them. The Stalag was a camp in which violence had earlier been exhibited and prisoners had been beaten by guards and subjected to harsh treatment, ordered by the *Kommandant*. Kerr felt that it was a strange kind of poetic justice which led to the main players in this drama paying with their lives or liberty for what they did, while those who were truly guilty of trading, most of whom the Kriegies found friendly and helpful, went scot-free. But as the Germans were frequently to say as a sort of excuse, '*Krieg ist Krieg*'.

LOW-LEVEL ATTACK

In the Nissen hut which served as 460 (Australian) Squadron's briefing room, four crews learned that their target for that night, 29–30 May, was to be the Gnome Rhône aero-engine works at Gennevilliers near Paris. Theirs would be four of twelve Wellingtons which were to bomb from 2,000 feet and light up the target for 60 heavy bombers which would follow at 8,000–10,000 feet. This was something new and the procedure was, in fact, one of the experiments which preceded the formation of the Pathfinder Force.

Sergeant Calton Younger and the other three navigators plotted their courses together. Later, Younger attended an ENSA concert. Towards midnight the four Wellingtons took off. The crews had been told the target was only lightly defended, but Younger, in 'R' Robert, had a premonition and, as they flew over a moonlit Northampton, he suggested to the wireless operator, 'Go down to the bombsight and have a look at your home town.'

When they reached the target area, cones of searchlights reared up and streams of light flak criss-crossed the sky forming a vast multi-coloured tracery, beautiful but deadly. A blue beam, a master searchlight, picked up 'R' Robert and at once, like tentacles, other beams fastened on the aircraft. Younger took his place, prone, in the bombsight, saw vicious fingers of red tracer hurtling towards him and heard a crunching sound amidships. The intercom went dead and he went back to the skipper, P/O Russell Jones, to say that he would use red and green lights to give bombing directions. They heard the tail gunner, Sgt Godfrey Loder, firing from the rear turret. Loder was firing straight down the blue beam; he learned later that he had killed eleven Germans.

Another burst of flak appeared to go through the nose of the Wellington. Standing beside his skipper, Younger saw fire ripple along the starboard wing. Flames streaked past Loder's turret and he decided it was time to go. At that point, the aircraft was still flying straight and level. Meanwhile, Younger picked up Jones's parachute from its container and put it on his lap. He took a step forward and released the front gunner from his turret, opened the escape hatch and told him to jump. He returned to his skipper's side. Jones had managed to clip one side of the parachute on to the harness and Younger hastily fastened the other side before dealing with his own parachute.

'Is there any chance, Cal?' Jones asked. Younger glanced at the burning wing and said, 'No.' Suddenly the controls went, and the aircraft went into a screaming dive. Younger looked at his skipper whose face was extraordinarily tranquil. He was smiling slightly. Younger felt a kind of peace himself.

'Jump, Cal,' ordered his skipper. Time was passing in fractions of seconds. Younger saw that the front gunner was still standing by the open hatch, tugged his arm, saw that it was no use and jumped. He felt the heat of the fire, then the jerk as his parachute opened. He heard the awful roar as 'R' Robert and its bomb load hit the ground, then he crashed face-down on the earth.

About half an hour later, he came to, released the parachute, which was dragging him, and watched it blow away. Still woozy, he tore up the pages of an empty notebook and carefully hid them around the field of vegetables in which he had landed. Bombs were still crashing down and the flak was crackling noisily. Overhead he could see the heavies outlined in the moonlight and realised what an easy target, at 2,000 feet, 'R' Robert had been. He wondered what had happened to Loder and the wireless operator. Had they escaped? He knew there had been no time for the front gunner or the skipper to follow him. Russell Jones would never have jumped even if there had been time, unless he knew that he was last to leave.

It was some time before Younger found a way out of the field. He put on his cap, which had been tucked inside his battledress jacket, pulled his trouser legs over his boots and hastened away. Almost at once he met two Germans, who gazed at him curiously then offered 'Heil Hitler', to which Younger responded. Later, on an empty road, he heard the last of the bombers set course for home and felt unbearably lonely. In the early morning, after walking for about three hours, he reached Sevran where the market was being set up. He was watched and so turned into a side street and hid behind a hedge in the churchyard. He stayed all day with only Horlicks tablets and rain off the leaves to sustain him.

In the evening he was discovered by an old lady throwing dead flowers on to a nearby rubbish heap. She thought he was a drunken German and bravely approached to drive him away. When he explained who he was, she told him to wait. Soon her daughter, Hélène Buvelot, who spoke English better than he spoke French, took him into her apartment above a clinic. He had the evening meal with the family, then was sent to bed. An hour later, he was awakened. Hélène's husband, Jean Buvelot, had arrived, bringing news that the Germans had found Younger's parachute and were searching for him. Hélène produced a civilian raincoat and a beret. She had also packed a haversack with some food and a half-bottle of brandy. Jean Buvelot and his friend Jean Lelong took him to some woods and told him where he would find an empty house in which he could hide. It was after curfew and they were running a tremendous risk. Younger lost his way in the dark wood and never found the empty house. Years later he was to learn that the Buvelots had searched for him the following day.

He was on the run for eight days, walking at night and hiding, mostly in barns, during the day. One French farmer brandished an axe at him when he asked for food, and a woodcutter invited him to come back later to share with him his meagre lunch. A Belgian farmer gave him food and showed him how to wear his beret and walk like a Frenchman. On another farm he was taken into the house and dined with the family. The village barber was summoned to shave him, a kindness which caused him some apprehension when he was questioned about his activities on the loose. He walked through the town of Provins before curfew but missed the road he wanted and, on retracing his steps, was arrested by French police and handed over to the Germans.

When he revisited the town in 1949, having tried to repeat his wartime adventure. Younger learned that he should have been handed over to the Resistance and flown to England by Lysander, as were scores of airmen.

Driven to Paris, Younger was taken to *Luftwaffe* headquarters and interrogated. The German officer told him that only he and Loder had survived. Another Wellington from 460 Squadron had been shot down. The rear gunner, Sgt John Holborow, was the only survivor. Four Wellingtons, a Halifax and a Stirling had been downed. Forty-one aircrew lost their lives, three were captured. Younger was taken by train to Germany escorted by the same guard who had taken Loder and Holborow a week earlier.

MILLENNIUM AND BEYOND

For weeks there had been a feeling of suppressed excitement spreading through the Bomber Command Station at RAF Linton on Ouse. A kind of sixth sense pervaded 35 Squadron aircrew in particular, an awareness that something 'was on', perhaps a daylight raid or a special target. Flight Sergeant Bill 'Shiner' Higgs, the fair-haired flight engineer of a Halifax II, noticed that normal flying had been partially curtailed and feverish preparations made to ensure that all the squadron's aircraft were serviceable.

It was unusually early in the day when, on 30 May 1942, the crews were told that operations were 'on' that night. As they assembled for briefing, Higgs was surprised to see the American crew of a Liberator sitting against the wall in the briefing room, probably as observers. The US Air Force had arrived in Britain in small numbers so far and had not yet bombed Germany, but their presence must mean that something special was afoot.

When the curtain was drawn back, the ribbons and markers on the wall map led straight to the target, the inland port and industrial Rhine city of Cologne. Many crews had been to Cologne before; it was heavily defended and near the Ruhr 'Happy Valley'. The area was always a monstrous firework display of concentrated flak fired from thousands of guns and approached through swarms of radar-directed nightfighters. No one was pleased to be going to Cologne, but why was this trip so special that every recent indication seemed to have been leading up to it?

The usual briefing went ahead, with the latest information about the weather, the routes, defences and bomb loads, until the moment when the CO quietly announced: 'Well over 1,000 bomber aircraft will be attacking this target.'

There was a moment of almost stunned silence before the briefing room erupted into an excited, cheering, hat-throwing crowd. Amid the sudden babble of noisy chatter Higgs glanced across the crowd at the Americans. They were silent, with looks of utter astonishment on their faces. These were not the phlegmatic Englishmen they had expected to see.

Higgs, like many aircrew men, felt that he was at last going to give the Germans 'a good hiding'. Higgs was a Londoner whose girlfriend and her father had been injured and bombed out of their home. While a member of a fighter squadron ground crew, he had been dive-bombed, high-level bombed and machine-gunned throughout France and the Battle of Britain. Now, he thought grimly, it was his turn to give something back.

Sir Arthur Harris had been determined that Bomber Command should make its mark. He knew the command was under threat from the Admiralty, who wanted a force of long-range bombers for anti-submarine duties. He recognised the propaganda value of a large, devastating mass attack on a German city, and thus the idea of a thousand-bomber raid was born. The first target selected was the city of Hamburg, but weather conditions caused it to be changed to Germany's third largest city, Cologne.

Bomber Command alone could not raise that number of service-able, crewed aircraft. The Admiralty had refused to allow Coastal Command to participate so the Operational Training Units and even Flying Training Command were pressed into service.

More than 1,000 aircraft in three waves left for the cathedral city. The raid was planned so that the force was over the target for only 90 minutes.

Take-off for Flt Sgt Higgs and his crew was at 11.30 p.m. They were to arrive at Cologne midway through the one-and-a-half-hour raid. Their job with their five 1,000lb bombs and 4,000lb of incendiaries was, as Higgs said succinctly, 'to stoke up the fire'.

The flight to the Dutch coast was uneventful but there the crew were puzzled by what appeared to be an enormous glowing fire ahead. 'It is on course for the target,' the navigator reported but, as they were still some 150 miles from Cologne, they assumed it to be a decoy target. They were wrong, Cologne was already burning furiously.

Higgs saw few anti-aircraft guns fired, just half a dozen search-lights pointing immovably and vertically upward. The inside of his Halifax was brilliantly lit by the red glow from the burning city below. He could see three other heavy bombers nearby, almost in formation, apparently looking for the same clear, flame-free spot on which to unload their bombs.

The crew of a Lancaster which was to bomb during the last twenty minutes of the attack could also plainly see the burning city before crossing the Dutch coast. Wireless operator John Banfield was pleasantly surprised to discover that there was practically no heavy flak. The guns below had been firing continuously since the first aircraft had appeared over the city and now, as the raid was nearing the end, the gun barrels were too hot for use. Losses in the third wave of bombers were considerably fewer. The defences were saturated and overwhelmed by bombs, smoke and fire.

Operation Millennium was an outstanding propaganda success throughout Britain and the world. The amount of damage, dislocation and disruption exceeded that of any previous raid. All main services were seriously affected, more than 40,000 people were made homeless and 200,000 were evacuated. For the first time the extent of a raid could not be concealed, even though Göring flatly refused to believe first reports. Fifty-two Bomber Command aircraft were lost, including eleven which crashed on return. Fifty-nine aircrew were taken prisoner, one hundred and ninety-two were killed and six evaded capture.

Despite the losses, morale among the Bomber Command aircrews had never been higher than after this devastating raid. Gone was the feeling that yours was the only aircraft flying over a heavily defended target. Instead, each airman knew that he was part of a powerful and expanding war-winning force. The Cologne raid was a turning-point and the Germans must now know that they were, to quote Flt Sgt Higgs again, 'due for a hammering'.

Sir Arthur Harris received congratulations from Winston Churchill, General Arnold of the US Air Force and General Golanov of the Red Army. Harris had scored a triumph for Bomber Command and the Royal Air Force. He wanted to continue with the successful formula, so on 1 June he set up another attack of similar size. Although he was unable to find the same total of aircraft as he had used against Cologne, the raid was nevertheless set for Essen and listed in leaflets dropped on Germany as having '*Mehr als 1,000 Bomber Auf einmal eingesezt*' and carrying a warning that the RAF offensive '*in ihrer neuen Form hat begonnen*'.

The second so-called thousand-bomber raid was, in comparison, a failure. Essen was covered with haze, bombing was scattered and 31 bomber aircraft were lost. One who made a parachute descent that night was an RAF officer of lengthy experience who had served in the First World War. Group Captain Herbert Massey knew what it was to be shot down in flames, wounded and then have the hospital ship bringing him home torpedoed. Shot down again and wounded in Palestine, Massey imperturbably carried on with his career. Now for a third time he had been shot down and was to become a prisoner of war and the Senior British Officer in Stalag Luft 3 Sagan. He should have been on his way to Washington to help organise a four-engined bomber training unit but the thousand-bomber raids intervened and Massey just had to be part of it. He was captured, with a severe leg injury, hiding in a chicken run. As SBO in Germany, however, he was to continue serving with the distinction as characteristic and notable as he had when free. He was repatriated in 1944, his injury having never healed.

SCRAPING THE BARREL

Harris was often accused of 'scraping the barrel' for using aircraft from the Operational Training Units with scratch or untrained crews, but this was not the case. Well over half of the aircraft taking part in a 1,000-bomber raid on Bremen on the night of 25–26 June were Wellingtons, many from OTUs, but an example of the crew make-up is that of a Wellington Ic from RAF Harwell. The five-man crew consisted of the captain and pilot Sgt Jack Paul, three other instructors, plus one pupil, 'pulled out of the hat'.

Apart from the pupil, this crew comprised operationally experienced men, men so valuable for the training of future aircrew that their loss, when they crashed following a Messerschmitt 110 attack, was a serious blow, and there were others like them. Only the rear gunner baled out from this crew in time and survived to travel down an escape line to Gibraltar. Three members of the crew died in the action or subsequent crash and Jack Paul, who survived the crash, endured months of treatment in several German hospitals.

These heavy raids brought large numbers of fully trained and partly trained men into the prisoner-of-war camps who had not been allocated to an operational squadron and consequently were not considered as having taken part in any campaign. The Bremen force suffered a loss of 51 aircraft, 30 of which were Whitleys, Wellingtons and one Hampden from 15 Operational Training Units. For many their first trip on ops was their last. They were in a kind of limbo, not fully trained, yet thrust headlong into the fury of war. Although the losses were considerable, Sir Arthur Harris reported that OTU men took part in only seven raids.

On 11 August 1942, the Pathfinder Force was formally established and on the 15th it was formed with a squadron each from Nos 1, 3, 4 and 5 Groups. A squadron of Mosquitoes was later added from 2 Group. The name was chosen by Harris. His hope that aircrew of the new force would have a lift in rank was nullified by the Air Ministry who agreed only that they would have enhanced promotion prospects. The special badge was never to be worn on operations.

To command the force, Sir Arthur personally selected Wing Commander Donald Bennett following his release from the Falun internment camp and a hair-raising daylight flight to Leuchars.

WALLS *DO* HAVE EARS

January 1942 was a month of heavy snow and snarled public transport in Britain. Because of the delays, Sgt 'Batch' Batchelder, due back from a weekend leave, missed his return train to his base in Yorkshire, arrived

112

late and was 'docked' a day's pay. It was a trivial affair which Batchelder had forgotten, until he was shot down the following June and arrived at Dulag Luft for interrogation. On the third day of his sojourn in the Dulag cells he was confronted by the pseudo-Red Cross representative. The name, rank and number routine had become an impassable stumbling block, so the German decided to throw in a 'bombshell' to try to 'shake' Batchelder. He told his prisoner that he knew about the 'Absent Without Leave' charge of the previous January and said that the Germans received daily information, including the names, squadrons and personal details of all the people who had been reported missing as a result of the previous night's operations: also that Batchelder had taken off on the first operation since the squadron had returned from the satellite to the 'new' airfield at RAF Topcliffe. When he was shown a clear aerial photograph of Topcliffe, resplendent with its new runways, Batchelder, despondent and not a little demoralised, knew well that someone, somewhere, had been doing plenty of talking. He decided that the government were wasting time and money with their posters and slogans of 'Careless Talk Costs Lives' and 'Walls Have Ears'.

PRAYER AND PROVOCATION

Apart from the usual 'goon baiting', another method of demoralising the German staff was a show of unity among the prisoners. Kriegies were the despair of German officers who insisted that they should dress and act like 'soldiers'. They should, asserted the German officers, be amenable to discipline and smart in their dress, not lax and sloppy. The lower ranks of the *Luftwaffe* employed in the camps were generally scruffy, not only those necessarily in overalls. Nor were they helped by the poor quality of their uniforms. The officers, however, were always 'band-box' smart. The Kriegies countered that they, RAF men, were not mere soldiers but a different and exalted breed; they were aircrew and the *Luftwaffe* should know better.

Just occasionally, the Kriegies would stagger the opposition, as when a National Day of Prayer was proclaimed. If the German authorities knew of such a proclamation beforehand, they would place obstacles in the way, but the Kriegies were not to be denied. Sunday 9 August 1942 was to be such a day. Word had been passed round that everyone was to turn out for *Appell* as quickly and as smartly dressed as possible and be prepared for an outdoor service.

The Sagan Germans were suitably taken aback. Kriegies left their huts 'at the double' to the call of the *Appell* whistle, as if attending an AOCs' parade. It was soon apparent to the German officers that the counting of prisoners was incidental to the true purpose of the parade. Every man seemed to have been able to beg or borrow the main elements of an RAF uniform. Previously unseen shirts and ties appeared. In the officers' compound the parade snapped smartly to attention at the SBO's order.

In the NCOs' compound the men jumped to 'Dixie' Deans's command, as if on a barrack square in Britain. Polished boots and shoes slammed down in unison on to the compacted earth, raising a cloud of surface dust over trousers that had been laboriously pressed by home-made smoothing irons, fashioned from flattened tins filled with sand and heated on a stove. Others had been carefully stretched out all night beneath flea-infested palliasses.

When the Germans had finished their count and were leaving the compounds, the Kriegies remained properly at ease until called once more to smart attention. Hymns were sung, prayers for victory said and, as the National Anthem was forbidden, 'Land of Hope and Glory' was roared out with a gusto and confidence that left the camp Germans looking back in wonder. Was this the same disorderly rabble that they had so much trouble in keeping under control? Why was it that all their stamping, pistol-waving, raging and shouting had so little effect when, in the NCO's compound, Deans, a mere sergeant, had only to call out one single word to turn the unruly mob into a manageable, cohesive and well-trained corps? It was beyond them.

FRIENDS AND ENEMIES

Sergeant J. 'Bas' Downing, flight engineer on 149 Squadron Stirlings, found himself on aircrew through a 'friend' volunteering for flying duties and submitting his name at the same time.

He had been quite happy as a corporal fitter on Wellingtons but, as the news of the application spread rapidly throughout RAF Lakenheath, he found it difficult to 'back out'. He was also excited at his promotion and change of role from groundcrew to aircrew. Later he found himself in the unusual situation of having to journey to RAF Cardington for an aircrew selection board after having already completed ten operations. He had neglected to have a medical examination because the Wing Commander of 149 Squadron had immediately pressed him into being a flight engineer. At Cardington, Downing found it almost impossible to convince the authorities that he was entitled to wear the FE brevet because Cardington had not blessed his transfer from groundcrew.

Frankfurt-am-Main was the target of more than 200 aircraft of Bomber Command on the night of 24–25 August 1942. For the second time Pathfinders led the raid. 'Bas' Downing was not the only crew member who was relieved when the captain, Sergeant Doug Baker, headed their Stirling for home.

The attack on the Stirling by the Messerschmitt 110 came from behind and below with complete and sudden surprise. To Downing the stream of bullets and cannon shells which ripped through the fuselage were a deafening shock, it was as if he had been sitting inside an oil drum that rowdies outside were hitting with sledgehammers. A second and third attack wounded 'Bas' in the right arm and filled the aircraft with smoke and flame. With the 'bale-out' order he snatched his parachute from the stowage rack, struggling to clip it to his harness. Only his left hand was usable.

Throwing himself into space from the front escape hatch, Downing felt himself helped on his way by a boot in the back of the neck. The jerk of the canopy opening had almost taken off his flying boots and his head was trapped between the harness straps. With his right arm hanging uselessly, he was unable to ease himself in the harness or release his trapped head.

A heavy landing in a cornfield sent searing pain through Downing's right leg and completely winded him. He lay still for a while, collecting himself. His right arm and right leg were agonisingly painful and although thankful to be alive, he knew he was in urgent need of medical attention. Pushing his parachute under a cornstack, Downing crawled on his left side towards the edge of the field. Corn stubble tore at him and a cabbage patch was hardly more comfortable.

At last he struggled to a road and house near a rail crossing. Reaching up with his left arm, he hammered at the door. A dog inside barked loudly, the door opened and his plight was seen. Quickly Downing was dragged inside by members of a Belgian family. His wounds were tended. A young member of the family went to ensure that his parachute was well hidden and to call a doctor. A telephone call to the local *Bürgermeister* appealing for help brought instead a car-load of Germans. Bursting through the door, steel-helmeted soldiers forced Downing to hop to their car. Two armed guards sat on either side of him and two others stood on the running boards as the car roared off at high speed.

At a farm he was transferred to an ambulance where he was confronted by the appalling sight of his crewmate, mid-upper gunner, Vic Woods. Woods had a bloody and swollen face where a bullet had grooved his forehead. A heavy parachute landing had broken a leg. An interminable journey over rough cobblestones took them to a hospital used by the *Luftwaffe* in Brussels.

RETALIATION AT LAMSDORF

In early October 1942, a hardening of the already harsh attitude of the Germans had been evident at Lamsdorf 8B. On the third, Sgt Harcus and seven other NCOs were taken to the guardroom, without explanation, and made to stand facing the wall. Harcus was sure that they were to be shot but they were eventually returned unharmed to the compound. The supply of Red Cross food parcels to the RAF compound was stopped on 8 October and mail was held back. Both were vital to Kriegie morale. The so-called reprisals took a sinister turn on the eleventh, when an order was made that the RAF men were to have their hands bound from 8 a.m. to 11 a.m. and from 12 noon to 9 p.m. Reprisals, it was said, because of treatment German soldiers had received at Dieppe and others captured during a raid on the Channel Islands.

The 190 men in Sgt Harcus's room, a third of them sleeping on the floor and the others in bunks above them, regarded the tying as just a nuisance at first but, by the end of the month, Harcus thought the restriction of exercise was showing effects. He was continually tired and other men found their hands swelling. Some men's rope bonds were replaced by chained manacles. Harcus found them more comfortable. The eighteen inches of chain between the manacles made movement easier, giving a greater freedom, but they were much heavier.

The German rulings were inconsistent. Some mail and Red Cross food was allowed into the compound and, without reason, stopped again. Then the chains were taken off for the occasional morning or afternoon to allow men to do their washing and cleaning of the huts. At an army band concert in the compound, the RAF Kriegies found it awkward to clap the spirited performance. On Christmas Eve they were unchained at 4 p.m. and manacled again on Boxing Day, but the compound gates were opened, enabling the RAF men to visit other compounds.

The Kriegies suffered frequently from diarrhoea, and the manacles added considerably to their discomfort, misery and difficulties when attending the draughty and public 'forty-holer' in temperatures of minus 30 degrees Centigrade. Some tasks were impossible without the help of another. Even walking or eating was awkward, and the parades in the snow, with hands chained in front of them, were a torment. Such communal punishment was contrary to the Geneva Convention but the Germans used the convention only when they needed it. Sgt Harcus was sure that another such winter would bring on suicidal tendencies.

MISTAKEN IDENTITY

Not all swaps made by airmen with soldier prisoners at Lamsdorf had happy results. Flt Sgt Jack Lawrence, who had been in several different camps and attempted escape from them all, reasoned he would have a better chance if he took the identity of an army private able to get outside the camp on working parties. He swapped and settled in with the soldiers to await his chance. One morning, without explanation, he was ordered to report to the *Revier*. To his surprise, a medical orderly handed him a razor and ordered him to shave. Not wishing to cause trouble that would disclose his true identity, Lawrence shaved his beard and moustache. When the orderly returned, he was furious. 'Not there,' he shouted, 'shave immediately – down there!' Lawrence was about to be circumcised.

The soldier with whom he had swapped had reported sick in Crete and, after many months, his papers had followed him to the prisoner-of-war camp, where the 'so correct' German medical team were about to carry out the delayed operation. Jack Lawrence knew that his cover was about to be 'blown'. He could not even prepare for the operation, the briefest examination would show the bare truth that the proposed procedure was unnecessary; it had been carried out many years earlier. Delaying tactics managed to put off the 'op' until at last the doctors were so busy elsewhere that the matter was dropped.

BACK TO BARTH

There had been a 'latrine rumour' among the NCOs at Sagan that a move was about to take place but, when one morning 'Dixie' Deans announced on *Appell* that he had been asked for 50 volunteers from the NCOs to return to Stalag Luft 1 at Barth, there was some surprise. The Kriegies were told that the camp at Barth was empty, had been enlarged and that the 50 were wanted to form the basis of the new camp.

There was an immediate buzz of interest. Would it be easier to escape; would there be a chance on the journey? At Barth it was known that tunnelling was difficult because of the high water table but the Baltic ports were near and there had been escapes that way. Burton and Shore had made it. To some it was worth a try – the airfield was close and Barth was nowhere near the war zone. To others any change was worth leaving the monotonous misery of the close boundary of dark firs and pines at Sagan. At least one was able to glimpse the world outside the wire at Barth.

To other aircrew Kriegies (all volunteers) the RAF maxim of 'never volunteer for anything' ruled. Were not aircrew already in deep enough trouble for volunteering? To leave Sagan would mean abandoning camp leader 'Dixie' Deans who had their confidence and trust. Nevertheless, 50 were found and embarked on a train journey north on 20 October 1942. Among them were Sgt Bill Baird who, when newly captured in February 1941, had told an incredulous 'Dixie' about the new four-engined Stirling, and Sgt Ron 'Ackers' Akerman who, in November 1940, had parachuted down to very wet reclaimed polder land and into the middle of a startled herd of cows. Luft 1 Barth, the original permanent camp for RAF prisoners of war, was filling up again.

DIARY OF A GERMAN GUARD
It was a troublesome lot of Kriegies who occupied Barth when it was reopened, as a selection of entries in a guard's diary testified. The first entry records that he received his posting to Stalag Luft I as an interpreter by telephone. He left Bremen on 28 September and arrived at Barth at nearly midnight the same day. The diary goes on: .

15 October: Arrival of the first Tommies.

24 October: Escape attempt by Sgt Gillespie in a sack of straw (a palliasse).

29 October: Sgt Blair caught escaping, dressed as a Pole.

5 November: Sgts Adams and John Sommerville caught midday in a tunnel. Sgts McKay and Taylor hauled out of the ashes wagon. Sgts Oliver and Wood caught. Oliver dressed as a German *Unteroffizier* escorts Sgt Wood to the kitchen in order to escape from there. Sgt Oliver speaks good German.

27 November: 1,000 Russians arrive.

8 December: Escape by Sgt Thompson. Caught by PJW.

16 December: Christmas party.

19 December: Mention to *Kommandantur* Order and Four days special leave.

24 December: Sgt Adams escapes in kitchen wagon
Christmas Day: To Catholic church with 35 Tommies.

26 December: Sgt Sommerville caught in a tunnel under the barracks. Concert in the evening by the *Flak-Kapelle* (Band). Theft of three caps.

27 December: Two roll calls. Caps returned at midday.

The diary continues until August 1944 and the pattern did not change. In 1943 the officers' compound was opened and they were as relentless as the NCOs. The guard-interpreter would seem to have deserved his promotion to *Obergefreiter* in February 1943 and to *Unteroffizier* in April 1944.

MONASTICISM DENIED

With the autumn nights, General Kammhuber had increased the depth of the nightfighter defences to counter their being swamped by the bomber stream. Once more, Bomber Command's losses started to rise.

As RAF man John Jones's train for Dulag Luft ran alongside the beautiful Rhine, he was escorted by an English-speaking, garrulous, armed *Feldwebel*. The *Feldwebel* claimed to have been a monk at a monastery on the east bank of the Rhine from where he was drafted into the *Wehrmacht*.

At Frankfurt-am-Main station the pair waited outside for a tram to Oberursel. Near the tram-stop the airman was closely and silently studied from a few feet by a nine-year-old boy. After a while, the *Feldwebel* had had enough. Shouting across the RAF man, he ordered the boy to 'clear off'. Backing away a short distance, the boy continued his wordless study. The *Feldwebel* lost his temper. The slow retreat by the boy appeared to the guard to be some form of resistance to the authority vested in him by virtue of his uniform, rank and pistol. In an explosion of ill-tempered roaring, the *Feldwebel* fumbled at his holster and, as his pistol was withdrawn, the boy, now thoroughly frightened, swung round and ran. Jones instinctively placed his hand lightly on his escort's shoulder who turned on him aggressively. Their eyes met but neither spoke, the boy kept running, the pistol was replaced in the holster and the tram for Oberursel arrived.

At Dulag the *Feldwebel* handed his prisoner over to the *Luftwaffe*. Then the one-time monk, stiffly at attention, turned to Jones, saluted and left. Not a single word had passed between the two from the moment the boy had drawn near.

REPATRIATION?

In late 1942, a commission of doctors from the Swiss protecting power visited the hospitals and camps, examining the severely wounded prisoners with a view to their repatriation. The criteria which the repatriation board had to satisfy were stringent, and although there was a strange envy among many of the comparatively fit Kriegies, none would have wished to change places with any of those selected. It was believed, though, that at least two Kriegies successfully feigned insanity.

On 29 October 1942, Bill Legg received his visit from the doctors. Nineteen months after miraculously crash-landing a blazing Wellington, in which he had been left for dead, Legg no longer had reason to feel self-conscious about the overpowering odour caused by his wounds, and he unequivocally gave credit for his recovery to the skill and dedication of fellow prisoner Doctor Chatenay. Legg was able to smile a confident greeting when Sagan's SBO, Group Captain Massey, visited him, but he was still troubled by the hole that had been in his back, for although it had healed over completely, intestinal leakage had caused an abscess to form. Bill was soon again in hospital at 9C, where the wound was cleaned and a rubber tube inserted, leaving a permanent hole which prevented the flesh healing over it.

From his bed in the sick quarters Legg watched a nearby compound fill with emaciated and starving Russian prisoners. The cigarettes thrown over the wire by French and British prisoners were immediately eaten. Guards prevented what little food the other prisoners could spare from being thrown to the Russians. Legg and the others were rooted with horror as the Russians tried desperately to escape by climbing up the barbed wire, only to be mown down by machine-gun fire. As the dead and wounded lay there, some caught up by the wire, others crumpled on the ground, a horse and cart was brought and those Russians still alive were forced to load the cart with the bodies. It is certain that the remainder did not last long under the cruel regime of their tormentors. During the following week, Legg calculated that 300 Russian prisoners died from shooting and starvation, including those shot for attempted cannibalism.

It was a relieved Bill Legg who learned that he had been passed as suitable for repatriation. It was not only the anticipation of liberty and home that excited him, it was the prospect of being away from surroundings of starvation and slaughter. But the exchange of prisoners was called off and it was to be two more years before the outstretched arms of his loved ones would hold him and he could once more breathe the air of freedom.

ELECTRONIC AFFLUENCE

Since their first tentative efforts at Barth, the radio makers had reached a state of positive radio component affluence. Having ingeniously converted a first aid cabinet into a secure hiding place for receiver components*, they had now to decide where a newly acquired sixteen-microfarad electrolytic condenser should be hidden. The solution was to bury it in an Allenbury's Invalid Food cardboard container, which enabled the condenser to have special connectors fixed to the positive top and to

*Not All Glory!, pp. 51, 55, 63

the negative bottom. The condenser could then be used without the lid being opened.

Other parts and valves arrived at random, some potentially useful, others not, but the acquisitive team were quite unable to refuse anything. Tobacco tins had the bottom flange removed after heating over a margarine lamp, some of the contents removed, a valve inserted, the base resoldered and the label replaced without any trace of the tampering. The difficulty now was remembering who held the tins, remembering what was in them, and reminding the owner which tin had the contraband in relation to the others on his shelves. Any kind of list-keeping was dangerous.

With the coming of winter, Bristow's steamboat had fallen into disuse, so the boiler was removed and the centre-section tie-rod replaced with their first-line replacement radio valve. Not all valves and parts were in tins. One valve was between a double bladder wall inside a rugby ball which was inadvertently used in a game. The valve emerged unscathed. A skilled leather-worker invisibly stitched a heavy and not very useful mains transformer inside a medicine ball which immediately went back into service. Small pieces of hardware were dropped into a tin of melted dubbin which was then allowed to set.

By November, a smooth routine was established, with the midnight BBC news being taken down by Stubbs at 1 a.m. local time. Stubbs and Bristow were confident they could pack up in a few minutes if need be, but the greatest danger was an early morning search before the portable components could be dispersed to other blocks. The bulletins were prepared in the camp office and read at lunch-time by an army of readers, each of whom was assigned to a different room from day to day. The news from Britain was improving daily, British forces were victorious in North Africa and Stalingrad was almost surrounded by the Russians. For security reasons, any really sensational news items were held back until some inkling of the event had been announced by the Germans.

As the days shortened inexorably, the room lighting was far from adequate, and even the occupiers of top bunks found it difficult to read. Larger bulbs were 'racketed' from the Germans and a number of unofficial extensions appeared in some bottom bunks. They were of little use as the increased load seriously reduced the line voltage. The voltage drop in the external power distribution on inadequate cross-section steel cables would probably have been excessive, but what was needed for more light were lower voltage bulbs, not higher wattage.

For a change from radios, Bristow decided to build a model car using another gramophone motor as the motive power. This motor had a good spring but the governor was faulty. Bristow and Young spent hours designing and building the independent suspension and steering gear. Four rubber balls, compressed between small tin lids, formed the wheels and an aluminium wish-bone, and coil springs served as the suspension. The motor was at the rear and the drive from the turntable shaft was coupled to the wheels through flexible disc universal joints. Young averred that, fully wound, the machine could be lethal, tearing along at about 30mph. As with the boat, the Germans were intrigued, their less welcome attentions diverted.

FREEDOM POSTPONED

When the Kriegies heard of the American landing in North Africa on 8 November 1942, there was earnest discussion in the camps. Every armchair-general could see how the war was to progress. The second and main Battle of El Alamein had taken place only four days previously. It was obvious, they said, that the Germans would be shovelled out of North Africa and a landing made in what Churchill called the 'soft underbelly of Europe', somewhere along the Mediterranean coast of France or even on the shores of Italy.

Maps were amended to include the areas of possible conflict and the Kriegies settled back confidently to wait for an invasion of Europe. At last it seemed that the Allies were making a big effort. The Kriegies were not to know that 'Operation Torch' had taken so much equipment and men from other possible operations, and from Bomber Command, that any invasion, frontal or on the 'soft underbelly', had been seriously delayed. In the Pacific the US Navy had taken the offensive and was in need of urgent supplies. On 7 August 1942, the Americans had landed on Japanese-held Guadalcanal and were about to begin their incredibly courageous and costly 'island hopping'. All the landing-craft it was possible to make were needed there. The invasion of *Festung Europa* would have to wait.

Pointlessly, the German camp authorities did their best to forbid or discourage any church service or celebration which might be construed as giving encouragement to Allied arms. So it was on 11 November 1942 that the customary armistice service was held in Stalag Luft 3 and other camps, despite German opposition. They could hardly stop midweek prayers or private thought, although that was the Nazi intention among their own people.

Forbidden, too, were wall maps which indicated any retreat or defeat of the *Wehrmacht*. The Battle of El Alamein had begun on 4 November 1942, and the pinned strands of wool marking Montgomery's pushing back of the *Afrika Korps* had been steadily moved westward.

Even when a German reverse was obvious, the Kriegies had to be careful about revealing what they had learned from the illicit radio. Germans were reluctant to admit to any *Wehrmacht* movement other than an advance or the occasional 'strategic and temporary withdrawal'. Only a victory like Dieppe was rapidly broadcast, usually by the oily Lord Haw Haw. 'Operation Torch', the landing behind Rommel's men, was glossed over until it could no longer be denied. The ominous fact that six Russian armies had broken through the German lines, north and south of Stalingrad, and joined forces behind the *Wehrmacht*'s Sixth Army was minimised but that, too, was marked up exultantly by the Kriegie cartographers.

THE BLOODIEST BATTLE

From the daily news bulletins Kriegies in all camps had plotted the inexorable German advance of over a thousand miles, deep into Russia. They had followed the *Wehrmacht* drive on their maps with a mixture of awestruck, grudging admiration and horror. They had seen the evidence of the hordes of prisoners that the Germans had sent back as slave labourers and had heard their triumphant announcements on the *Deutschlandsender* radio. That the Germans had achieved some overwhelming victories could not be denied, but of late there had been a subtle change in their boasts. The '*Untermensch*' were, it seemed, fighting back with success. The news that German armies were about to capture Leningrad and Moscow had been premature and now von Paulus's 6th Army was surrounded at Stalingrad.

Names, strange at first to western ears, became familiar to the Kriegies from their secret bulletins. Russian marshals and generals such as Yeremenko, Rokossovsky, Timoshenko, Malinovsky, Zhukov and Chuikov became as familiar as Montgomery and Eisenhower were to become. These were the men that 52-year-old *General* Paulus and the *Wehrmacht* were facing at Stalingrad. The titanic struggle in the '*Kessel*' or cauldron was a forlorn one and Kriegies were, in a way, fortunate to hear both sides of the propaganda war. For once, many of them felt a slight pang of sympathy for the *Wehrmacht* fighting in such appalling and hopeless conditions.

Despite the promise by Göring that the *Luftwaffe* could and would supply the 6th Army from the air, it proved impossible.

In a temperature of minus 31 degrees Centigrade, Paulus, a broken man, labelled a coward by Hitler, was forced to surrender.

First the Battle of Britain, then El Alamein and now Stalingrad. Each German reverse was a turning point, and such a crushing defeat to German arms as at Stalingrad was unsustainable. In Sagan and Barth, in Lamsdorf and Mühlberg, and other camps throughout Germany and Poland, the Kriegies brought out their hand-drawn wall maps and updated the pin and red wool markings; the front line was now moving steadily westward. The guards and interpreters did not seem to mind, they shrugged, accepting the inevitable and were already losing heart. Everywhere the myth of German invincibility had crumbled.

Again there was no hope of the Kriegies being home for that Christmas, but it looked a distinct possibility for Christmas 1943. Meanwhile they made the best of things.

Ice-rinks were laid down by flooding areas where low earth dykes had been raised to retain the water which quickly froze. Angle-iron was taken from hut corners and underneath forms and laboriously fashioned into skates. Hockey sticks were made from any wood available and Canadian ice-hockey players, some of whom were skilled performers, provided exciting entertainment.

""Can't a fellow get any privacy?"

PART 4

1943

A SPARK OF CIVILISATION

At Lamsdorf the temperature hovered between minus 30 and minus 40 degrees Centigrade for the first three weeks of January 1943, and lack of proper food and exercise caused the RAF men there to feel dispirited. Concentration became difficult and thoughts returned constantly to home and loved ones. Wrists ached from the chafing restriction of manacles. The importance of the morale lift given by music was demonstrated by Sgt Harcus's description of a performance by Jimmy Howe's band on a bleak January night as, 'like a spark of civilisation'. But at Sagan, although extra double bunks were squeezed into odd spaces to accommodate the few prisoners arriving, their numbers were insufficient to disrupt the parcel distribution and the Kriegies continued on a full issue. Without the Red Cross parcels life would have been bleak indeed.

As a member of the Sagan officers' compound theatre club, Sqdn Ldr Ken Campbell was able to cross on parole to the NCOs' compound to attend a performance of *Aladdin*. He thought it the best Kriegie production he had ever seen but Sgt David Young, with commendable restraint, described it as 'an extravagant production, which, had it been put on in Britain, would have been banned and, as a pantomime, would have been quite unsuitable for children'. Nevertheless, the pantomime played to packed houses and was thoroughly enjoyed by those officers allowed to visit the NCOs' compound.

A means of marking the target other than by incendiary bombs and flares had been needed to make the Pathfinder Force a viable unit and on 16 January 1943, target indicators (TIs) were used for the first time. Made up with some 60 red, green or yellow pyrotechnic candles fitted into a 250lb bomb case, they were ejected by a pre-set barometric fuse cascading to the ground and burning brilliantly for three minutes. Each candle had its own built-in ignition and the vivid ground pattern varied in diameter depending on the height above ground at which the barometric fuse was set; at 3,000 feet the spread would have a diameter of approximately 100 yards and set at 1,500 feet it would be 60 yards.

That night, Ken Campbell, working in the theatre in the Sagan officers' compound, was heartened by the sound of a raid in the direction of

Berlin. The cast and stage crew had just completed their final production of *Treasure Island* when the siren sounded its wailing alarm and the lights throughout the camp and the boundary were extinguished. Flak and bombs could be heard exploding in the distance. Over in the NCOs' compound, men peering through cracks in the shutters could clearly see a distant cascade of brilliant sparkling lights. Everyone could feel the ground vibrating. The far sound of bombs and flak shells exploding was drowned by the cheering of the Kriegies.

The following night Berlin was raided again, and once more cheers were heard throughout the compounds, but as an aircraft fell from the night sky like a flaming comet, a hush came over the watchers. The Kriegies knew only too well the cost in men on such a raid.

'Poor buggers', someone murmured.

PLUMBER'S MATES

Kriegies' metal-working facilities in the compounds at Sagan received a sudden and unexpected boost by the arrival of a plumber and accompanying guard to repair a leaking pipe in a wash-house. As soon as the plumber settled to work he was surrounded by inquisitive and acquisitive Kriegies bidding in cigarettes for any item in his tool-bag. The armed guard was an elderly *Luftwaffe Gefreiter* who seemed quite uninterested. When the plumber had finished the repair he, risking court martial, opened a kind of ironmonger's stall and sold his entire tool-kit. He walked from the camp with his armed guard and a tool-bag stuffed with cigarettes.

ODOROUS TALE

Bill Goodman and Errol Green at Sagan gave up crocheting weird 'bobble' hats from old socks for a while in order to concentrate on promoting their hair growth. The methods used brought first ridicule and then ostracism. They cut off their locks, shaved their pates and immediately earned the names of 'Flarepath' and 'Pathway'. It was when they decided to massage into their scalps olive oil to nourish the hair roots that the temporary banishment, until they were odour-free, took place. The only source of olive oil was from tins that had contained sardines. What was even more galling was that neither treatment worked. The 'oil plan' was forcibly discontinued by general consent of those living nearby.

For his birthday Bill Goodman's father had given him a handsome silver cigarette case and, strangely, he still had it at Sagan. It was during one of the frequent outbreaks of dysentery that Bill had to pay a hurried visit to the multi-holer, and in the panic his treasured case disappeared into the sludge below. Bill judged by the level that soon the little man with his horse-drawn cylindrical tanker would be round to empty the pit and distribute the contents over the surrounding fields. When the small, sad German appeared, Bill was ready. By sign language and gesture he conveyed his willingness to pay the German cigarettes for the recovery of the lost item. Soon the tanker man commenced raking among the filth and stirring up revolting smells. Then he stopped, plunged in his arm to the elbow and withdrew it, holding up the case for approval. After dousing the case and his arm under a tap, the little man was duly rewarded, with Bill standing well back as he watched the sludge running from the holes in the man's thigh boots. The case was restored by rubbing with cigarette ash but still bore the scars of its immersion, two dents where it was struck by the little German's 'muck raker'.

A MAN'S CONSCIENCE

Alec Burton, by his own admission, had been a rotten service 'copper'. Remustered to aircrew, Stuttgart was his first bombing objective in late 1942. He had been horror-stricken by the sight of the city in flames; to him it looked like a huge fairground smothered in coloured lights, with great bonfires everywhere. At the thought of what they were doing, he wrote: 'It hit me in the pit of the stomach with the worst shock of depression that I have ever experienced. Somehow, I thought that none of us deserved to get out of it alive.'

They nearly did not. Tearing across western Europe 'right down on the deck', they were three times hit by flak and had two engine fires by the time they got home to Lincolnshire.

On the night of 17–18 January 1943, Burton navigated his Lancaster to Berlin for the second consecutive night. More than 200 aircraft had raided the 'Big City' twenty-four hours before, using a route over Denmark, across the Baltic to Stettin and then south to Berlin. The return journey was a similar route in reverse. When at briefing the crews were told that the target and route were to be a repeat of the previous night, there was a murmur of discontent and dissent. Surely this was madness, a desk planner's aberration and a flyer's nightmare. The defences would easily pick them up and be waiting for the bomber stream. Despite the misgivings of the crews, they had to go, but they flew into the night tired and apprehensive.

When the bomber stream reached Stettin, there was cloud below. Gun flashes could not be seen, but the shell-bursts were visible among the aircraft. Muffled crumps were heard above engine noise and shrapnel whipped through fuselages. The steel supports of Sgt Burton's seat

127

were sliced through, the hot steel screaming on to smash the radar set. Seconds later the bomb aimer cried out that he had been hit in the eye. The cabin filled with smoke as the flight engineer scrambled down to bandage him. Despite his wound, the bomb aimer insisted on carrying on with the actual bombing. The action over Stettin was to cost him the sight of his left eye.

On the return flight from Berlin to the Baltic the defences unerringly fixed on the stream. Every few minutes Alec Burton would hear ominous thuds and clangs beneath the aircraft. The Lancaster would dive and twist as Burton scrabbled on the floor, searching for his navigation instruments. Landing back in England after ten hours of tense flying, they were diverted to an airfield far to the north of their home base. Burton reckoned they had just enough fuel in the tanks to fill a cigarette lighter.

Richard Dimbleby was shaken by the ferocity of the defences when he recorded a commentary on that night's Berlin raid. He was flying as a supernumerary in a 106 Squadron Lancaster captained by Wing Commander Guy Gibson.

The men who did the flying were right, it was a folly to send the stream of bombers on precisely the same route for two nights in succession, especially to the 'Big City'. The price of such stupidity was paid with the blood of some 150 men and the loss of 22 aircraft compared with one aircraft and its crew on the previous night.

By now, ex-RAF 'copper' Alec Burton was a seasoned airman and had started 'to secrete a thin layer of cynicism', possibly as a protective covering. He could not visualise completing a tour of 30 operations and still remain in one piece.

On Sunday morning, 14 February, Burton reported for briefing and was told that the target for that night was Milan. The crew were still tired from the previous night's attack on the U-boat pens at Lorient. Burton had returned on Friday evening from a week's leave, during which he had married; now he was back into the swing of almost nightly operations.

The outward flight to northern Italy went smoothly, his navigation was accurate and the snow-covered Alps were a beautiful sight in full moonlight. Not a shot had been fired at them. As they neared Milan, it was a blaze of light; streets and buildings were clearly visible. They bombed accurately, then as they turned to make a course for home, the aircraft began to shake violently, hit by incendiaries from a bomber above. One incendiary smashed through the nose and demolished the pilot's instrument panel. Others damaged the tail controls and the Lancaster began to career uncontrollably. On the order to 'bale out', the bomb aimer pulled up the nose escape hatch and dived out. Burton would

Above: Interior view of a hut.
Below: Packing case furniture in a hut, Lamsdorf.

Above: A game of cards. (photograph of drawing)
Below: Bed time, Heydekrug. (photograph of drawing)

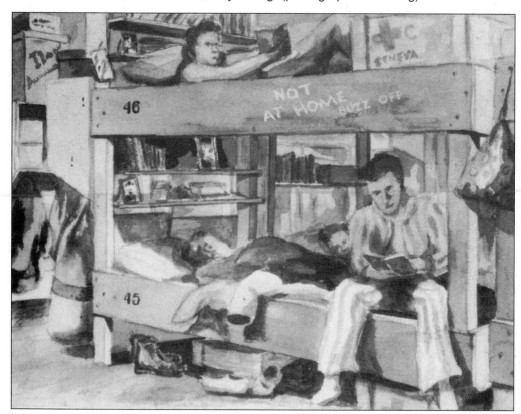

Above: Christmas 1943 in a hut, Lamsdorf.
Below: Opening Canadian Red Cross parcels.

Above: Watching issue of 'gash', swede peelings, Fallingbostel.
Below: Soup issue, Fallingbostel.

Right: Artist Bob 'Smudge' Coles, model Johnny Culpan, Cookhouse, Fallingbostel.

Right: Hiding tools.

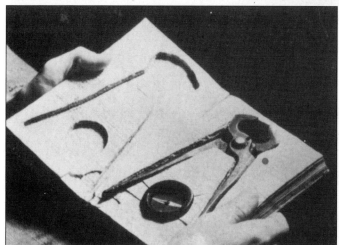

Right: Home-made imitation of German rifle.

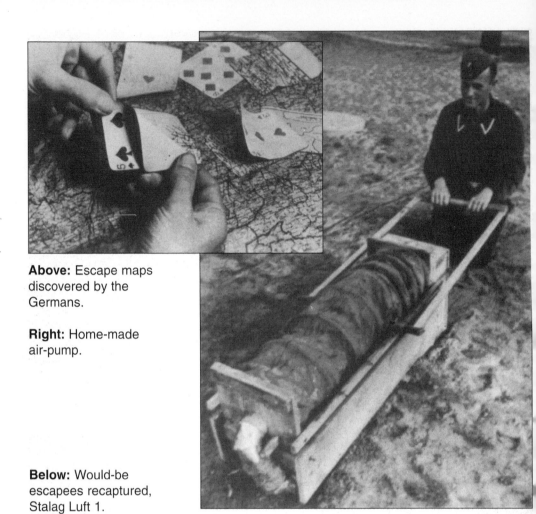

Above: Escape maps discovered by the Germans.

Right: Home-made air-pump.

Below: Would-be escapees recaptured, Stalag Luft 1.

Above: 'London Arcade' swap-shop, Fallingbostel.
Below: Water from a frozen static tank used to make a skating rink,
Sagan. (photograph of drawing)

Above: Watching USAAF Liberators and Fortresses en route for Hanover, Fallingbostel, 12 September 1944; below left, W/O Hurlestone (left) and Bob Hale.

have been a closer second than he was, had he not become wedged against the hatch framework, likening himself to a 'picture in a frame too small for it'.

As he struggled to free himself, Burton saw a view strangely like a huge blackboard covered with vari-coloured, flickering electric light bulbs which were being tilted and rotated before his nose. As the aircraft twisted, Burton was thrown out into the night. He tugged at the 'D' ring of his parachute, then he was hanging 'as if in the grip of some massive chucker-out, held dangling by the scruff of the neck and the seat of my pants'.

Burton's parachute descent was not silent. The four Rolls-Royce engines had seemed almost soundless compared to the noise coming up from what looked like Dante's *Inferno* below. He was aware that masses of shells were being hurled at aircraft above, only to descend again in smaller, jagged, red-hot pieces. Burton expected at any moment to be perforated by a shell on its way up, or shrapnel on its way down, and if he survived that, to drop into one of the raging fires immediately below. He closed his eyes and later said that he pretended he wasn't there.

Gradually the noise diminished, so Burton forced his eyes open and saw that he had drifted away from the city. He appeared to be coming down on a tarmac road between pine forests. What he thought was a road was a ditch and suddenly Burton was thrashing about, up to his ears in freezing water. He scrambled out, soaked and dripping but overwhelmed with relief at being alive and unhurt. He knew he was lucky and even the thought of his uncertain future could not depress his soaring spirit.

Squeezing water out of his clothes, Burton set off briskly northward, making a wide detour to avoid the lights of Milan, assuming that the natives would be unlikely to be friendly to one who had just bombed their city. Trudging towards Switzerland, he calculated that the odds against him reaching there were some million to one against.

With sudden, chilling terror, Burton realised he had walked blindly into the main street of a village. Chattering people were all around, gazing and pointing at burning Milan. His stomach seemed to freeze, his legs turned to jelly. He could only walk brazenly through the crowded street and hope for the best. Someone spoke to him, he ignored them. Further down the street somebody shouted after him. He wanted desperately to run but, looking neither left nor right, he walked steadily onward. He felt so conspicuous that he could as well have been carrying a banner announcing his identity. He was not challenged again until, after about six hours of slogging through irrigation ditches and swampy fields, he heard the unmistakable Italian equivalent of 'Who goes there?' The rattle of a rifle bolt and his surrounding by enemy soldiers convinced Sgt Burton that he should surrender. He had walked unwittingly into a searchlight unit and was now a prisoner of the Italians.

The searchlight crew were very friendly and one man, an obviously confirmed anglophile, appointed himself Burton's personal valet. A bunk was provided for him to rest, his uniform was dried and brushed clean, and bread and wine were brought. In return, he had only to admire photographs of the man's wife and *bambini.*

At a prisoner-of-war camp for officers at Chieti he was received with jubilation by the news-hungry inmates. Burton could do little to help, feeling that his knowledge of current affairs was minimal.

Chieti was small, barely 200 yards square, surrounded by a 15-foot wall with sentry boxes and searchlights at strategic corners. Into this restricted space were crammed some 1,200 army officers with just a leavening of RAF. Despite the lack of room, Burton was astonished by the presence of experts in almost every branch of knowledge who taught the varied curriculum at the 'Chieti College'. The camp also had a flourishing theatre, a symphony orchestra, a dance band and a marionette show. Burton thought they were doing well for themselves.

His sly digs at everyone found expression in a camp wall newspaper entitled 'CLAP-TRAP'. Here he could allow full rein to his ability to find the satirical word to reduce pomposity and stupidity to laughter. The hiring of a film projector at an extortionate price allowed the prisoners to see some American films in the courtyard. The dialogue was dubbed in unintelligible Italian and the films were poorly projected, with ten-minute intervals for reel changes. This produced the quip in 'CLAP-TRAP': 'Well, thank God they can't translate Carole Lombard's figure into Italian!'

Neither friend nor foe was safe from Burton's 'barbed wire wit'. Inevitably 'CLAP-TRAP' was banned by the Italians. 'FREE CLAP-TRAP' was then issued in a cardboard folder and carried the following editorial.

'CLAP-TRAP BANNED BY AXIS'

Verboten by Axis edict; her presses broken up; and her foreign correspondents in Berlin, Paris and Tokyo put to death or worse; 'CLAP-TRAP' continues to work underground to bring 'TRUTH' to the oppressed peoples of the world. The staff of the new 'FREE CLAP-TRAP', working under the ever-present threat of the firing squad or the concentration camp, have pledged themselves to print on, to the death!

The hand-written paper continued to lampoon the Italians, Germans and even the attitudes of some of the army officers in the camp. Burton was, of course, overstating the possible penalties for his perseverance in continuing to supply real news, but ridiculing the Axis propaganda and flagrantly disobeying the Italian commander's orders could have had serious consequences for him.

DOWNED AND DRILLED

There was much guesswork in forecasting the weather, but great efforts were made to gather as full information as possible by the use of specially fitted aircraft, such as the Hudson from St Eval which took off at 7.30 a.m. on the foul-weather morning of Wednesday 10 February 1943. It headed blindly through cloud to the Bay of Biscay. The height of the Hudson was determined by barometric pressure, but was on average 2,500 to 3,000 feet. The course took it to within 40 miles of the hotly defended port of Brest where it was necessary for the aircraft to descend to below 50 feet for low-level readings.

Sergeant pilot C. Glover was feeling his way down through the cloud, so that navigator F/O M. Buttler could get a fix, when the aircraft emerged at about 250 feet over a convoy protected by three flak ships. Bursting flak immediately struck the aircraft and the Hudson dived out of control, crash-landing in flames on the nearby beach. All four members of the crew were badly wounded; three were unconscious inside the stricken Hudson. Despite orders from German soldiers to keep away, two Frenchmen, Le Roy and Cornac, pulled the four men out of the blaze. Their heroism failed to save the pilot, who died less than two days later, but the other three survived severe wounds and burns.

After five weeks in German hospitals in France, the two wireless operator/air gunners, Sgts Ernest Winfield and Roy Gilbert, were sent to Dulag, although their burns were still raw and the bone-breaks still mending. One week later they were off again on a miserable three-day journey, in a train with wooden slatted seats, to Stalag 8B Lamsdorf to join the 1,000 airmen in the RAF compound already there. At Lamsdorf the idea of the *Straflager* or punishment camp, for the 'bad boys' persisted.

Despite the camp's reputation, a propensity for 'mickey taking' surfaced when the German *Major* in charge decided that one hour of foot drill every day might instil some discipline into the scruffy and slack Kriegies under his command. Bob 'Smudge' Coles observed that, with their usual unquenchable humour, the Kriegies set about inventing a series of outrageous drill movements loosely based on ballet. Change step was performed with one hand on the hip, right foot forward, pause, stretched to the right, pause, then back, pause, then forward march and so on. It was practised in squads and performed with serious zest, solemn demeanour and military precision, to the great satisfaction of *Herr Major*. He thought it a bit strange, but Alan Morris explained that RAF drill was quite different from that of the army. The same *Major* complained that he was not saluted when he entered the compound. He spoke no English, so when he came in, an NCO would shout, 'Squad – Load of Shit' and then salute with his hand behind his ear, while surrounding Kriegies stood to attention. *Herr Major* returned the salute quite happily.

AIRMEN IN CHAINS

On the same night that Sergeant Burton was flying to Milan, Sergeant Norman Leonard was operating the radio of a Wellington X bombing Cologne. As the pilot, Flight Lieutenant Kirk, banked the plane towards the Pathfinders' sky markers, it was attacked by fighters from the rear. Immediately, cannon shells smashed the hydraulics, the navigator was killed in his seat and the aircraft was blazing. Kirk ordered the jettisoning of the bomb load. The incendiaries fell from the bomb bay already flaring. With the 'bale out' order the bomb aimer and Sgt Leonard dived out of the forward hatch into ten thousand feet of darkness. Pilot Officer Mason, the second pilot, had been in the astrodome and had left his parachute in a rack. It was destroyed in a fire extending from the main spar to the tail. Kirk struggled unsuccessfully to crash-land the burning Wellington; its wreck was later found near Ostend.

To Sgt Leonard the parachute descent was a blank; he was unconscious from the moment his canopy snapped open to the moment when he awoke looking up the barrels of several rifles held by soldiers of the *Waffen SS*.

After a few weeks in hospital and Dulag, Sgt Leonard was sent to Lamsdorf, where he found the RAF men still manacled. He joined them. Sgt Harcus had been moved out of the compound with 50 others to make room for a new intake and said a thankful goodbye to the 'chain gang'.

On 1 March the German authorities decided that the RAF Kriegies at Lamsdorf should be chained only on alternate days and that the Australians and New Zealanders could be unchained altogether. The response of the 'Anzacs' was immediate; they would remain chained like the others until all were freed of manacles. Such solidarity puzzled the Germans who were continually trying and expecting to drive a wedge between the Commonwealth men and the British. 'Why do you fight for England?' they would ask. 'You owe her nothing.' The enemy was always England, never Britain. The same question was asked of some Scots and

Welsh, and in particular, of Irishmen. The invariable rebuff constantly surprised the Germans.

MOVES AT SAGAN

On the far side of the *Kommandantur* a new compound for officers was in the course of construction at Sagan and volunteers were asked to help. Giving their parole not to escape, the Kriegie working parties were nevertheless extremely interested in, and watching for, any possible means of escape. The drainage system was given close attention but the visible manholes gave no indication of the size of the follow-through pipes.

A move in March found most officer Kriegies happy at the prospect of smaller rooms with fewer occupants, and of pine trees inside the compound. Les Ford thought it a vast improvement. The compound was larger, had the luxury of clean flushing lavatories and washing facilities but the four to a room was soon raised to six and then eight. The NCOs, however, continued with their 20- to 40-holer *aborts* and 60 men to a room.

The pleasant change of trees growing in the compound did not last. The Germans thought the trees gave cover for escape activities and, because the Kriegies refused to chop them down, they were not allowed the wood for burning. Russian prisoners were sent in to fell the trees and cart away the logs in lorries.

But the Russians and the lorries inside the compound gave some Kriegies the chance to indulge in a few impromptu escape attempts. While others distracted guards in the *Posten* boxes, they climbed to the roofs of the huts near the gate and, as the lorries passed, they jumped down and burrowed into and under the loads of pine foliage. Few got further than the gate. Guards thrust long spikes and pitchforks deep into the foliage and loud yells of pain revealed hidden prisoners. The few that did get beyond the wire were caught and returned to the camp and the 'cooler' within two days.

There was consternation among the Germans when a Kriegie dressed as a working-party Russian attempted to pass through the main gate. He spoke Russian and had revealed his identity to the workers. Despite the enormous risk, the Russians were determined not to give him away. The party successfully passed through the first gate but, at the second, the guard, after several counts, still found that he had one Russian more than had been admitted to the compound. The Russians entered whole-heartedly into the masquerade. Eventually, the English-speaking *Lager* officer who knew the Kriegies well, identified the man as an inveterate escaper. The Kriegie was led away to his spell in solitary confinement.

The *Kommandant* of Stalag Luft 3 Sagan was an Oberst, the equivalent of a colonel. Friedrich von Lindeiner-Wildau was a patriotic and staunch German of the old school. He had replaced the first *Kommandant, Oberst* Stephani within a month. Stephani had no experience with prisoners and, unlike von Lindeiner, could not speak English. Whenever von Lindeiner was seen by Kriegies he was always immaculately uniformed and carried himself with an upright military bearing. His behaviour was never less than courteous and gentlemanly. Many Kriegies secretly admired him but were equally willing to see him harried, disgraced and sacked. Yet it suited them for von Lindeiner to be in charge; he would always listen to complaints on behalf of the prisoners from Herbert Massey or 'Dixie' Deans and he would help where possible.

Oberst von Lindeiner was not a member of the Nazi party. His years in the Colonial Service and three wounds received in the First World War when he was an aide to Kaiser Wilhelm's youngest son, Prince Joachim, had tired him and he left the service in 1919. For years he worked abroad in Europe, North and South America and, when living in Holland, he married a Dutch baroness.

Business brought von Lindeiner back to Germany where he found it necessary to rejoin one of the services. There was little doubt that the *Luftwaffe* was the branch least infiltrated by the Nazi party so, to avoid party membership, von Lindeiner took a job as a member of Göring's personal staff. He was exhausted by strenuous duties during the overrunning of the western Allies and when he was denied retirement he found the running of a prisoner-of-war camp a comparative relief.

From the spring of 1942 von Lindeiner believed he had found a niche in which he could safely shelter, which would see him through to the end of the war and the Nazi party. But von Lindeiner's 'sheltered' niche was becoming increasingly noticeable to 'higher authority'. Prisoners, particularly RAF men, were a growing nuisance. Their escapes and escape attempts involved thousands of searchers being taken from productive work and the control of the increasing number of inmates meant more sophisticated means were needed than barbed wire and guards. Also, prisoners were filling the *Luft* camps to a bursting point where the capacity safety valve was about to blow.

The longer-term Kriegies had gained in experience and ability over the years. They were able to contain the inexperienced keenness to escape of those newly taken and direct their enthusiasm into productive, sensible and mutually useful channels.

In almost every camp, despite rigid German controls and watchfulness, tunnels were proliferating so that the earth beneath was like a rabbit warren. The discovery of one tunnel would sometimes satisfy the Germans, causing them to overlook others that were being vigorously burrowed.

THE HORROR OF KATYN

The Kriegies thought there was 'something up' when the Germans almost deluged them with copies of the *Allgemeine Zeitung*, the *Völkischer Beobachter* and their propaganda rag 'The Camp'. Early in April 1943 the Germans had discovered a mass grave that had not been dug and filled at their instigation. Radio Berlin solemnly and sensationally broadcast the first news of a massacre and mass grave at Katyn Wood, near Smolensk. A Russian peasant, whose conscience had troubled him, told the *Feldgendarmerie* that Polish officers sought by General Sikorski to make up his new Polish army, had been shot and were buried on the Hill of Goats in Katyn Wood.

The Germans realised that here was a hell-sent opportunity to split the Allies and were quick to let the world know of the perfidy of the 'Reds'. With a complete disregard of what was happening to Poles and other nationalities at Auschwitz and other concentration camps within the power of the Reich, Goebbels had a Polish commission set up to investigate and publicise the crime. As if with clean hands, he accused the Russians of mass extermination of the Polish officer cadre. All the bodies found had their hands tied behind their backs and had been shot through the back of the neck or head. Cold-blooded and calculated killings had taken place on a huge scale.

The Kriegies were subjected to a continuous barrage of newspaper and radio reports and every guard and interpreter brought up the subject of the type of people with whom Britain was allied. The assumed shock and horror of the Germans was a cynical ploy but the Kriegies were relieved when the Russians had retaken the area and the whole question of who committed this terrible crime was postponed until after the war's end.

'YOU ARE IN INVASION – YES?'

Peter Hall, who, since joining the RAF Volunteer Reserve with his brother-in-law in 1939, had flown many different types of aircraft, heard of a marvellous new aeroplane operating from RAF Bircham Newton, the Mosquito. He immediately applied for a posting. At that stage, however, the Mosquitos (Mossies) at Bircham Newton were part of the meteorological unit and consequently unarmed.

In March 1943, Flight Lieutenant Hall was posted on to RAF Oakington. First-hand weather information would help the Pathfinders to improve on the good job they were already doing. The Met pilots at last felt they were doing vital work. Their afternoon destinations indicated where the big raid was to be that night and the information brought back could have a positive bearing on the success or otherwise of the night's operation. On a flight over the Baltic, they took photographs which were believed to show the first indication of the flying bomb laboratories and factories at Peenemünde.

On Sunday morning, 9 May 1943, the Met/Pathfinders were ordered to fly straight to the Ruhr and back. Unfortunately, the sky was clear all the way. On the return flight over Den Helder at 27,000 feet, they were 'bounced' by four Fw190s. Hall could not avoid them and was unable to retaliate. Rapidly both wings of the tailplane were shot away, and in a typically RAF understatement he wrote: 'There did not seem to be much future in remaining with what was left.' Hall saw that navigator Bill Woodruff was apparently going out by the bottom exit hatch, and decided to opt for the small hatch over his head.

As he floated down beneath his parachute, Hall watched the air-craft getting smaller as it neared the ground and, after what seemed ages, a puff of white parachute showed that Woodruff was out. He had left the aircraft when it was close to the ground so that, in spite of a westerly near-gale, his parachute had barely opened when he landed in the same field as the plane wreckage. Hall, blown several miles inland, hoped that the pilots of the victorious Fw190s flying in close circles around him, had good intentions.

He landed safely and the first person he met was a young Dutch boy who asked in English, 'You are in invasion, yes?' Hall was flattered; he could not pretend that one petrified RAF officer was an invasion, but the desperate people of Holland were inclined to clutch at any straw.

He had never really considered the possibility of being shot down. Yet here he was, on a lovely May evening, sitting in a patch of Dutch brussels sprouts, bewildered and fearful at a time when he should have been sitting in the mess having a cup of tea before going home to his wife and young son at Cotterham.

Told to stay out of sight by the Dutch boy, Hall joined the hens in a fowl pen. The next morning the same boy brought him a set of overalls and asked him to change out of his uniform and accompany him on a cycle ride. Hall's first mistake, quickly rectified, was to ride on the left but the German soldiers they passed did not seem to notice; they were too busy searching for him in the ditches. Alongside a dyke they came to a small hole, already cramped with two people. They were Jews who had fled from Poland and had been there for months, sheltered and fed by the

Dutch family. Only then did Hall realise the incredible bravery of the Dutch people. If any of those in hiding had been found, the entire family would probably have been shot, yet they were prepared to add to their problems by also taking him in.

Throughout the daylight hours, the trio squatted in the restricted, insanitary conditions in the hole. After dark, despite the curfew, the farmer brought them a bottle of milk and a loaf of bread. One night he took them back to the farmhouse for a wash. The whole time Hall was on edge, alarmed for the safety of this brave man, his young wife and children.

The Germans were still searching for the '*Luftgangster*' and combing the areas around the dykes. The fugitives had to move and were taken to a large field of rape where they were hidden among the two-and-a-half-feet-high stalks topped with yellow flowers.

One night Hall met a Dutch parson who spoke fluent English. He had heard stories about escape organisations and asked the parson if he could hand him on to one of them. Returning later that night, the parson brought the sad news that the escape organisation people he knew had all been caught recently and immediately shot.

It was clear to Hall that he had little chance of getting home and that while he stayed with his Dutch and Polish friends they were all in great danger. Not wishing to be shot as a spy, he asked for the return of his uniform. Luckily, it had been buried and not burnt. Before leaving, he asked his new parson friend to look after and keep his gold pocket-watch. Next day he quietly walked away.

One last effort to escape was made by offering a barge owner ten thousand guilders to get him across to England but he was told that he could not possibly get past the guards on the coast.

Hall was hungry. The only place nearby where he could purchase some food was the Hotel Schmitt. He decided to take the risk but was told by the owner that he had been seen by a local policeman in the pay of the Germans. His presence would have been reported. Within minutes the policeman came through the hotel door, beckoning Hall to go with him. At the policeman's house he had a much needed and morale-lifting wash and shave, but it was when the cell door clanged shut in Amsterdam jail that Hall realised what was happening; he was a prisoner-of-war.

During exercise Hall met an RAF sergeant who had recently been captured wearing overalls, not a uniform. Unless he could prove his identity he would be shot as a spy; if he revealed where his uniform was, and who gave him the overalls, a good Dutchman would be shot instead. Hall was very thankful that he was not in the same predicament.

The next morning thirteen prisoners with five guards left by train for Dulag Luft and solitary confinement. In the tiny and roastingly hot cell No. 41, Hall worried about his family's anxiety rather than his own plight.

The 'heat treatment' was in operation. The electric 1.5kW radiator was set at its hottest. Even when stripped to his underpants, Hall found perspiration rolling from him. There seemed to be no way of turning off the gruelling heat, although he later heard that a prisoner further down the row of cells had managed to blow the fuse by urinating on the equipment. When Hall heard of the exploit, he reckoned that he would have been too scared of electrocution through a vital part of his anatomy.

It was a relief to be taken to the office of his interrogator, *Oberleutnant* Koch. Koch was another smooth character whose office wall was covered with RAF quarter-inch maps which showed the location of every RAF station in Britain with squadron numbers clearly marked. Astounded, Hall quickly decided that Koch knew very much more about the RAF than he. Name, rank and number was all they were going to get. The 'soft treatment' was then tried. Hall was moved to a pleasant room in a nearby house and supplied with clean sheets, good food and cigarettes. Small children played in the garden in an atmosphere of homely peace. Hall was unimpressed, and as he claimed to know nothing about a new torpedo, the Germans lost interest in him. Their easy acceptance of his lame story of having lived on raw potatoes and milk direct from cows while on the run surprised him. It was a relief to move on and meet old friends at Sagan.

THE *OBERST'S* TOURER

In the north compound at Sagan, as the officer Kriegies were being dismissed from morning *Appell*, they were excited to see a large open-top Tatra tourer drive through the main gate into the compound. From the car stepped an elegant *Oberst*, a *Wehrmacht* inspector of prisoner-of-war camps, who disappeared into a hut. He was no doubt proud of his impressive, chauffeur-driven vehicle but incredibly foolish to believe it would remain untouched in an RAF prisoner-of-war compound.

The Kriegies drifted from the parade ground and settled like a huge swarm of interested bees around the car. The alarmed *Gefreiter* chauffeur began to raise the hood. Scores of willing Kriegie helpers at the same time removed all loose items from the interior of the car.

When the *Oberst* returned he climbed importantly into the car which drove off at speed, accelerating to demonstrate the performance. After a short distance the car screeched to a halt. The *Oberst*'s police pass

138

was missing; he would not get far without it and had a good idea where it was. A polite request was sent for its return.

A copy had already been made by the 'forgers', so the escape committee agreed to return the pass but not before it had been endorsed: 'Examined by members of The Royal Air Force. Signed ... Winston S. Churchill'.

The *Oberst* no doubt had some explaining to do, but the Kriegies heard that he took the incident well and kept the pass as a reminder of an embarrassing indiscretion. A guard or 'ferret' who had been as careless would have found himself in very serious trouble.

THE MEN FROM THE YMCA

Henry Söderberg was a Swedish representative of the Young Men's Christian Association whose particular concern was the welfare of prisoners-of-war. He made his home in Germany and visited camps such as Stalag Luft 3 and Stalag Luft 6 as often as his busy schedule allowed. Prisoners had much for which to thank him, for his influence was considerable. The Germans liked him. Tall, serene, handsome and fair, he was in their eyes the perfect 'aryan' type that they so greatly admired. Söderberg's linguistic abilities put him at ease in any company and his dedication to his chosen, dangerous duty was total. He was a man to whom the succour and welfare of men of any race, religion and culture was of supreme importance. The contrast between dull, miserable, poor, frightened Germany and brilliantly lit, cheerful Sweden, which he visited when he could, struck him forcibly.

Söderberg was not alone in this work and he still has great admiration for his colleague, Christiansen, from the Danish YMCA. Christiansen worked in northern Germany, visiting, among other camps, Stalag Luft 4 and Stalag Luft 7. When the Russians entered Berlin in April 1945, they suspected Christiansen of being an American spy and he was incarcerated for a year in a Soviet prison. He devoted seven years of his life to prisoners-of-war and related his experiences in a book published in Denmark and, in translation, by University Press, Ohio.

Söderberg noted that *Oberst* von Lindeiner, *Kommandant* of Stalag Luft 3, had a fairly open aversion to the Nazi hierarchy – a dangerous characteristic. He recognised, too, that the German staff at Sagan were nervy, edgy, convinced that the prisoners were tunnelling but unable to pin anything down. They were sure the Kriegies were planning a big escape. The 'ferrets' searched nervously for signs of tunnel sand, poked the compound earth with long steel rods to find shallow tunnels and did their best to sneak up to overhear conversations which suddenly ceased at their approach.

The guards had paid particular attention to the officer Kriegies' 25-strong shower parties. The camp staff suspected that the Kriegies might attempt a break using the party as a cover. They were right, the 'X' organisation did have a plan, a two-pronged plan. Six senior officers, escorted by a bogus guard and supposedly on the way to visit the *Kommandant*, were exposed at the second gate, engaging the full attention of the delighted security people. Meanwhile, 26 Kriegies in a party on their way to the showers, again with one of their own disguised as a guard, made good their escape. All were soon rounded up.

THE LIONS' DEN

The flight to Duisberg, the great inland port and industrial centre, had been one of shot and shell. Sergeant Ken Goodchild, the wireless operator/gunner, was glad to be on the way home. The flak had been concentrated and powerful but the crew felt they had done a good job. Pathfinder marking had been clear and the bombing accurate. They knew that they had sustained some flak damage, but the crew suddenly found themselves in even more desperate trouble when they were attacked again by a Fw190 and a Ju88. The Halifax was badly damaged and would not make it home, The captain gave the 'bale out' signal.

Ken Goodchild marvelled at his good fortune. His parachute descent had been uneventful and his landing gentle and soft in an opened haystack. It was 3 a.m. and quiet, so after disposing of his parachute he walked quietly towards a dirt road nearby. Stiffening suddenly, Goodchild heard a gentle footfall and saw a shadow moving along an almost parallel path. The rustle made by another person was unmistakable and, with pounding heart, Goodchild tried to edge away. For nearly an hour this cat-and-mouse game continued until, in a brief moment, he caught a glimpse of a bulkily dressed figure. It was Sergeant 'Pop' Knight, his flight engineer.

It was a relief to both to have company; never is a man so lonely as when he is alone and hunted in a strange, hostile country. Both men had seen a *Luftwaffe* aerodrome when they were descending by parachute and, in the light of the first flush of dawn, they headed in the direction of the airfield hoping that they could hide up during the day and steal a plane at night.

Passing a farmhouse, they glanced up when they heard a woman open an upstairs window, and saw her lean out and point along the same dirt road. Making off in the direction she indicated, they came to a five-barred gate which stretched across the road. On the gate there were notices printed in several languages but they conveyed little to the two airmen. In a field to the left of the road stood a wooden building which they took to be a large tool-shed. As the area seemed deserted, they decided that the shed would be a safe place to hide for the day. Crossing quickly to the door, Goodchild turned the handle. It opened easily. The inside of the hut was lit and rousing themselves from sleep was a company of ten German soldiers, the guard detail for a frontier post. The airmen had walked into a lions' den.

There was no escaping now but the German soldiers, after recovering from their first amazement, were friendly. They took the airmen in and shared with them their coffee and black bread. Goodchild learned that, just two weeks earlier, the Germans had taken over the post near Poppel between Holland and Belgium because of frontier pilfering. Goodchild realised that the woman waving from her window had been trying to warn them, but they had misunderstood her signals. Now the two airmen were travelling the well-trodden road to Dulag and the inevitable grilling.

A DISDAIN FOR DANGER

On the night of 16–17 May 1943, 617 Squadron carried out the famous 'Dams' raid that captured the imagination of the British public. Led by Wing Commander Guy Gibson, the Lancasters had released a flood of water like a tidal wave into the valleys which, although not appreciably reducing the water supply to the Ruhr, had a devastating effect on German morale. The Kriegies were thrilled and to a man would love to have been part of the raid, despite the heavy losses – eight Lancasters, fifty-three aircrew dead and three prisoners. The Germans tried to play down its importance, accusing the RAF of a deliberate attack on the women and children drowned in the resultant destructive wave.

'What else can you expect,' asked the *Völkischer Beobachter*, 'from these *Terrorfliegers* and *Luftgangsters*; these murderers of innocents?' In some prisoner-of-war camps water supplies were deliberately cut by the Germans in retaliation.

On the same day, the *SS* blew up the main synagogue in Warsaw and completed the destruction of the Ghetto they had created. The Poles who survived the onslaught of the Germans were rounded up and sent for 'resettlement' to Treblinka on their way to Auschwitz and the crematoria.

FLYING FOOD

The 600-aircraft attack on Wuppertal, on 24 June 1943, was aimed at the half of the town that had been little damaged by a heavy raid at the end of May.

Sergeant Reg Cleaver was flight engineer on a 419 Squadron Halifax from RAF Middleton St George. His home in Coventry had been bombed in 1940. Now he was a veteran of many operations, but on this night Cleaver was flying with a different crew. Approaching the target, the Halifax was attacked by three Fw190s. Shells from the first hit the starboard inner engine and badly wounded the navigator. The next fighter set the whole wing ablaze. The third Fw190, for some unaccountable reason, did not attack but just sat astern as if waiting for the Halifax to go down. The *Luftwaffe* pilot made a fatal mistake; the Halifax's rear gunner sent a blast of tracer at the fighter and it turned away, blazing.

The Halifax flew on, although the starboard outer engine seized and literally fell off the wing. For some time the crew nursed it along on the two port engines, hoping they could make the North Sea and ditch. Everything movable was thrown overboard, but the Halifax was losing height and it was soon too low for the crew to bale out. Flying through a row of very large poplars, the aircraft crashed on a Dutch farm. There was no fire and the crew survived.

A Dutch girl, Corrie van Oord, ran to Cleaver and two other crew members to try to get them away but an *SS* Battalion had seen the aircraft crash. The airmen were captured, taken to the prison in Amsterdam and interrogated. Locked in a windowless, pitch-dark underground cell, the RAF men were not allowed to leave it even to relieve themselves. When food was brought, the plate was proffered but, as they reached for it, the contents were thrown over them. For three weeks this treatment continued until, to their relief, they were sent to Dulag. The officers were despatched to Sagan, the NCOs to Heydekrug.

JARMANY CALLING

Sergeant Kenneth Bowden was the kind of person who should have been 'born in a trunk'. The stage seemed to be his natural home and that was where he was, one special night in 1943, when a concert was put on in the camp theatre by the Kriegies in honour of YMCA man Henry Söderberg. The German camp officers were seated in the front row on either side of 'Dixie' Deans, Söderberg and the *Kommandant*.

Bowden had been doing impersonations and had taken his applause, bowed and exited left when producer Alan 'Tubby' Dixon pushed him back on to the stage for an encore; the next act was not ready. The encore over, faced with another delay, Dixon propelled Bowden back on with instructions to pad out his performance a little longer. Only one voice remained in Bowden's repertoire but he usually reserved it for British audiences. Looking at the German officers, he took a breath and launched into the voice of William Joyce (Lord Haw-Haw), reading the *Deutschlandsender* news with a tale of how his father's grave had to be moved to build a sewer. Puzzlement, then shock, showed on the Germans' faces and their hands moved towards their holsters. But the humour filtered through to them and slowly, taking their cue from the *Kommandant*, they began to smile and laugh. Gradually, Bowden's palms ceased their sweating and his heart its pumping.

After the show the *Kommandant* told Bowden: 'That was very brave ... but it was very funny.'

Another of Bowden's tricks was deliberately to cause confusion during roll-calls so that escapers would not be missed. A Kriegie wearing a very long overcoat would button it over his head so that he was completely covered while Bowden would push his head beneath the other's arm. The 'head tucked underneath the arm' pose was very effective, causing enough momentary confusion for someone to sneak down the middle row to be counted again.

YIPPEE!

From the beginning the Germans had been unable, or unwilling, to devise a better means of constructing or of emptying the primitive latrine pits in the NCOs' compounds. Watching the flexible pipe being lowered into the heaving mess, the Kriegies at Heydekrug were intrigued to see a new man on the job. He seemed a little unsure of himself and his two-horse team, whereas the Kriegies, as observers, were by now theoretically expert. When the German poured rather more than usual benzine into the pump, their interest was thoroughly aroused. They waited for the lighted match to be applied. The resultant 'bloody great bang' and the crashing down of the flap valve on top of the tank startled the horses, which bolted with the little German standing on the cart-step frantically pulling the reins and shouting. But the suction had already begun and, as the horses ran, the flexible pipe was pulled from the pit, the contents spraying in all directions. The watching Kriegies, anticipating this, had retired to a safe distance. There they cheered heartily with cowboy 'whoops' at this extempore German attempt at a rodeo.

DANGEROUS CROSSING

It was natural that, even under such trying circumstances, the American prisoners in Sagan should want to celebrate Independence Day. Brews made from raisins, currants and prunes had been laid down earlier and allowed to ferment. Eventually the bubbling liquid was illicitly distilled to produce a fiery, fiercely intoxicating liquor. The infectious *joie de vivre* of the Americans spread throughout the camp. Cares and close confinement were forgotten for a few hours and inhibitions cast aside, causing several senior officers to be thrown unceremoniously into the central fire pool.

When the block doors were closed at 11 p.m. some officers found themselves locked in the wrong huts. In such a rare and happy condition they decided to defy German orders and make their way through the windows back to their rooms. Among those to attempt this dangerous crossing were the acting SBO, Wing Commander Harry Day, and the SAO, Colonel Charles Goodrich. They were fortunate that they were only caught by a patrolling guard with a bristling Alsatian who escorted them to the 'cooler' for the rest of the night – much to the delight and amusement of the prisoners in the compound.

In another incident Squadron Leader Ken Grant thought he was about to be attacked by one of the Alsatians and took refuge in the communal lavatory. A guard's assurances that the dog would not attack brought Grant outside, but as he and the guard neared the gate, the dog appeared to other Kriegies to be biting the officer's arm. Grant made a dash for a hut but the guard drew his pistol and fired three shots. A bullet struck the squadron leader and for a week he was on the danger list.

Because of these incidents the *Kommandant* forbade the making of inebriating brews and in a search the guards destroyed all the stills they could find.

PANIC AT THE 'ALL CLEAR'

The mildness of the summer weather and the now almost nightly stream of bombers over the camp at Luft 1 Barth gave Sergeant Arthur Minnitt an idea for an escape. The effluent board led through a trapdoor from the hut toilet to the *abort* outside, if he could get through the trap then crawl under the wire during the darkness of an air-raid alert there was a chance of an escape. Two other NCOs decided to join him. The night came when all the camp lights went out as a bomber stream rumbled past overhead. Quickly the three went through the trap and up to the wire. With the cutters snipping, they were frantically bending back the wire when suddenly the small bomber stream passed over, the 'all clear' siren wailed and died away. All was quiet, when the high-power lamps around the perimeter flooded the area with dazzling light.

In an undignified rush the three tore back to the hut. Two dived through the flap but Minnitt's trousers caught and held him with his head and torso inside the hut being pulled by three men. His legs were outside in the brilliant compound lighting. Expecting to hear the roar of gunfire and

144

to feel bullets ripping into his exposed legs at any moment, 'Arf-a-Mo Min-nitt struggled and scraped through, his trousers severely torn and minus several inches of skin. But relief that the *Posten* had not seen him took over, the strain passed and the mood of relief changed to one of laughter and ribald comment about the recent danger to Sgt Minnitt's lower half.

'HANDS UP, ENGLISHMAN!'

Sergeant Les Blanchard, a bomb aimer of 77 Squadron, had been on the run in Belgium since 11 June. The mayor and people of the town of Her-stal had provided him with civilian clothes and a bicycle and told him to follow a guide. If he was caught he was to show no signs of knowing the man and to say that he had stolen the bicycle.

Blanchard remembered his instructions, but when he heard a car coming from behind, he instinctively wobbled over to the left side of the road. For a heart-stopping moment the car slowed down. The German officers in the car shouted at him with the arrogance of conquerors and drove on.

At the end of his cycle ride Blanchard was hidden for two days at a fire station before being taken by a priest to Liège. There he stayed in a house with two wanted Jews, also being sheltered. Ten days later, he was reunited with the mid-upper gunner of his Halifax, Sgt Dennis Burrows, who had also evaded capture. They were both passed into the care of a man in whose car they were to travel to Brussels. The airmen became sus-picious that the man could be a double agent. In the centre of Liège, where a swastika flew over the town hall, the car apparently broke down. It was immediately surrounded by armed soldiers, but the agent pro-duced a bundle of documents and the soldiers were marched away. The agent said that he had told the officer that the passengers were members of the Swiss legation.

More RAF escapees, Belgian agents and a Jew with a price on his head joined the party in Brussels, which then set off by train to Paris. It seemed that their guide had been instrumental in avoiding their being searched and some confidence was restored.

The next day, 5 July, the entire party were told they were going on a train journey that would lead to Spain and freedom. Mixed emotions and fears, hopes and doubts, raced through the fugitives' minds, but on a sudden command pistols were whipped from the pockets of plain-clothes men. The party was surrounded by shouting, gesturing *Gestapo*.

A pistol jabbed painfully into Blanchard's back as a voice in his ear growled, 'Hands up, Englishman, take your hand out of your pocket very, very slowly. If you pull it out fast you're dead.'

145

As he was climbing into a car at gun-point, Blanchard, with disappointment falling over him like a black cloud, heard the *Gestapo* man ask: 'You are English, aren't you?' When there was no reply he continued, 'I can wait, we have means of getting you to tell us.'

At Fresnes prison the prisoners were taken in pairs to be questioned. Blanchard, handcuffed to Burrows, was particularly worried. He was pretending to be a Belgian commercial traveller and carried false identification papers which bore his photograph.

At first, the *Gestapo* would not accept his protests that he was an RAF flyer. To them he was a spy and could be shot. After ten days of solitary confinement, starvation rations, continual interrogation and threats, the *Gestapo* interrogators reluctantly believed his story and he was returned to his cell. Two months later he was sent from the horror of Fresnes to Dulag Luft.

CARPET OF FIRE

Worries about presenting the Germans with the secret of 'Window' – the fine metallic strips of foil designed by the young scientist R. V. Jones to confuse German radar – were finally dispelled on 23 July 1943, and Sir Arthur Harris lost no time in putting it to full use in a raid on Hamburg on the night of 24-25 July.

At first the radar stations on Sylt and Heligoland were staggered when their screens registered an approaching raid consisting of some 11,000 bombers. The impossibility made them try harder to separate the bombers on their screens but 'Window' had made their radar screens useless. Radar was swamped and it was impossible to send directions to the circling nightfighters.

From the view of Bomber Command and its chief, 'Operation Gomorrah' and Window were a great success. To the people of Hamburg they were, in the words of Goebbels, 'a catastrophe'.

On the night of 27-28 July a follow-up raid on Hamburg fuelled the famous fire-storm. Hamburg, easily picked out on the river by the H2S screen, became a vast carpet of fire, the network of streets etched in flaming red. Air gunner Geoff Parnell felt sorry, on this one and only time, for the Germans.

'We could see a street map drawn in fire. A great bubbling, festering, incandescent mass with more and more incendiaries pouring in – Hell could be no worse,' recalled Parnell in awestruck wonder, 'You could read a newspaper at 14,000 feet and feel naked in the unaccustomed brilliance.'

Seventeen aircraft were lost to the newly introduced *Wilde Sau* methods despite the use of 'Window'.

There were four heavy raids, one producing the hugely lethal and destructive firestorm. It had drawn oxygen away to feed the fire, causing hundreds of people to be suffocated in the air-raid shelters, and had left Hamburg a battered, burning shell with a smoke pall covering the city and obscuring the target indicators on the last raid. Kriegies could see the glow of the fires as far away as the prisoner-of-war camps near Hanover and stories of the appalling havoc came from 'tame' guards. In one week as many people were killed in Hamburg as had been killed in all the raids on Britain.

Armaments Minister Albert Speer wrote that another six such attacks would put Germany out of the war.

WILD BOARS

Losses in Bomber Command were rising. The night of 3–4 July 1943 had seen the birth of a new tactic by the German defenders. *Luftwaffe Major* Hajo Herrmann had long pressed for day fighters to be allowed to attempt to shoot down the bombers by the light of any illumination available, such as searchlights, flares, target indicators or the reflection of fires below. At last his No. 300 Fighter Group was given its chance during a heavy raid on Cologne. Despite the opposition of *General* Kammhuber, Herrmann's *Wilde Sau* (Wild Boar) Messerschmitts went into action. The RAF lost 38 aircraft that night, at least 14, probably more, to nightfighters.

More than 700 bombers, led by Pathfinder aircraft raided Berlin on the night of 23–24 August. With the route marked by Mosquitoes and a master bomber in charge, the bomber force found its way to the 'Big City' without difficulty but, on this occasion, the Pathfinders, even with the help of the sophisticated H2S navigational aid, were unable to identify the target area. Added to this, the main force arrived late and, in cutting corners, frequently bombed open country. This raid, the beginning of the Battle of Berlin, cost Bomber Command 56 heavy bombers. To surviving aircrew, losses on this scale were patently unacceptable. There were so many faces missing from the bars and the armchairs in the mess anteroom. Graves, known and unknown, and the prisoner-of-war camps were filling.

BBC commentator Wynford Vaughan-Thomas flew with this attack on Berlin and, like Richard Dimbleby, was clearly alarmed as all around he saw the brilliantly coloured Pathfinder flares, the flak and fighters' tracers flashing past and aircraft flaming. At last, people back home had some idea of the terrifying intensity of the air war in the night skies of Europe.

HORSE LAUGH

Sergeant Wilf Sutton was the flight engineer of a Halifax of 35 Squadron which took off at 10.15 p.m. from RAF Gravely on that same occasion to mark the route and target for the bomber stream. Climbing to the operational height of 22,000 feet, the pilot set course for Berlin. Because they were leading the way, and the entire stream was behind, any aircraft that approached within 1,000 yards caused 'Monica' to bleep.

'Monica' was a rearward-looking radar which gave a warning of fighter or other aircraft in a 45 degree wide cone. A series of bleeps into earphones increased in intensity as the range closed. 'Monica' became unpopular with the crews because of false alarms from friendly aircraft in the bomber stream. As 'A Able' crossed into Holland in heavy cloud, the crew decided that an hour of bleeping 'Monica' was enough – they switched off the warning radar.

Just east of Hanover, the Halifax came out of the cloud and, within minutes, a Junkers 88 had straddled it with 20mm cannon shells. As the attack started, Sgt Sutton was at the flare chute to push out 'Window' foil strips. The pilot 'corkscrewed' the Halifax into violent evasive action. He succeeded in evading the fighter, but when the plane was righted, Sutton could see the extent of the damage. Cannon shells had ripped through the fuselage, within an inch of the flare chute position, and torn the starboard wing apart. The two starboard engines were on fire plus the tank containing 1,000 gallons of high octane fuel. Miraculously, the seven crew members were unharmed.

In desperate circumstances one is sometimes driven to extraordinary and incomprehensible measures. Wilf Sutton uncoupled his oxygen and intercom leads, went to the centre of the plane and grasped a tiny fire extinguisher. He realised immediately the futility of trying to douse the roaring flames from 1,000 gallons of burning fuel against a 250mph slipstream, so he made his way back to the flare chute and reconnected his oxygen and intercom leads in time to hear the skipper calling the crew to abandon the aircraft. Every item that had not been securely fixed inside the Halifax had been whirled around by the corkscrewing; luckily Sutton's parachute had thumped down near him. Quickly clipping it to his harness, he opened the rear hatch and jumped into the moonlit night.

The potato field was soft and Sutton's landing was easy. He buried his parachute among the potatoes, then searched the sky, found the North Star and headed towards Stettin in the hope of stowing away on a Swedish boat. It was a warm, still, summer night when sound carries over long distances. Just as Sutton was crossing a field, a noise on his right startled him. For a few seconds he felt paralysed, and then he ran and ran until he slumped to the ground gasping with exhaustion. He was so winded that he had passed beyond worrying about who was chasing him. Slowly recovering his breath and wits, he looked around him and saw, not a soldier or a farmer, but a horse. And it was on the opposite side of a wire fence. Sutton started to laugh, and continued laughing until that, too, exhausted him. He crawled into a copse to regain his equilibrium and, within a matter of seconds, leaning against a tree, he was fast asleep.

Sutton was woken next morning by the voices of German labourers on their way to the farms. As the copse gave only minimum cover, he filled his water bottle with rain-water and purifying tablets, took the RAF markings from his battledress, cut the top from his flying boots to make them look more like shoes and set off to find better shelter until dark. As he walked along a country path, the landscape was so much like that at home that he found it difficult to accept that he was in Germany. Even passing farmers called out '*Morgen*' which sounded very familiar. Sutton felt confident that he could make his escape without too much difficulty. Ten minutes later, he was disillusioned when three shotgun-armed farmers challenged him. They shouted '*Flieger*'. Sutton knew what they meant and replied '*Ja*'. From that moment they were convinced that he spoke German.

At a *Luftwaffe* barracks Sutton joined about 90 other RAF men taken prisoner from the previous night's raid. Losses had been the heaviest in one night so far in the war. Dulag Luft was never so crowded.

ON DANGEROUS GROUND

Leutnant Eberhardt, an interrogator at Dulag Luft reception centre, was an oily character. Alternately smooth and bullying, he nevertheless stopped short of physical violence. Veiled threats of extended solitary confinement, mixed with appeals for reason, and the suggestion that the captured airman could be handed over to a less humane authority, were his stock-in-trade. With one prisoner he had no trouble. Michael Joyce was a member of the crew of a Hampden which crash-landed in Holland on 26–27 August 1940. When the rest of the captured crew were sent from Dulag Luft, Joyce stayed behind. He had agreed to Eberhardt's suggestion that he spy for Germany.

Joyce spied on his fellow prisoners within the camps and at other times. Wearing German uniform, he interrogated British prisoners in North Africa. Finally, he reverted to his RAF identity and with the cooperation of the *Gestapo* joined an escape line in order to infiltrate and betray its members to the Germans. Reaching Gibraltar, Joyce was repatriated to England, his story of courage and daring during his 'escape' earning him a commission in the Royal Air Force and a Military Medal.

It was when Eberhardt himself was captured and interrogated that Joyce's treachery became apparent. Interviewed, he at first denied the charges but eventually broke down and confessed. In June 1946 he was stripped of his medal and resigned his commission shortly afterwards. He was never court-martialled and returned to Ireland, where he died in 1976. His treachery remained generally unknown until author Alan Cooper, in the course of his researches, uncovered the shameful story.

Some crew members of the 44 aircraft lost on the Peenemünde raid survived to become prisoners-of-war. Lancaster air gunner Sergeant Raymond Hughes from Mold in North Wales was one. He found himself 'cattle-trucked' to Dulag Luft, where he was interrogated by smooth *Leutnant* Eberhardt. Hughes's story was that he professed ignorance when questioned about 'Monica', and that when he refused to fill in the usual bogus Red Cross form with more than rank, name and number, Eberhardt threatened to hand him over to the *Gestapo* and then proceeded to fill in most of the form himself. When asked by Eberhardt if the form entries were correct, Hughes replied, 'If you say so they must be.' Then Hughes filled in the names of his crew and signed the form as asked. Hughes was on dangerous ground. His story continued that when he had been visited by an American and a Pole who asked him if he had considered escaping, he found his cell door left unlocked. From then on, although locked in at night, Hughes was able to walk in and out of the building freely.

A few days later, a German officer asked Hughes for his assistance in getting Red Cross interrogation forms completed and told him that he had better be known as *Herr* Becker. From then on, Hughes says, he was always referred to as Becker by the German staff.

He was later taken to meet Sqn Ldr Boyd-Carpenter and Norman Baillie-Stewart. Baillie-Stewart, the notorious 'officer in the Tower', had been cashiered from the Seaforth Highlanders and jailed for selling official secrets to Germany. He was now an Austrian citizen. Hughes was also introduced to other men connected with the British Free Corps. Boyd-Carpenter warned Hughes that the Germans would try to get him to broadcast and he was on no account to do so.

Hughes was given a small office and instructed to write talks for broadcasting, principally about Jews and Russia. Advised to maintain amicable relations with the Germans, Hughes, with help, wrote three or four talks on the lines of those by William Joyce, also obtaining much material from the book *John Amery Speaks*. His scripts were rejected as poor, but he was offered a commission in the British Free Corps. He was told that 2,000 men were waiting to join the corps, which would be commanded by Brigadier General Patterson from Crete, and that Amery was the head. Hughes says that in order to find out the names and make-up of the Free Corps he expressed an interest.

But it was when Hughes visited the Radio Metropole station at Wannsee, Berlin, that he took a step towards committing treason. His version of subsequent events was that he suggested to the Germans that he should broadcast in Welsh to the Welsh regiments serving in North Africa and, following 'Land of my Fathers', read the Lord's Prayer. Knowing the Germans were unfamiliar with the language, he would introduce in the middle of the prayer, 'You know where I am: give the Sports Palast a good clout. It is being used as a place for talking over the air.'

Although Hughes was provided with accommodation in Berlin and a salary, he claimed that his true purpose in hobnobbing with the Germans was to obtain as much information as possible and eventually to escape with it, to destroy the British Free Corps and to carry out sabotage. In evidence at his court-martial in August 1945, he stated that he had misled the Germans concerning Bomber Command tactics, sabotaged street telephones and wrecked a train. He told defence counsel Mr T. U. Liddle that he had never been a traitor but was proud of his efforts for his country.   Mr Liddle described Hughes's activities as 'a campaign for assisting his own country and not assisting the enemy'.

On six of the eleven charges Hughes was acquitted. Found guilty on the other five counts, he was sentenced to five years' penal servitude.

A FOOT IN THE BACK DOOR

On 24 July 1943, the Italian dictator Benito Mussolini was deposed and, on 8 September, armistice terms between the Allies and Italy were published. The fourth anniversary of the start of the war had seen the last of the programmed raids on Berlin. The three major attacks had cost 123 heavy bombers and their crews. The air war against Germany was costing Bomber Command dear, but at least Germany's Italian ally was now out of the war. Montgomery and the 8th Army had landed on the toe of Italy. Allied troops were on the mainland of Europe. The Germans under Field Marshal Kesselring reacted swiftly, disarming their former allies and taking over the defence of Italy.

In the Italian prisoner-of-war camps there was confusion until orders were received from British headquarters for the prisoners to 'stay put'. In Chieti the British colonel in charge told the prisoners that they must stay and threatened a court-martial for those who made a bolt for freedom. It was a strange decision; it condemned the prisoners to an unknown future and further incarceration in the harsher regime of German prisoner-of-war camps. There was help outside the Italian camps, provided a man on the run did not fall into the hands of German troops or pro-Axis partisans. Some did run and eventually reached Allied lines, some died in the attempt, but most prisoners would like to have tried.

Alec Burton in Chieti felt that the remainder waited like sheep until, on one depressing morning, they awoke to find khaki-clad, blonde youths of a *Fallschirmjäger* unit manning the sentry posts. A nightmare journey in the usual box-cars followed, ending for Burton at Sagan.

Burton had founded another satirical wall-paper burlesquing the camp newspaper 'Scangriff'. He called it 'Slangriff'. The paper consisted mainly of wisecracks subtitling illustrations clipped from the German press. An editorial example was:

Once again 'Slangriff' brings you last year's news and views, in accordance with our famous slogan: 'What the *Völkischer Beobachter* prints today – we tear into convenient squares tomorrow! Any resemblance in these pages to any real persons, whether alive or dead, will be a pleasant surprise to the Editor.

Not every jibe was directed against the Reich however, for example:

HOME NEWS
We hear, in a letter, of the dumb blonde who thought that a
'Static Charge' was a British attack on the Italian Front.

TODAY'S HAPPY THOUGHT
What do they know of England who haven't been back
since the Yanks landed?

The quips reflected the struggle the Allies were having against the Germans in Italy, a country perfect for defence, and the prisoners' ever present worry about the effect the money and nylon-rich American troops were having on the feminine population of Britain.

'AS BALD AS COOTS'

The Battle of Berlin continued. On the night of 31 August more than 600 aircraft raided the city, but heavy cloud and ferociously effective German defences caused the bombing to be ineffectually spread. Forty-seven of the bombers were lost, mostly to nightfighters who used the light of flares dropped by *Luftwaffe* bombers into the bomber stream to illuminate their quarry. This was another of Herrmann's ploys. The navigator of a 51 Squadron Halifax, Sergeant Tom Nelson, knew that his aircraft had been attacked by a fighter, but the subsequent violent explosion took the crew by surprise. The three members in the nose section, who had clipped on their parachute packs, were blown out and all managed to pull the rip-cords. The other four members of the crew died. Such was the loss of height from 18,000 feet that the parachutists and the plane came down into an area no more than 100 yards across.

As Tom Nelson was falling, he saw his parachute pack, which had pulled out of its shoulder harness, floating five feet in front of him. In the deliberate way that some people are able to deal with a life and death emergency, Nelson reached out, drew the pack to him and pulled the 'D' ring. Five seconds later, he landed and ran off into the darkness. The bomb aimer and wireless operator were captured immediately and compelled to remove the four bodies from the wreckage. To their distress, they saw that the body of the pilot, P/O Larry Cates, was severely burned all down his left side.

Nelson evaded capture for two days, then, after a fitful rest in a wood, awoke to find a farm worker holding a pitchfork to his throat.

Prison camps for RAF men were grossly overcrowded so, after Dulag, Nelson was one of a group sent to Stalag 4B near Mühlberg, close to the east bank of the Elbe, and 120 kilometres due south of Berlin. Stalag 4B was another of those camps which since 1941 had housed French and Belgian Army prisoners, many in transit. In due course, Russians, Serbs and, later still, Italians arrived.

At Mühlberg Nelson underwent what he described as a crowning indignity. A kind of 'sheep shearing' machine with a hand-wheel at one end of a flexible tube and a set of clipper shears at the other was operated by two men. With this primitive tool one turned the wheel while the other cut the hair from the next man's head. 'All ended as bald as coots,' said Tom Nelson, 'with morale at rock bottom.'

Red Cross parcels had been almost unheard of at Mühlberg and the German rations were of the usual starvation quantity and quality. Three weeks later, 5,000 Allied soldiers arrived. They had been taken prisoner in North Africa, had spent about a year in Italian camps and had been rounded up with their former guards, who were now also prisoners of the Germans. It was a recipe for friction. The Italians were from a mountain regiment and wore green capes and Tyrolean hats. None was more than five feet tall. For some time Tom Nelson thought all Italians were as diminutive.

Conditions improved when Red Cross parcels began to arrive regularly. Men could take an interest in subjects other than food, but their feeling of well-being was marred by seeing the abominable treatment the

Germans dealt out to the Russians. It was a favourite winter game of the Germans to catch a Russian in some minor misdemeanour and punish him by forcing him to stand at the main gate facing into the east wind with his bare hands out of his pockets. In a temperature of minus 10 to 20 degrees Centigrade it usually took less than twenty minutes for a man to fall unconscious. The Kriegies donated as much food as possible each week to the Russians, but it could only go to the sick and the dying.

IDENTITY CHANGE

Persistent escapers were frequently transferred to a place the Germans thought more secure. Stalag 8B Lamsdorf and Oflag 4C Colditz were selected, Lamsdorf because the RAF compound was surrounded by other compounds, which made tunnelling to the outside almost impossible, and Colditz because it was a castle built on a hill of solid rock through which pneumatic drills would be needed to carve a tunnel. With masses of barbed wire, searchlights and guards, both prisons would be escape proof, or so thought the *Luftwaffe*.

Lamsdorf contained many thousands of army prisoners who, by the terms of the Geneva Convention, could be made to work for the Germans. Working on farms, factories, quarries and mines meant the prisoners leaving the confines of the huge camp, and it was inevitable that the RAF men should sometimes be allowed to enter the other compounds and mix with the army prisoners. Getting outside the *Luftwaffe*-run camps was extremely difficult, but with the army working camps a swap with a willing, reasonably look-alike working soldier took a potential escaper outside the wire. Once there, his problems were enormous but at least the first step was over. Many men took this route, some successfully.

After ten attempts at escape, big, bluff, RAAF Flight Lieutenant Alan McSweyn contrived somehow to swap identities with an army orderly at Sagan and deliberately behaved so badly that he was sent to Lamsdorf. On 19 September 1943, dressed as a French workman and furnished with identity card and sick leave papers, he scrambled through a tunnel with a companion, New Zealand Army driver F. Williamson, a fluent German speaker. McSweyn's poor French accent was covered by the illness shown on his sick leave pass, tubercular laryngitis. The pass and their courage led them across Germany and to the Resistance.

Their hazardous travels had taken them through Mannheim during a heavy RAF raid. McSweyn and Williamson stayed silent in a crowded air-raid shelter while the Germans beside them discussed just what they would do to an airman who fell into their hands.

Driver Williamson was sent on ahead by the Resistance and, to McSweyn's distress, lost his life as he struggled in deep snow to cross the Pyrenees. During a dangerous and trying journey, McSweyn himself crossed the Pyrenees into Spain and went on to Gibraltar and England.

Fred Turner was a corporal, a Londoner in the KRRC, taken prisoner during the invasion of Crete. Flight Lieutenant Rex Reynolds was a journalist who had worked for the *Sunday Times* in Johannesburg and was an 80 Squadron Hurricane pilot. The two men met briefly during the forcible removal by the Germans of Allied prisoners from Italy to camps in Austria, and there they swapped identities. Reynolds believed that he would have more opportunity for escape as a soldier than as an RAF officer, so to the Germans Turner was Reynolds and Reynolds Turner for the remainder of the war.

The flight lieutenant was a determined escaper and made several attempts from working parties while masquerading as a soldier. Captured in Libya, he had already established a reputation for dash and courage when he landed his aircraft in the desert and picked up a crashed pilot.

Fred Turner carried off the impersonation perfectly and with courage. Few in the camps other than the SBO and one or two who had known Reynolds in earlier days knew of the swap and they were sworn to secrecy. Turner could have been in very serious trouble with the Germans had they discovered his true identity. Turner, alias Flt Lt Reynolds, was sent to Sagan's north compound.

'ALLES TOT'

It would have been strange if Sergeant John Dennis had not been considered a 'jinx'; two of the Halifaxes in which he had flown had been written off through crash-landings. On his last operation Dennis, the mid-upper gunner, and the rear gunner had succeeded in shooting down a Junkers 88 and possibly a ME110. In the action four of the crew were wounded and the other three, including Dennis, were sent on leave. On returning from leave, Dennis was 'spare' and, when asked if he would fill the place of a sick gunner, he agreed, but was shaken to discover that this was to be the crew's first operational trip. The target was Hanover, a city that had not been heavily raided for two years.

Nearing Hanover, Dennis saw a Halifax coned in searchlights, hit by flak and go down like a bright meteor. Dennis's aircraft dropped its bombs and turned for home. Just as they cleared the target area, he saw two flares dropping behind the Halifax and yelled a warning of fighters

155

to the skipper. As on a previous operation, Sgt Dennis heard that frightening rat-a-tat-tat but this time, as he twisted round to look, flames were roaring from the starboard wing and growing fiercer every moment. There was no sign of life from the front so he climbed from his turret, uncertain what to do. The Halifax was going to crash, that was sure. Dennis rammed his parachute on to the chest-harness clips, ran back and kicked out the escape hatch. Before jumping out, he felt he had to make sure whether the rear gunner was still alive. He tried to open the turret doors but the aircraft went into a dive, knocking him to the floor and holding him down by the 'G' force. Unable to move, Dennis lay helpless. This was it, he thought and said a prayer, hoping that the end would be painless.

As the aircraft struck, he was thrown from the horizontal position on the floor through to the front of the aircraft. His left knee struck the midships step and his parachute pack hit the framework of the mid-upper turret. It saved his life. Exactly at that point, the fuselage split open and Dennis, unable to move, lay half in and half out of the fuselage. The fire blazed higher, there was a tremendous explosion and he lost consciousness.

Slowly his senses returned. Lifting his arm, Dennis looked at his watch. It was five minutes past five, morning or afternoon he did not know. Foggily, all he could think of was that, if he could get to the pigeons in the Halifax, he could send a message home to England so that people would know they were still alive. It seemed sensible then, but he could not move and drifted off again into oblivion.

John Dennis's next recollection was of strange voices and soldiers in unusual uniforms looking down at him. He turned and saw that the Halifax had cut a swathe through some trees. Again he tried to get up but could not move. As *Wehrmacht* men lifted him out of the wrecked aircraft, he could see that the front was charred to a cinder.

'What about my comrades?' he asked, A *Wehrmacht* officer looked straight at him. '*Alles tot*,' he said simply.

Dennis slipped in and out of consciousness as he was taken by ambulance, first to one hospital and then another, where each decided that his injuries were too serious for it to handle. As he came out of one spell of dark numbness he saw a man in a white coat boring a hole in his kneecap with what looked to him like a plumber's drill. He slipped into painless black oblivion again. When next he regained consciousness he was on his back; a plaster cast covered him from the shoulder blades to below his groin and down his left leg to beyond his ankle. The only apertures in the cast were those necessary for his natural functions. He felt the need almost at once. Pressing a bell-push nearby brought a nurse, a nun. As Dennis tried to explain that he needed a bed-pan, the nurse said 'Ja, ja' and was back seconds later with a glass of water. He realised that he had to learn some German pretty quickly. When they understood his needs, he had to be lifted on and off the bed-pan – a procedure of indescribable agony.

The first thing that John Dennis had seen as he regained consciousness was a crucifix. It convinced him that he was in Holland. Propaganda had it that Hitler had abolished the church and there was no such thing as religion in Germany. Therefore, he reasoned, the aircraft must have crashed beyond the German–Dutch border. Already, despite his crippling injuries, he was thinking of underground movements and escape, but he was to lie in that plaster for nearly three months. He was wrong, too, about his location; he was in the St Marien hospital near Oldenburg – in Germany.

Dennis described the surgeon who operated on him as 'a charming fellow,' but his deputy was a man twisted by personal tragedy, the loss of his wife and two children in a cellar in Hamburg. When Dennis was alone this man would repeatedly tell him that they were 'incinerated'. Staring malevolently for long moments, he would say: 'Ah! Sgt Johnnie Dennis, the Bolshevist baby killer. And how is our gallant sergeant today? Have you killed any babies recently, sergeant?'

He would ask Dennis if he had been on the Hamburg raids and go on to tell how those cellars, full of sheltering people, were white-hot for days after the raids. Producing a photograph of his wife and two children, the deputy surgeon would thrust it in Dennis's face, forcing him to look. He would then ask if Dennis felt proud of how the gallant RAF were bombing the women and children of Germany. To assert that the *Luftwaffe* was carrying out the same thing in England would only send the deputy surgeon into a rage and he would start pacing rapidly around the bed. Helpless in his plaster cast, Dennis was sure that the enraged man would do him further injury. To the nursing nuns it was unimportant who he was or how he came to be there. He was just another patient needing their help. When in their care it was hard for him to believe he was a prisoner of war.

During his stay in the hospital, John Dennis became a favourite of the nurses and his own personal *Luftwaffe* guard, a man named Joseph but called Yop by everyone. Guard and prisoner became very close friends and, when they were alone, they had discussions about Hitler and Churchill. Yop told Dennis that when Hitler began to obtain power, the Germans had nothing. Hitler offered them work and some kind of a future, whereas previously they were just wallowing about like a ship without a captain.

For three months, John Dennis's only contacts were the nuns and Yop. For hours he would count the seconds between the quarter-hour striking of the local church clock. When RAF bombers passed overhead, everyone went to the shelters but Dennis could not be moved. He was sure that during alarms he was the only person above ground in the hospital.

Throughout his stay, Dennis had asked what was wrong with him, why he had the encasing plaster and why he was not allowed to sit up in bed. He knew that his right leg was broken but, when he tried to discuss his condition, the nuns and Yop pretended they did not understand.

When Dennis was allowed to get up for a while in November he saw 'that damned clock' for the first time, and saw, too, the many German wounded in the hospital, most of them amputees on crutches. Yop told him that most were suffering from frostbite incurred on the *Ostfront*.

One morning in December, the Mother Superior came to see Dennis. She was obviously upset when she told him that he was to leave the hospital that night, concerned about the journey to the prisoner-of-war camp and how he would manage. During that day the entire staff came to say '*Auf Wiedersehn*'. John Dennis was moved near to tears; he had made many friends there.

The faithful Yop did not leave Dennis that day; he was a friend from whom parting was a wrench. Dennis tried to cheer him and said, 'Don't worry Yop. I shall be all right and, when the war is over, I will come back with my wife, find you and buy you a bottle of Schnapps.' That was too much for Joseph. Overcome, he could only say, 'Ya, Ya, Yonny'.

At the station Yop said goodbye and hurriedly left.

The journey was a nightmare. The wheelchair in which he had been taken to the station had to be returned; somehow he had to manage without it. Standing was a torment; his huge plaster cast seemed to attract the bitter cold. The train arrived drawn by a snorting monster locomotive bearing the slogan *Ein Reich, Ein Volk, Ein Führer*. Painfully, Dennis struggled aboard, with little help from his guards.

When they changed to the Cologne express, the train was full and a *Feldgendarmerie* policeman roughly ordered everyone out of a compartment into the corridor, so that Dennis and his escort had the compartment to themselves. Thereafter, the expelled passengers spent the journey to Frankfurt glaring at them. Next stop was Dulag Luft and then a hospital run by British Army prisoners. There, his plaster was at last removed and John Dennis realised that his left leg was now one-and-three-quarter inches shorter than the right. He was to have a club foot for the rest of his life.

When told he must persist in trying to walk with crutches, Dennis complained of the pain in his leg and back. The Medical Officer, Captain Willie Smellie, who had been taken at Dunkirk, retorted: 'The trouble with you, Sergeant Dennis, is that you think you are the only man who has ever been wounded, and you should have all the attention. There are chaps in this hospital who are in a far worse condition than you, but they don't come whining to me saying they can't walk. You want to pull yourself together man and think that you can walk and not give up at the slightest twinge of pain.'

John Dennis was stunned by this speech. He was furious and swore under his breath, 'You bastard! Even if I'm dying I won't come near you again.'

Yet when his anger subsided, he was glad to see the MO again before leaving the hospital. He knew that the speech was instrumental in bolstering his determination to succeed in walking, and many other actions he had thought impossible.

Sergeant Ron Bence, a Channel Islander who had lost a leg after being shot down in a Blenheim in 1940, was fortunate in coming into the care of Arthur Weston, a soldier taken in France. Weston had cajoled the Germans into allowing him sufficient tools and wood to fashion artificial limbs and he had set up a workshop near Lamsdorf. One of Weston's early jobs had been to make a jointed and articulated leg for Ron Bence. An elated Bence had taken his first faltering steps on crutches in September 1940 and was now, in the autumn of 1943, walking with just a stick.

THE GARDENER

Matt Clarke had been working in the small garden plot at Stalag Luft 1 Barth since his arrival at Easter 1943. The rewards were minimal. His friends thought him crazy, but Matt had a long-term plan. Now, at the end of September, he surveyed the pile of weeds, the result of spring and summer weeding, that he had systematically tossed beneath the stilts of the *Posten* box. Unobserved, a great mass of undergrowth had sprung up around them. One night, he hid in the compound after the evening *Appell*. In the dark he cut his way through the wire into the undergrowth that he had so assiduously nurtured and then snipped through the outer wire. He was soon returned to the camp for a sojourn in the 'cooler', his half-year of work and planning fruitless except for the satisfaction of 'having had a go'.

A DARK HORSE

All the prisoners at Sagan were delighted and thrilled by the escape of three officers from the east compound. Day after day, they had been carried outdoors, encased in a wooden vaulting horse. They had excavated a hundred-foot tunnel beneath and beyond the wire. The play *French Without Tears* was scheduled to begin in the camp theatre at 6 p.m., precisely the time when the tunnel was to break. The camp guards and security staff had been invited to attend the play. Most accepted and were ushered to seats in the front row. There they could be watched throughout the vital period. The cast carried on with their lines, every moment expecting to hear rifle or machine-gun shots echo throughout the camp. None came. A few days later, Peter Tomlinson, who produced and acted in the play, received a letter from Group Captain Maycock, RAF air attaché in Sweden, which stated simply: 'We had three friends of yours here yesterday. They are well and send you their regards.'

The Germans were furious. The *Kommandant* called in 100 fully armed *Soldaten* to restore order at the subsequent riotous *Appell*, and *Oberfeldwebel* Hermann Glemnitz angrily kicked over a chessboard, scattering the pieces in all directions. It was 'checkmate'. Codner, Philpot and Williams were safely home in England and the Germans did not like being beaten.

There had been changes at Stalag Luft 3. The latest prisoner in the North Compound was the highest-ranking American airman captured so far. On 12 August, Colonel Delmar T. Spivey was shot down in a B-17 during a daylight raid on Bochum. Spivey was equal in rank to the Senior British Officer, Group Captain Massey, and at that time American flyers were imprisoned in the same compound as the British, but on 1 September 700 American airmen moved into the centre compound, once occupied by RAF NCOs, with Spivey as their SAO.

WINDS OF CHANGE

The Kriegies at Stalag 3A Luckenwalde had a fair view of Berlin raids despite the preventive efforts of the camp Germans; those in Dulag had a prime view of the raids on Frankfurt. Watching the massive coloured waterfall of the target indicators, and feeling the rumble of exploding bombs was a new and awe-inspiring experience to some 'new boys', but the long-term prisoners took it in their stride. The way things were going, the consensus opinion was that they would definitely be home for Christmas 1944. The unknown factor was how and in what manner freedom would come. There was a feeling that at the end it would be every man for himself. The Germans were unlikely to give in easily. An air of resignation set in, the Kriegies would face that test when it came, the sooner the better, and until then survival was the name of the game.

A relaxation was the Kriegies' theatre where, at most camps, the prisoners produced plays, musicals and concerts. Sergeant Harcus and appreciative new prisoners enjoyed *French Without Tears* at Lamsdorf, the female parts convincingly played by slim, soft-featured young men. However, the British Medical Officer put a stop to the 'dances' occasionally held in the camp in case they encouraged 'bad habits'. Harcus thought the MO's decision the right one. Also banned were 'dips' in the 'cesspools', as the two fire pools became known. They had become stagnant and slimy, and there had been three cases of typhoid in the camp.

Those who were moved out of the Lamsdorf RAF compound earlier were told to move back on 3 September and the chains were removed for everyone. It was a profound relief, not only to the Kriegies, but also to many Germans, who regarded the whole business as a useless farce. They knew that the prisoners had rapidly found a way of opening the ratchets of the manacles: also that Kriegies frequently held their hands in their pockets, clutching the handcuff section with the chain spread across their fronts as if still shackled. Large numbers of manacles had found their way into the unfathomably murky depths of the 40-holers in which they disappeared forever.

September was an exciting month, Italy had collapsed and now the congestion in the barracks at Lamsdorf had become almost unbearable. More than 4,000 prisoners from the Italian and Sicilian campaigns were squeezed into the RAF compound, 60 extra to a room. The concrete floor was crowded with straw palliasses. Sgt Harcus dreaded the winter months when they would be shut in after dark. 'God help us then,' he worried as he contemplated the stifling, smelling crush of bodies. It was always a relief to get outdoors into the compound to breathe freely.

Among the newcomers was a tough bunch of Paras, who quickly settled in and were soon almost running the compound, taking life as it came and making the very best of it. James Howe's Stalag 8B dance band was back in camp and October brought feverish excitement as the 'repats' entrained for home. Strangely optimistic, many Kriegies expected the war to end in November.

December brought two serious cases of rat-biting in the 40-holer. Being bitten by rats on a sensitive part of the anatomy was a constant fear for Kriegies, yet frequent visitations to the noxious place were a necessity. A rat-hunt week was organised with prizes offered.

Snow had fallen during the night of 15 November at Lamsdorf. Bitter cold wind blew into rooms through the broken windows. *Appells* were from then held in the barrack rooms. The Germans did not like standing out in the snow for hours any more than their prisoners. Despite wearing all their clothes, the Kriegies spent freezing nights huddled under their thin blankets.

On 15 December, at Mühlberg Stalag 4B, the *Kommandant* strode out on morning *Appell* to warn the assembled Kriegies that if the Russians were not stopped they would overrun Europe. He then asked for volunteers for a military unit called The Legion of St George to fight the communists. There were no takers.

Bill Garfield was part of a large fatigue party which headed for the railway sidings at Mühlberg to collect a delivery of Red Cross parcels. Garfield was apprehensive but adults in the streets watched the Kriegies with an apathetic lack of emotion. It was different with the children, who were openly antagonistic, spitting and swearing and jostling the prisoners. There was little the Kriegies could do but swear back beneath their breath.

Despite the shortages and privations at Mühlberg, the Kriegies found initiative and energy to form a flourishing camp amateur dramatic society (CADS) to add to the many clubs organised from the countries of origin. It became a craze for club members to sport a badge, fashioned from tin, to represent the particular club. This gave some of the more irreverent members of CADS an opportunity not to be ignored. Those CADS members – willowy, baby-faced lads – who played female roles in the shows were always the objects of crude jokes and some suspicion. Their badges were made in the form of a question mark, with a hole puncturing the dot at the base. On being asked what club this badge represented, they would immediately adopt a limp-wristed posture and pout, 'The Queeries dear!' Anyone not completely taken aback by this answer would then ask about the puncture and receive an even more lewd reply.

The Kriegies continued to receive great encouragement from the BBC news bulletins. The German broadcasts, on their rudimentary public address systems in the camps, gave the usual German news in English, but were less enthusiastic now about the war. German-language broadcasts still featured the occasional *Sondermeldung*, combining fanfares and impressive military music, but the special announcements had undergone a radical change from the earlier triumphant-shout days. Now they often referred to a Russian town or district which had been evacuated 'according to plan'.

The growing menace of US Army Air Force daylight attacks had engendered another routine radio transmission stating the number of enemy aircraft over Reich territory, where they were heading, and who in the population should be making for the air-raid shelter.

Prisoners at Heydekrug near the Lithuanian border were little concerned with American bombers; a greater interest was taken in the map of the Eastern Front. Rokossovsky's troops were making rapid progress and the Kriegies were beginning to have visions of release and repatriation.

In November 1943, the NCOs who had been sent from Sagan to reopen Barth, and most of those who had been shot down and sent to Barth after that, were transferred to Stalag Luft 6 Heydekrug. There, from 5 October, they were housed in 'K' Lager which rapidly filled. Heydekrug then became the main camp for Air Force NCOs. Barth thereafter became an officers' camp for Allied airmen.

Despite its northern latitude, the winter of 1943 at Heydekrug was mild, with just an occasional dusting of snow. Inside the camp huts it was warm. Red Cross food was plentiful at this time. Potent brews, made from Canadian raisins and sugar, had been laid down in good time for a celebration for what the Kriegies hoped would be their last Christmas behind the wire.

Black-out shutters were unnecessary. Air raids were not expected at that distance from the fronts and there was little of strategic importance nearby. The long evenings the prisoners spent in the huts were probably the envy of the guards patrolling the perimeter wire outside.

At Sagan, unlike the mild weather at Heydekrug, it was bitterly cold. As a concession for Christmas and the temperature, the Germans did not call for a roll-call until 11 a.m.

'KEEP YOUR CHIN UP'

From the time that letters from Britain had begun to trickle through, the words, 'Keep your chin up – it won't be long now', intended to boost morale, had engendered scepticism.

The turn of the year from 1943 to 1944, however, seemed to contain a germ of real hope. It was accentuated by a Christmas card that most prisoners of war received.

Christine Knowles had been indefatigably supplying Kriegies with Bibles and prayer books for years. To many the gifts were a source of great spiritual comfort, to others they were a supply of thin paper useful for rolling cigarettes with tobacco from butt-ends. Her Christmas card for 1943, addressed 'For All Prisoners and Captives', read:

> For a few of you this is the fourth Christmas, for some the third and for others the first Christmas 'behind the wire'. But on sending you our Christmas wishes and New Year Greetings we see clearly that next Christmas you should be in your own homes wherever they may be – Canada, Australia, New Zealand, South Africa, India, England, Scotland, Wales, Ireland, Malta, Cyprus, West Indies, USA. Each individual conjures up for himself the particular city, town or village, the street, the house and the loved ones which combine to make a home. Your courage in action continues to be matched by an amazing spirit of patience under restriction which wins for you not only the proud admiration of your own kith and kin but also that of other nations. May God bless and protect you till we meet is the heartfelt wish of one who is proud to serve you always.
>
> Your faithful friend, CHRISTINE KNOWLES.

For a few 1943 was, to quibble, their fifth Christmas behind wire but everything pointed to this being their last. Certainly Miss Knowles thought it likely but few could guess when freedom would come and what lay ahead.

As 1943 ended, on a bitterly cold night, in most camps there was deep depression and homesickness among some Kriegies. Morale rarely flagged but ahead was danger, hunger and tighter control. The war in the camps against the Germans was stepped up. While the Kriegies provided their own entertainment in the theatre, debating society, classes and sport, escape was an essential to lift spirits. The year's end had been inconclusive, cold and miserably crowded and a New Year always brought the hope that, 'We'll be home this year'.

PART 5

1944

A QUESTION OF COLOUR

The New Year did not start well for Bomber Command. Twenty-eight Lancasters were lost in an unsuccessful raid on Berlin on the night of 1 January. Flight Sergeant Archie King was a Lancaster flight engineer who had parachuted from a flak-destroyed aircraft. He had serious leg injuries. The severity of his wounds caused the Germans to send him immediately to the Hermann Göring *Luftwaffe* Hospital at Gotha.

Dubliner Archie, at 34, was more mature than most aircrew and could readily assess the awful circumstances of his situation. Lying alone in the small room, in constant pain, he felt lonely and miserable, full of worry about his wife back home, and desperately hungry. With dramatic dumb show gestures Archie managed to convey his state of near starvation to an Austrian sister, who would come at night and push a handful of black bread under the sheets. It was unpalatable, but overwhelmingly welcome.

The kindness of the sister was further demonstrated when, after checking that the coast was clear, she escorted two very young *Luftwaffe* pilots through the door marked '*Eingang Verboten!*' to sit with Archie while she stood guard outside. Archie got used to the two young men coming into his room at night, bowing low, clicking their heels and presenting him with a cigarette each from their ration of seven per day.

The visits were a welcome diversion. One of the Germans had been a crew member of the liner *Bremen* and spoke perfect English. Both showed Archie photographs of the appalling conditions suffered by those at the Russian Front, and he was hardly surprised when they referred to the Russians as 'those savages'. Archie mused on the strange consequences of war. When he and his wife Doreen were married, they had spent their honeymoon sailing the beautiful Rhine, and the ex-*Bremen* sailor was an absolute gentleman whom he liked. War was a swine.

On their last visit, one of the *Luftwaffe* men asked Archie if the RAF had many negroes flying on aircrew. Archie laughed at the suggestion. Coloured men were rare in the RAF. Later, he remembered that on 218 Squadron there had been a Jamaican doctor who trained as a navigator in Canada. He wondered vaguely why the *Luftwaffe* man had asked and dismissed it from his mind.

After a spell in the *Obermässfeld Lazarett*, Archie was sent to Barth with instructions to attend the 'sick' hut and see the RAF doctor there about treatment. It was the Jamaican who flew with 218. Archie guessed that the *Luftwaffe* men were nightfighter pilots who had shot down the coloured navigator and his crew.

THREAT OF THE ROPE

The Kriegies in all the *Luftwaffe* camps felt a distinct change in the attitudes among the guards. The devastating air raids, the reverses in Russia and the Mediterranean, made some of them almost obsequious, as if they had a need to ingratiate themselves because the red-light of future danger was flashing. The prisoners were not slow in fostering this lack of spirit among defeatist guards. A further change was noticed among younger *Luftwaffe* guards who, through wounds received on the Eastern Front, were no longer fit for fighting service and had been posted as prison-camp guards. They were frequently openly aggressive, sullen and 'trigger happy'. The Kriegies knew it was a dangerous situation; RAF men were in increasing danger as the raids intensified. It was known that shot-down aircrew had been hung from trees or lamp-posts. At least one man still had a rope weal on his neck when he arrived at Heydekrug. He had been saved by soldiers who had happened to pass.

Australian Flight Sergeant Alan McInnes, a schoolmaster by profession, was the bomb aimer/radar operator of an 83 (Pathfinder) Squadron Lancaster shot down by a nightfighter on the night of 21 January 1944. The crew, captained by Tasmanian F/O Ken Hutton, a notable athlete, had been to Berlin on the two previous nights. This time the target was Magdeburg and the crew had been allotted a special marking job. At the time, McInnes explains:

> It was found that many of the bombs did not fall on the target, but tended to fall short of the marked spot – caused by over-anxious bomb aimers dropping their bombs a second or two early in their desire to be off again. This meant that much of the attack was wasted. To overcome this, special crews were sent in at about one third and two thirds of the way through the attack, with instructions to re-mark the target and so try to draw the attack back to the vital spot.

The nightfighter attacked as the Lancaster approached the target area and a cannon shell exploded behind McInnes's shoulder, wounding him.

166

The aircraft was on fire amidships and one wing was ablaze. The controls were damaged but somehow Hutton held the machine steady as he gave the order to bale out. McInnes describes the moment vividly:

> Kneeling on the edge of the opening, I glanced down, and there, far below, were the fires, the red and green markers, and the flash of bursting bombs. It took more courage than I believed I had to roll forward into space and start that 17,000 foot descent.

It took a long time to float down and McInnes's parachute jerked constantly as bombs burst below. He landed in a tree, slid down bruisingly and set out vaguely towards Switzerland. 'My spirits reached their lowest depths as I heard the last plane fade away into silence,' he recalls, 'for although it could be of no possible help to me, yet it was a friendly presence. Then all was quiet. God, how quiet!'

Seeking a detour round a village, McInnes encountered a group of villagers who seized him and kicked and punched and pushed him along the moonlit track leading to the village. Twice he fell to the ground. A rib snapped and his wounded shoulder was agonising. As they went, more men joined in. Eventually McInnes was pushed into a lighted barn and soon was joined by his Irish wireless operator, F/O 'Paddy' Houston. They were two of the four survivors; Hutton and the two gunners had perished.

It seemed unlikely that McInnes and Houston would survive much longer. The angry villagers conferred and a rope was produced. The reason for it was clear. However, the young wife of a *Luftwaffe* airman, perhaps envisaging her husband in a similar plight, realised what was happening and ran to fetch the local policeman. After a heated argument in the barn, the law won. The two airmen were chained together by the wrists and led away, their original captors following and raining blows on them.

MÜHLBERG SURPRISE

Early in the New Year Stalag 4B Mühlberg received its most remarkable intake. Four hundred Polish women who had taken part in the Battle of Warsaw were pushed into the adjoining compound. Tom Nelson knew that most of the Kriegies had not seen a woman for two years and, to them, these Polish girls looked like Betty Grable and Rita Hayworth. Packets of food, chocolate, cigarettes and the occasional love-letter were flying backwards and forwards across the wire, and when the Germans informed Nelson that his commission had come through and he was transferred to Oflag 7A at Eichstätt, he was almost sorry to leave.

During the second week in January 1944, more than 500 RAF officer prisoners were sent from Stalag Luft 3 to a camp at Belaria situated on a small hill overlooking, and just three miles west of, Sagan. It took the Kriegies a very short time to find that tunnelling was going to be difficult. Temporarily designated Stalag Luft 4, the camp soon became an annexe of Stalag Luft 3 and the designation of Luft 4 passed to the camp near the Baltic at Gross Tychow.

A BET IS A BET

The weather at Sagan was bitterly cold and in room 2, hut 66, the officers were enjoying a frugal lunch of a bowl of watery kohl-rabi soup and two thin slices of black bread, when the friendly discussion turned to the subject of sport. P/O Maurice Butt rashly made a wager that he could give F/L Harrison-Broadley a start of 60 yards and still beat him in a race around the circuit, a distance of just over half a mile.

'Perhaps,' said Butt, 'we could put in a few training sessions and run the race in March or April when the weather has improved.' 'No chance!' said a room-mate emphatically. 'A bet is a bet,' said another, 'The race must take place immediately.'

There was no time to change, the race would be run in boots and battledress – now.

Out on to the circuit went the eight men from room 2. The snow was hard and compressed. Time-keepers and judges were appointed and the 60-yard start carefully measured. Other Kriegies, getting wind of the wager, joined them around the circuit, shouting encouragement.

Over the first 400 yards P/O Butt had gained very little but he could tell that Harrison-Broadley was beginning to tire and, at 100 yards from the finish line, Butt managed to overtake and then won by some 20 yards. The time was hardly up to Olympic standards but the prize was duly presented with ceremony. Butt enjoyed the two squares of chocolate.

'OUI M'SIEU, JE PARLE FRANÇAIS'

Flight Sergeant Hal 'Horizontal' Croxson always stretched out and closed his eyes when the other airmen in the mess were reading or playing cards, but his alert manner when flying as rear gunner in a Lancaster belied his nickname. Wide-open eyes and constant attention were necessary to survive but even that was sometimes not enough. The *Luftwaffe* had perfected their angled, upward-firing 20mm cannon (*Schrage Musik*); the crash of shells into the aircraft was often the first that the bomber crew knew they had been attacked, then it was too late.

For two anxious, back-breaking hours after an attack the crew had fought to keep the Lancaster flying; everything possible had been jettisoned to reduce weight, but the crew was fighting a losing battle. On the Berlin raid of 29 January 1944, the Lancaster dived towards the earth and 'Horizontal' Croxson made a hurried vertical leap into space. His parachute had barely opened when he tumbled to the ground on a hillside. His canopy and shroud lines collapsed on him. With his heavy, thick flying clothing Croxson described himself as feeling like a Christmas parcel that had come undone.

Although out in the quiet of the country, Croxson was quite sure that the 'whole of Germany' knew he was there and would shortly come to collect him. He watched a faint glimmer from a leaking blackout and, when the door opened and a shaft of light momentarily flooded out into the dark night, he thought, 'This is it, will they come to murder or help me?'

Hal Croxson always carried a .38 revolver and, to be prepared to defend himself, he checked that it was loaded, put it by his side and waited – expectant, ready. But nobody came.

Eventually, so confident was he that 'they' knew he was there, that Croxson took out a cigarette and lit-up without making any effort to conceal the flame. He remembered from blackout drills that someone lighting a cigarette can be seen for three miles in those conditions. Still nobody came. Lying back, mentally and physically exhausted, Croxson, still in his flying suit and parachute harness, dropped into a troubled sleep.

Waking 20 minutes later, Croxson concluded that the whole of Germany had not seen him arrive. With his Bowie scout knife he sliced off the lower part of his flying suit, pulled out the kapok from the pockets and collar and wrapped the whole in his dark-coloured electric inner suit.

For the first time, he saw that two fingers on his right hand had been deeply cut during his scrambling escape from the rear turret. His snow-white parachute was liberally stained with blood. Croxson cut a two-inch strip of parachute fabric to bandage his wounds.

Then, to his dismay, he saw that one boot was missing, but he had to press on. Stuffing his helmet and unwanted gear into a bush, he sliced the fur-lined top from his one flying boot and, using the parachute shroud lines, he formed a kind of shoe for his other foot. Ever a practical man, Croxson carried a pocket compass, so he set off in a westerly direction.

Feeling through his pockets, he found a bar of chocolate, some Horlicks tablets, a tube of condensed milk and seventeen cigarettes. Croxson reckoned he was reasonably well equipped, although a walk from south of Frankfurt across hostile Germany and over the Rhine to an already occupied France or Luxembourg seemed a forlorn prospect.

The next day he travelled carefully, planning to make up time and distance through the night. As he climbed out of another ditch, and collided with yet another fence, Croxson concluded that the instructions that one should travel by night had been given by instructors who had never had to do it themselves. He decided that it was necessary to see ahead and move in daylight.

On the third day, he was studying his compass, deciding which route to take at an intersection of deer trails, when he saw a group of 'country yokels' approaching. They carried twelve-bores and had dachshunds at their heels. Croxson determined to bluff it out in French.

'*Parlez vous français?*' he asked, deciding that they did not look a very bright lot and that he might, perhaps, pass himself off as a French worker. He had reckoned without the local schoolmaster, a tall thin man with steel-rimmed glasses.

'*Oui, m'sieu,*' he replied. '*Je parle français.*'

His bluff was called. With a twelve-bore pressed to his midriff, Croxson was relieved of his .38 and knife and whisked to a *Luftwaffe* station near Hammelberg.

The *Luftwaffe* men were puzzled. Although well hidden, Croxson's abandoned gear and bloodstained parachute had been found. They had captured two crew members and discovered the remains of four others in the aircraft wreckage. With Croxson that totalled seven. The *Luftwaffe* were sure that there must have been an eighth man on the aircraft. Croxson had said that he was not wounded, yet here was that bloodstained parachute and a helmet emblazoned with the name 'Horizontal' on the rim. Where was the wounded 'Horizontal'? A further complication was that the *Feldwebel* interpreter was bluffing the interrogating officer that he could speak good English when he certainly could not. The situation was such a comedy of errors that Croxson found it difficult not to laugh.

'KEEP YOUR HEAD DOWN'

A constant 'bind', particularly among some regular RAF officer Kriegies, was the reduction in their chances of promotion and awards. Junior officers would be promoted into positions that should have been theirs. For career officers such as Wing Commander Day or Squadron Leader Bushell prospects of promotion were drastically reduced when they became prisoners. 'Wings' Day obviously had no chance of commanding an RAF station from Germany any more than Roger Bushell had of commanding a fighter wing. Flying Officer Ted Chapman, who was not aircrew but had commanded an Air Sea Rescue boat, knew his promotion to flight lieutenant was still in papers floating around 'detachments and attachments' when he was taken prisoner while doing someone else's job for a 24-hour emergency stint. He was to have taken over a new base in Gibraltar as a squadron leader, but when he came home four years later, he was still listed as a flying officer. Whatever was claimed to the contrary, promotion prospects for the majority were negligible once inside a prisoner-of-war camp.

A similar situation prevailed where awards were concerned. Sgt John Dennis was the rear gunner and the only unwounded member of a crew that between them had shot down a Ju88 and driven off a Bf110. Sgt Pilot Alf Kirkham, though wounded and losing blood, brought the Lancaster back for a crash landing at Bradwell Bay. He was deservedly awarded the DFM. The navigator was badly wounded and lost an eye, never to fly again. He, too, was awarded the DFM, as was the mid-upper gunner who had a slight flesh wound. Rear gunner Sgt Dennis, who was unscathed and immediately flew on operations again, was shot down, taken prisoner and, as far as awards were concerned, was overlooked.

For most Kriegies, however, the main concern was not promotion or reward but simple survival: to cope, to get by from day to day and survive the inevitable chaos at the end of the war. Prisoners knew that the Germans would not give up easily. They feared the machinations of the *SS* and *Gestapo* and their desire to have complete control of the camps. They feared, too, Hitler's irrationality and unpredictability. His direction of the treatment of those in his power was shown graphically by the bestial starvation, shooting and hanging of Russian prisoners. Unable to accept that defeat was of his own making, he flailed about searching for scapegoats and revenge. The '*Terrorfliegers*' and '*Luftgangsters*' of the RAF and USAAF in his camps were the handiest undefended target.

'Keep your head down,' was the prisoners' dominant theme.

EMBARRASSMENT AT HEYDEKRUG

On the lighter side, there now being a regular supply of Red Cross parcels, food was adequate and no longer the main topic of discussion at Heydekrug. Women, their attributes and desirability, resumed their accustomed prime place. The results of such thoughts to young, virile men deprived of female company were sometimes an embarrassment.

A volunteer party in the *Kommandantur* on a mission concerning mail, were passing down a corridor when they saw a rare sight, a girl typing in an office. A girl, any girl, would have occasioned comment, but the sight of an attractive *Fräulein* brought forth a rash of coarse, suggestive remarks. The Kriegies carried on openly and bawdily discussing the young lady, confident that she would not understand, until she looked up and asked: 'Would you mind closing the door please?'

They should have learned their lesson. Many a Kriegie had found himself swiped with a rifle butt for smiling and at the same time calling a guard a 'square-headed bastard.' English was the second language in many German schools.

READY FOR BED

When Liverpudlian Flight Sergeant Eddie Scott-Jones had an early briefing for a raid on Lens railway yards, he reckoned he had plenty of time to return to the sergeants' mess for a shower. The projected raid would seem to be an easy run compared to the tough targets 428 Squadron Halifaxes had recently visited. They would be away only a few hours, the night was mild and maximum height would be about 15,000 ft.

Scott-Jones's mistake was that, after 29 operations, during which he had carefully observed all airmen's superstitions, keeping to the same ritual, such as urinating on the tail-wheel and so on, he was about to do something unusual. Scott-Jones should have known better than to break with tradition.

Returning from his shower, he noticed his pyjamas lying on the bed. It struck him that, if he wore them under his aircrew sweater and battledress, no extra flying clothing would be needed apart from boots, and on his return from the short trip to Lens it would be a case of 'heave ho into bed'.

The pilot of a Focke-Wulf 190 interfered with his plan, shooting down the Halifax in which Scott-Jones was flying. Parachuting safely to earth, he spent four days hiding under Belgian hedgerows until captured and sent to Dulag still wearing his, by now, grubby pyjamas.

PURR OF A MERLIN

Far to the north, in Luft 1 Barth, Gwilym 'Taffy' Peake walked round the small compound, thinking of pleasant Easter Sundays he had spent at home near Wrexham. Suddenly, he stiffened. That noise, the purr of Merlin engines, was unmistakable to an RAF man. Two Mosquitoes were flying low up the inlet from the Baltic; curving inland, they flew over the airfield at Barth. The reverberation of exploding bombs and cannon shells echoed over the compound. Circuiting Kriegies stopped dead, turned and stared. Their astonishment gave way to joy. Here, in front of their camp-jaded eyes, was action: the RAF was at work.

A huge, roaring cheer arose from the Kriegies. The guards, fearing a diversion for an escape attempt, ran into the compound, but the cheering was unstoppable. Laying about them with rifle butts and bayonets, the angry, ill-tempered guards shouted to the men to be quiet but it was too late. Whilst dodging the outnumbered Germans, the men carried on cheering until the Mosquitoes flew away to the west. There were a few bruises and cuts to mark the day but it was worth it. How the Kriegies envied the Mossie crews, wished them well and enjoyed the RAF's venture into this rarely visited area.

Shortly after this visit, on 22 April, the NCOs were moved to 'K' Lager at Heydekrug and Stalag Luft 1 was readied to receive RAF and USAAF officers.

'JE SUIS BLESSÉ – AIDEZ MOI!'

Bomb aimer Flight Lieutenant John Grimer and his fellow crew members felt bitter at being taken off German targets and credited with only one-third of an operation for attacking French targets. The night of 23 April 1944 was the 77 Squadron Halifax's third French trip. It was one of nearly 200 Bomber Command aircraft that were to attack the railway yards at Laon, an important marshalling centre and through-route to the French coast. Grimer was happy when able to call 'bombs away' and observe a 'bang-on' bombing of the marshalling yards. Immediately after releasing the bomb load, however, he saw a 'roman candle' tracer dead ahead. He clicked up his microphone switch to warn the pilot just as the Halifax went straight through it. The intercom went dead but the navigator's shielded light still shone.

As Grimer saw a Junkers 88 beneath them breaking away, the bombsight before him shattered. He felt a sharp pain near his right eye as a splinter opened a superficial flesh wound. Wiping the blood away, he watched with wonder as navigator Charlie Hobgen carefully folded his maps and raised his table and the collapsible seat to clear the escape hatch. Table and seat were both riddled with bullet holes but Hobgen was unscathed and cool. The wireless operator, though, had a foot almost severed. Grimer and Hobgen clipped his parachute pack to his harness and pushed him through the hatch. Flames were now roaring through the plane. Quickly Hobgen dived into the darkness, but Grimer's parachute pack had been hit and he was unable to secure it properly. He jumped with only one clip holding, but his fears were allayed when the canopy snapped open and checked his headlong fall.

The blazing Halifax crashed with a bright orange flash and an enduring glow. John Grimer's descent was smooth until his canopy snagged on a tree. Swaying gently in his harness, he peered below and could see stars reflected in water. Thinking that he must be hanging over a canal, Grimer turned the harness quick-release button, thumped it firmly, and fell. The unexpected fifteen-foot hurtling into a shallow puddle winded him and wrenched his back. After gathering his breath, Grimer decided to stand and look around him. Then he saw that below the knee his right leg was a shattered, bloody mess. Until that moment he had felt nothing.

Pulling himself together, he took his Benzedrine tablets, applied a tourniquet to his right thigh, and began an agonising crawl through a small wood and across several fields, until he reached a small village. Grimer had learned French from his Belgian mother and as he neared the houses, he called loudly, '*Je suis un aviateur Anglais – je suis blessé – aidez moi!*'

The responses were curses from windows thrown open angrily and shouts of '*Taisez vous!*'

Grimer was surprised and discouraged, but he crawled on through the village until he reached a small farmhouse. There he banged repeatedly on the door until it was opened. An elderly couple, seeing his plight, took him in and treated him with the utmost kindness, giving him brandy, hot soup and a bowl of raw eggs to sustain him. They sat him on a chair, propping his wounded leg on a stool. During his long crawl Grimer had loosened the tourniquet every half-hour and, as he did so again, blood dripped on to the stone floor. He was sickened as a farm dog lapped the blood.

The couple sent for a doctor, who bandaged and splinted Grimer's leg, telling him that he might be able to be moved or even walk with crutches in about six weeks. The elderly pair courageously offered to hide him in their barn until he could be moved to a safer place.

Despite their care, Grimer was soon running a high temperature and was racked with bouts of delirium. He asked his hosts to send for the Germans and tell them that they had just found him in one of their fields. They reluctantly agreed. A few hours later, two German soldiers arrived to collect him on a motor-cycle and sidecar. Grimer's hopes of being taken to a hospital were dashed. After a jolting and painful journey, he was carried into a prison and locked in a small cell furnished with a wooden board and a bucket. A shuttered judas-hole in the door was opened periodically, but for John Grimer, passing in and out of consciousness, time began to lose its meaning. During lucid moments he heard French patriotic songs being sung and once a volley of gunshots as if a firing squad was at work. He reached the utter depths of pain and despair.

Grimer had a vague recollection of being on a stretcher, driven in an ambulance, and laid on an operating table where the man leaning over him and working on his leg was referred to as '*Hauptmann Doktor*'. The German surgeon saved Flt Lt Grimer's leg and very likely his life.

DEAD CLEVER

Junkers 88s from a nearby airfield habitually 'buzzed' Stalag 4B and, on 30 May 1944, the inevitable happened – one came in too low. The prisoners were taking an evening stroll just within the compound boundary when the plane took away part of the barbed wire and staggered into the sky again, leaving two dead. Had the plane crashed, the death roll would have been crushing in such a small, crowded place.

From the end of August 1943 almost all captured NCO aircrew had been sent from Dulag Luft direct to Stalag 4B at Mühlberg. The Luft camps were full. Finally 4B held nearly 2,000 airmen. One of the strangest cases was that of Flight Sergeant Winston Barrington, whose mother lived in Germany with Barrington's stepfather, said to be an *Oberst* in the photographic section of the *Luftwaffe*. With the cooperation of the camp authorities, Barrington's mother visited him frequently, and is believed to have joined her son in the camp prior to the cessation of the fighting and to have returned to Britain with released prisoners.

POINT MADE

Pilot Officer R. 'Johnnie' Johnston, a Manxman by birth, had been shot down in May 1943 while delivering a 'Joe' and canisters of supplies to a secret rendezvous in central France. Johnston had lost his right leg below the knee in the action and spent a year at the *Luftwaffe* Hospital at Clichy, Paris, where the stump was cleaned up and a triple fracture of his right forearm set. When finally considered fit enough, he was sent by rail to Dulag Luft in May 1944.

It was night and the Kriegies and their guards were dozing in the train compartment when there was a rattle at the door to the corridor. As it slid back a *Kriegsmarine Leutnant* poked his head into the compartment and announced in faultless English, 'If any of you chaps have any overdue laundry we are now passing through the Siegfried Line.'

GARDENING AND MINING

The night of 31 May 1944 was windy and rainy. Huge thunder clouds filled the sky and deep penetration operations were cancelled, so Flight

Sergeant Verdon 'Bob' Cutts and his crew at RAF Methwold were surprised when they were called up for a briefing. They and another crew from 149 Squadron were to fly their Stirlings to do some 'gardening' near Knocke in the Scheldt estuary, sowing mines in the hope of bottling up some lurking E-boats.

The thunderstorm reached its wet, blustery peak as Cutts's Stirling lifted off the runway, left the friendly flare-path and headed for the Dutch coast. The bomb aimer complained bitterly that he had not had time to raise the hood on his Morgan 3 Wheeler. He felt a little better when, nearing the Scheldt estuary, the storm cleared.

Cutts and his crew could see anti-aircraft shells bursting ahead and guessed that the other aircraft was already in the target area. The defences were alert, yet all was quiet as their Stirling made its customary run-in at 600 feet, the height necessary to allow the parachutes on the mines to open. Five mines, with a five-second delay on each, meant that Bob Cutts was committed to a straight, level and seemingly eternal run during which flak guns had plenty of time to pinpoint their position. At the moment of the first release, the guns opened up on the Stirling.

As the last mine dropped from the bomb bay, Cutts threw the aircraft hard to port. He had to escape those accurate bursts from the guns. It was too late. A loud explosion, the port wing dropped with sickening speed and the huge aeroplane cartwheeled into the sea.

Cutts was violently flung round, his seat wrenching away from its fixings and trapping his right leg. The throttle levers remained a twisted bunch in his right hand and he was spattered with human remains which were washed away as the Stirling sank.

Fighting to hold his breath, Cutts wrenched his leg free and then, suddenly, he was outside the Stirling wreckage, inflating his Mae West and gasping on the surface. Hearing groaning, Cutts looked around him for other members of his crew, but the groans were his. Listening intently, he realised there was no sound other than the lapping water – he was alone. He swam towards a dark shape floating near him which gave some hope of flotsam to which he could cling. Unbelievably, it was the aircraft's rubber dinghy, inflated by its immersion switch. It was an answer to an unspoken prayer. Cutts climbed over the rim and flopped into the bottom.

The dinghy was leaking air but the emergency bellows were still in place. Throughout the night he pumped to keep the dinghy inflated. With morning light there was little more to see. He was sitting in the dinghy near a half-submerged aircraft petrol tank. There was no sign of the rest of his crew. Bob Cutts felt desolate and desperately lonely.

He could not understand how he alone had survived. The Stirling had a reputation for killing its pilots, who were sometimes unable to be strapped in as is usual in most aircraft. (The Stirling was built for two pilots, one of whom had to be able to reach some distant controls.) Cutts had been thrown about when the aircraft cartwheeled and that probably saved his life. Picked up by the last of three passing fishing boats, Cutts eventually arrived at Dulag – still worrying and wondering why.

STRIKING AT THE HEART

One morning in early June 1944, Lord Haw Haw smugly announced on the German radio that British miners had come out on strike. The Kriegies at Heydekrug were incredulous, certain that this was Goebbels's latest mad propaganda ploy to undermine morale. The strike was confirmed later by the BBC on Bristow's radio and was met at first with disbelief and then anger. John Dennis, who had been so severely wounded, voiced the feelings of many when he wrote:

> I shall never forget the feeling first of absolute incredulity and then impotent rage. Rage to think that Britain with her back literally to the wall, with the second front open, these loyal, patriotic British miners, safe and secure in their reserved occupational jobs, could even think of striking, but they had and were holding the country to ransom.

Ron Mogg, journalist and camp secretary wrote:

> We could not believe such action of our own countrymen. It was inconceivable that with millions of enslaved people looking to us to free them, even a small section of Britons could jeopardise the war effort for selfish reasons. Ninety-nine-point-nine per cent of the prisoners were bluntly in favour of shooting the miners...
>
> A few voices spoke in the miners' favour, saying that a right to strike was one of the freedoms for which we were fighting. They were shouted down by the majority whose opinion was that there was a time and place for everything and it was certainly not in the middle of a bitter life-and-death struggle.

That bad and good luck can rapidly alternate was proved to the crew of a 106 Squadron Lancaster on the evening of D-Day. Their target, bridges over the River Sarthe at Caen, was heavily defended and attacks by fighters killed two of the gunners in the plane. The remaining five crew men baled out. The wireless operator, Sergeant Bill Low, landed with sickening force on a roof, fracturing his spine in five places. The only good luck for him was that he was in the grounds of a hospital. Visits to many more hospitals were to follow. The other gunner was also taken prisoner but the skipper, Squadron Leader Sprawson, hid in Caen, survived the bombing, shelling and the front line passing over him, to be the first Britisher to be released by the troops invading Normandy. The other two members of the crew also made it home with the help of the French.

THE MUSIC MEN

A great morale booster, after the 'Canary' – an ingenious construction* of a radio receiver – was the written music department. In all camps efforts had been made to copy music from records, but this early department began life at Lamsdorf, flourished through Luft 3 at Sagan and reached its acme at Luft 6 Heydekrug. The moving spirit behind the department was H. W. 'Wally' Bradley. At Heydekrug often as many as five copyists worked together in a small room known as 'The Vicarage'.

Music was laboriously copied on to carefully drawn manuscript paper. Printed manuscript paper was later obtained from other sources. Music was provided for the symphony orchestra, the dance band, innumerable quartets, quintets and other combinations, light and classical, the church choir and the pit orchestras, of up to 30 players, for all the musical shows produced.

A few items arrived from the Red Cross in band-part form but, even with these, some parts had to be transposed for particular instruments that the Kriegies had obtained. Most of the classical music was written out from the miniature score, while numbers for the dance band were lifted, note by note and chord by chord, from Glenn Miller or Joe Loss records by John Fender or guitarist Ron Bush. The same procedure had been used by James Howe for the army prisoners at Stalag 8B.

The musical shows were probably Bradley's greatest headache. A self-styled composer would place a single line melody in front of him and cheerfully say, 'Would you mind writing an accompaniment to this? First rehearsal with the orchestra Thursday.' Probably Bradley's greatest feat was the orchestrating of the whole of *The Mikado* from the piano score. *The Mikado* was to have been produced after *Winterset* at the Heydekrug theatre, but the theatre was burned to the ground, sabotaged by John Bristow in order to conceal the theft of radio components.

* *Not All Glory!*, p. 55

One of Bradley's copyists was Doug Endsor. From his arrival at Lamsdorf in September 1941, he had resolved to keep his brain active. He began by teaching himself shorthand but then became engrossed in the musical life at the camp. He helped Bradley start the department of written music and later, with New Zealander Jack Murray, formed a church choir which soon began to work also in the secular field of singing. Choir practice took place virtually every evening and choral work played an important part in Endsor's life.

Music was always a fine diversion and across the warring lines in North Africa came a tune which was to be popular with both sides. Lale Andersen's recording of 'Lili Marleen' was broadcast by a German disc jockey from Budapest to the *Afrika Korps*. The song had previously had little success but suddenly Andersen was a star and 'Lili Marleen' so singable that an English lyric was exchanged for the German words. In Britain it appeared as 'Lilli Marlene' and Anne Shelton's version became popular. The song was soon being sung in the prisoner-of-war camps by prisoners and their guards, each in their own tongue.

Sometimes in the early mornings, the Kriegies could hear German soldiers marching in the woods. They sang in rounds and in the still air the voices sounded like a cathedral choir.

'GEORGE'

At Sagan the guards were increasingly 'trigger happy' since the mass escape in March when 76 prisoners emerged from a 348-foot tunnel – three making it home and the remainder being recaptured*. As a reprisal 50 were cold bloodedly shot. During air-raid alarms when Fortresses and Liberators were approaching the camp, the guards had orders to force the Kriegies into their huts and shut the doors and windows. The instructions were ignored by the prisoners until an *Obergefreite* drew an automatic and fired several shots into the compound. No one was hurt but the compound cleared rapidly. As the bombers were passing overhead, a rifle shot was heard from the area of the south (American) compound. When the Kriegies were allowed out of the huts after the 'all clear', they heard the story. An American working in the cookhouse had stood by a partially open door, looking skywards for the planes. A guard patrolling outside the barbed wire had rested his rifle on the wire, taken careful aim and shot the American in the head, killing him outright.

* *Not All Glory!*, p. 126–133

Perhaps the camp authorities hoped that the combination of intimidation and cooperation would make the Kriegies less troublesome in that summer of 1944. To keep them occupied they showed several films in the officers' compounds at Sagan. They included *Orchestra Wives* with the Glenn Miller Orchestra, *The Spoilers* with Marlene Dietrich and *The Corsican Brothers*. The NCOs saw none of these.

In mid-June the officers' escape committee decided to burrow another tunnel, despite the recent murder of 50 officers and huge German notices that declared, 'Escaping is no longer a sport'. Escaping was never considered a sport by the Kriegies. It was a serious and deadly business, a pitting of wits against the Germans in a struggle for freedom, and a matter of life and death.

'George', the new tunnel, would break in the Vorlager for use as an escape route when the reaction of the previous attempt had died down, or as a means to overpower the German guards and take over the camp. Recent information from tame goons had revealed that, as a result of the Russian advance, the Kriegies were to be massacred rather than allow them to be released. Swiftly Kriegies in the camp were secretly divided into defence divisions, companies and platoons. Officers and NCOs in charge were given talks on defence against German weapons, under the guise of history lectures.

On the night of 27–28 March, while the tense atmosphere gripped all in Stalag Luft 3, there was another drama taking place high in the night skies above Germany. When Sergeant Nicholas Alkemade scrambled from the rear gun turret of his burning Lancaster he saw his parachute silk frizzle in the flames and his hopes melt with it. There was no choice – he threw himself out of the blazing wreck, certain that he was about to die.

It was some time later when he awoke with the pain of shell splinters, facial and leg burns and a wrenched knee but no broken bones. He had fallen 18,000 feet without a parachute, crashed through tree branches into snow and lived.

There were at least two similar incidents during the war. One man fell 22,000 feet and Alkemade noted wryly that his record had been broken but that his injuries were less severe. The main thing, he said, was that they were both alive.

'GESTAPO! KOMM MIT!'

In a Britain bursting with Allied servicemen and packed with military might, it was evident that soon there would be an attempt at a breaching of what Hitler now called his 'west wall' of '*Festung Europa*'. Bomber Command had kept up attacks on communications targets, ranging all over France and Belgium, not concentrating blows in any one area, thus keeping the *Oberkommando die Wehrmacht* in ignorance of the selected landing place. As part of this 'transportation plan', the target selected for 2 June 1944, was the railway marshalling yard at Trappes near Paris. Of 128 aircraft on the raid, 105 were Halifaxes. They set off on that moonlit night and caused havoc in the target area but, of the Halifaxes, only 90 returned. Shortly after leaving the target, they were intercepted by night-fighters based at St André de l'Eure, and the moon helped the *Luftwaffe* fighters to a 'happy time'.

The pilot and the wireless operator died in one blazing Halifax as it crashed near the fighter airfield but the remainder of the crew para-chuted to safety and the arms of the Resistance. The navigator, Flying Officer Stan Booker, despite a twisted knee and facial cuts received from his parachute harness, felt he was in safe hands and was happy in the belief that the invasion would soon take place. General Eisenhower, despite pessimistic weather warnings, ordered the first convoys to sea on 2 June. Four days later, the Allied troops landed in force on the coast of Normandy.

By early July, Stan Booker had been allocated the identity of one Pierre Le Comte. Equipped with false travel documents and cards, Booker prepared to travel down the escape line to freedom. But there was an uneasy feeling that something was wrong in this Resistance group. His fears were horribly confirmed when he was roughly grasped, a gun was thrust in his back and the words, '*Gestapo! Komm mit!*' hissed in his ear. The French group had been penetrated.

Booker felt a shiver of apprehension. He knew he was in a desper-ate situation. Captured in civilian clothes, carrying false papers, and in possession of sensitive documents which he was to have taken on the Lysander back to England, there was little doubt that he would be con-sidered a spy.

The hard men of the *Gestapo* hurried Booker to Fresnes prison, where hundreds of French Resistance members and almost 200 Allied aircrew who had been caught trying to evade capture were held. Fresnes was notorious as a place of interrogation and torture, frequently followed by execution.

At Fresnes Booker was told that he would be denied prisoner-of-war status, denied any contact with the International Red Cross and forced to tell the *Gestapo* all they wanted to know before being shot as a spy. He was, at best, a '*Terrorflieger*'. Hitler had ordered in a directive in

May: 'Such enemy airmen who were shot down, should be shot dead without Court Martial and disposed of by the Security Services.'

The torture and brutality which followed was carried out with the sadistic cruelty of the ruthless with absolute power over the helpless. For Booker it began almost immediately. Repeated blows smashed into his face, leaving his nose crushed and his mouth a bloody mess. When he had not told the *Gestapo* men what they wanted to know, they transferred their torment by repeated blows to the genitals. Booker's agony continued until even the torturers tired and left him exhausted, a bloody, crumpled heap on the stone floor of the filthy cell.

Day followed day, when all count of time vanished. Time was punctuated only by the noise of the guards' heavy boots in the corridor, and the grating screech of the wheels of the metal food trolley as it ran along old iron rails, bringing a ladle of bitter acorn coffee to each of the prisoners at early morning and evening. Lunch was a basin of watery cabbage or swede soup and a small piece of black bread. Bouts of interrogation and torture and the agonised cries and screams of inmates were the only other interruptions.

Without warning, in mid-August, Fresnes was evacuated. The 2,000 prisoners, including 168 Allied aircrew, were crushed 80 to a box-car at the *Gare de l'Est*, Paris, to begin a harrowing six-day rail journey to the concentration camp near Weimar at Buchenwald. Two airmen were shot on the journey while attempting to escape.

Buchenwald concentration camp, established in 1938, deep in the Thuringian forest, seemingly miles from all civilisation, was enough to turn the strongest heart, mind and stomach sick with horror. Surrounded with barbed and electrified wire, and with brooding *Posten* boxes on high stilts looming over them, the shorn inmates, dressed in their striped pyjama-like clothes, shuffled aimlessly. Over the windowless huts and divided compounds hung an indescribable smell of decay, despair and death, aided by the continuously belching chimneys of the crematoria. One RAF prisoner compared the scene to a reopened grave and shuddered to think that the airmen were to join the hopeless thousands in this abominable place. Soon their heads were shorn, their clothes taken away and they were issued with the usual thin striped suits. The *SS* ruled throughout with whip, cudgel and gallows, with absolute and brutal authority.

The RAF and US airmen were segregated from the others and held in a quarantine area known as the 'Little Camp'. This camp had a fearsome reputation, due to its close proximity to the Medical Experimentation Block. The flyers were designated '*Terrorfliegers*' and as such were liable to instant execution on orders from Hitler. Their SBO, Sqdn Ldr Lamason, RNZAF, organised the airmen into flights, quickly recognising that their survival depended very much on their discipline and morale. Even barefoot, shaven-headed and dressed in striped concentration-camp garb, their courage and bearing impressed the inmates and guards. Executions took place almost daily. In late September and early October 1944, 31 SOE men were hung on hooks in the notorious and feared 'Tower' cells and left to die by slow strangulation. The 178 airmen designated '*Terrorfliegers*' expected a similar fate.

A precision daylight raid, on 24 October, by two waves of US bombers completely demolished the nearby Gustloff munitions factory, part of the *SS* domestic site and part of the camp. Large numbers of *SS* men, their families and luckless prisoners were killed. When called out, the flyer-prisoners thought their execution time had arrived as retribution for the air-raid, but they were wanted to help with rescue and rubble clearance.

The airmen remained in this atmosphere of death until the end of October when they were transferred to Stalag Luft 3 at Sagan. A nominal roll had been smuggled out of Buchenwald to a *Luftwaffe* aerodrome. The *Luftwaffe* demanded that the airmen should be in a prisoner-of-war camp. The Allied airmen had missed death again by a whisker.

Each man knew that he was lucky to be alive; few left a place like Buchenwald except, in the grim language of the place, 'up the chimney'.

SECOND TIME ROUND

Twenty-three year old Flight Sergeant Albert Bracegirdle was on his second tour of operations when he 'bought it'. Forty-four missions at that critical period of the war was quite exceptional so, although a shock, it could not have been much of a surprise when, approaching Wesseling to bomb the synthetic oil plant, a Ju88 shot away the Lancaster 3's rudder and starboard elevator. The starboard wing was badly holed and the control column jammed forward, so pilot Squadron Leader Steve Cockbain warned the crew to clip on their parachutes as the aircraft started to dive. The dive became vertical and Cockbain, his feet straining against the instrument panel, ordered the crew to jump. Gradually, he managed to haul the column back and, just as gradually, the Lancaster became controllable. At 8,000 feet Cockbain jettisoned the bomb load, live, and told the crew members who had not jumped to stand by. By then four had gone, their open parachutes clearly visible.

The bomb aimer and the rear gunner rapidly turned to other duties. Quickly the flight engineer, Flt Lt Walter Faraday, came forward to navigate, and with an H2S plot of Westkappelle and QDMs from West Raynham, they were able to get home to base. But Bracegirdle, two others of the crew and an 'under training' pilot on his first trip were down in the enemy heartland.

Bracegirdle fell heavily among trees, tumbling uncontrollably to earth amid confused blows and thumps that knocked the senses from him. For more than three hours, he lay unconscious in the woods. When he came round, he was weak, shocked and badly cut about the nose, eyes and ears. As he struggled to his feet, he found that he could hardly stand, an ankle was badly twisted and blood soaked his flying clothing.

An hour of painful staggering through the wood brought him to a house where he was seen and taken to a village police station in the front room of a cottage. In charge was a young man in Hitler Youth uniform. Bracegirdle had a blurred vision of a grey uniform covered in braiding and a red armband carrying a black swastika. This was Nazi Germany.

Taking no chances with his wounded prisoner, and with typical swaggering conceit, the *Hitler Jugend* member put a pistol to Bracegirdle's head with one hand and searched him with the other before sending him on to Dulag Luft.

THE FAILED PLOT

On 21 July 1944, the news of the attempted assassination of Hitler reached most Kriegies. They were disappointed but delighted. Here was further firm evidence that the Third and Final Reich was falling apart, not only being beaten back on all sides but rotten at the very core. Here was proof of internal strife which the Kriegies hoped would spread and lead to their being freed. Many 'tame' goons, interpreters, guards and even the odd *Luftwaffe* officer had hinted at anti-Nazi sympathies but most of them were spared the savage reprisals and penalties for those caught or suspected of being implicated in the assassination plot.

The failure of the plot meant a throttling squeeze on all security measures and the certainty that the Nazis would fight to the last. The planners had wanted to kill Hitler before an invasion by the Allies, so that an armistice agreement could be concluded with them before the German frontiers had been breached or, indeed, before an Allied soldier had set foot on the Continent. Germany would then have had an interim, pre-democracy government which would, with the agreement and cooperation of the Allies, have controlled an orderly retreat from the occupied lands. But the invasion had taken place and the Allies now insisted on absolute, unconditional surrender. Everything that could have gone awry for the plotters had done so; their mistakes and indecision had led them, inevitably, to their own destruction. The revolt against Hitler was over.

Hitler, determined after the assassination attempt to wield complete personal power, ordered that the service salute common to most armies would immediately be discontinued and replaced with the straight, raised right-arm Führer salute. A brief and completely unsuccessful attempt was made to introduce the salute to the Kriegies and for a while German officers gave the salute when taking *Appell*. Ribald laughter greeted the early attempts and, although some men spent a while in the cells for disrespect to the *Wehrmacht* and the swastika flag, the practice was soon dropped. A German who did not carry out the order was an object of suspicion but despite Kesselring's assertion, the disregard was so widespread that it would have been necessary to imprison a considerable portion of the German armed forces.

In most camps the summer weather had caused a huge increase of every kind of flying, crawling and scuttling vermin within the crowded conditions of the camps. Dysentery was rife and, after the typhus outbreak during the Russian campaign, the fear of diseases spreading beyond the Stalag confines concerned the *Oberkommando der Wehrmacht*. At Stalag 4B the *Kommandant* decided to fumigate the huts. The Kriegies were turned out for a couple of hours while the sealed rooms were fumigated with *Zyklon B* gas. It was effective. When the men returned to their rooms, the floor was covered with the corpses of vermin. The Germans knew that *Zyklon B* was efficient; the *SS* had used it in the gas chambers of Auschwitz.

GERMANY ALONE

Since the battles of Stalingrad and El Alamein, and the successful invasion of the European mainland, the German people had known that the war was lost. A few lost faith in *Der Führer* and descended into deep depression. Others demanded revenge for the bombing and the losses of their men in battle. There were only the unarmed and defenceless prisoners on whom they could satisfy their lust for revenge. Letters to the newspapers demanded the execution of the shot-down '*Terrorfliegers*' and '*Luftgangsters*' in German hands. The *Kommandant* of Stalag 4B issued a strong warning against escaping. Enraged civilians, he warned, were murdering Allied airmen captured during and after air-raids.

As August 1944 began, the troubles for Germany multiplied. On the fighting fronts the *Wehrmacht* was in desperate trouble.

Apart from their reverses in battle, there was internal disorder on a scale that made the ordinary soldier and the front line commanders realise that Germany was, as Britain once had been, alone and isolated. Germany's only reliable ally, Japan, was now in retreat and many thousands of miles away.

The attempted assassination of Hitler was still occupying the attention of the *Gestapo* and *SS*. On 1 August a decree announced that relatives of officers or soldiers found guilty of treason should share the responsibility and, therefore, the penalty for that act. The threat against families was a familiar method of the security forces to hold rebellion in check.

In France strikes were rife, the *Maquis* was active and armed groups were attacking the *Wehrmacht*. The occupying troops were nervous. In Yugoslavia, partisans were on the offensive, while in Germany some foreign workers were in revolt. Sabotage was common. Air-raids were night and day events, with great damage and loss of life, so that the *Soldat* at the front was always worried about his family at home and terrified by the enemy behind his back.

A major revolt was taking place in Warsaw. The Poles under General Bor-Komorowski were fighting hard against *SS* battalions. Some German soldiers, taking the risk of instant execution if caught, were collaborating or deserting to the enemy.

Kriegies felt the continual change in attitudes among their jailers. The older guards were often in conciliatory mood, heartily wishing the war over and concerned about their homes and loved ones, but some of the younger guards, whose wounds prevented their return to the front line, often took their anger out on the Kriegies. The trigger-happy guard had always been a danger but there were those who were looking for the opportunity to loose off a few rounds at unarmed and helpless men.

'JACKO'

The Reverend Arthur Jackson was no ordinary man. Although mild-looking, bespectacled and apparently well suited to his gentle profession, the reverend had fire in his soul. When the RAF Kriegies at Sagan asked the Germans to transfer a minister of religion to their camp, they fully expected to receive an army padre taken at Dunkirk or Crete; instead, they had the shabby, black-civilian-suited Arthur.

Jackson had been the minister of the Elimite Church in St Peter Port, Guernsey. With the German invasion imminent, he had sent his wife and family to England and continued his ministry, until one of his flock, a pregnant woman, was about to be led away for forced labour in

Germany. That was too much for Arthur; he begged, and was allowed, to go in her place. After a period in an internment camp, Arthur was sent as the requested minister to Stalag Luft 3, where he was at first suspected of being a German 'plant', but he was recognised by a former resident of Guernsey and fully accepted. From then on, he was to all the Kriegies just 'Jacko'.

When the NCO prisoners were sent to Heydekrug, 'Jacko' went with them. The camp theatre, a wooden barrack converted by the Kriegies, was used as a church on Sundays and his lengthy sermons on the Old Testament were popular, for 'Jacko', when he became excited, resorted to old-style histrionic arm waving and foot stamping. One Sunday, he preached 'on the hounds of hell which chased you down the street' – and so on. A German interpreter, sitting at the back, mistranslated and reported incorrectly that 'Jacko' was inciting the Kriegies to escape. He was immediately banished or 'purged' from 'A' Lager to 'K' Lager. The Germans allowed no contact between the compounds, so 'Jacko' was lost to 'A' Lager forever.

When, in July 1944, in the face of the Russian advance, the Germans decided to evacuate Heydekrug, they sent the Kriegies of 'K' Lager, crammed into the sweltering hold of a collier*, to Swinemünde. The traumatic voyage was followed by a terrifying and brutal three-kilometre 'gauntlet' run between guards wielding bayonets and rifle butts to Stalag Luft 4, the camp at Gross Tychow. 'Jacko' had to take part in this nightmare, the infamous 'run up the road,' and is remembered for the constant help and encouragement he gave.**

But for 'Jacko' the horrors were far from over. The *Kommandant* at Gross Tychow, *Oberstleutnant* Bombeck, when confronted with this shabby civilian without papers to prove his identity, was in no mood to listen to explanations and consigned 'Jacko' to the deathly hell of the concentration camps at Buchenwald and Dachau.

SUMMARY INJUSTICE

Flying Officer Charles Beeson was shot down and eventually sent to Dulag Luft. He had been short of food for weeks and the frugal meals were the high spots of his day. Beeson was surprised one day when, just as he was going into the communal dining room, the Senior British Officer asked him to hang back a little. Taking him to one side, the SBO explained that he wanted Beeson to stay within arm's length of an Aus-

* *Not All Glory!*, pp. 149–52
** Ibid, pp. 154–7

tralian warrant officer sitting at the table. Puzzled, Beeson agreed, but as he walked into the room, the reason for the SBO's concern was apparent. The young Australian was deeply distressed. Seating himself close by, Beeson watched with mute sympathy as the airman pounded the table with a clenched fist, repeating hoarsely to himself, 'I'm a traitor; I'm a traitor – I should not be alive ...'

Calming him, Beeson heard his story. The Australian had been shot down over Holland and had been in the underground 'pipeline' to be smuggled back to England, when it was infiltrated by the *Gestapo* and he was arrested. Under torture he revealed the location of the farm where he had been taken in by the farmer. It was enough; the airman was immediately taken back to the farm, where the farmer and his family were taken outside and shot in front of him.

ROCKETS

By early August the sojourn of the RAF men from Heydekrug at the army camp at Thorn was ending. In southern Poland the *Armia Krajowa* had been active in the area of the missile-testing site and were able to pass details of the composition and performance of the rockets. Finally they were able to send an almost complete A4 rocket on an RAF Dakota for examination. Another rogue A4 had crashed in Sweden and that too found its way back to the investigators. Scientists now had a good idea of Hitler's latest 'secret weapon'. Their horrifying conclusion was that there was no defence. The rocket carrying a ton of high explosive could not be intercepted and there would be no warning of its faster-than-sound approach. Since June the population of London and southern England had almost become used to the V-1 'Doodlebug' and were practised at diving for cover as the noisy motor cut out before the flying bomb pitched to earth and exploded. This new threat would be unnerving and a test of the forbearance and stoicism that characterised the Britishers' attitude to the Blitz.

The Russian army was crashing, cutting and exploding towards southern Poland. The rocket team had to move. The whole testing apparatus was transported to the Tugela Heide, an open area of heathland north of the town of Thorn. The test rockets were fired in a southerly direction.

From one section of the outside wire, between two huts at the Thorn Stalag, a road could be seen only a few yards beyond. It was fascinating to the RAF men, who had rarely been allowed to leave any camp or view the world outside. People walked past or rode by on bicycles, frequently calling out encouraging but often incomprehensible words. Not surprisingly, the fair-haired Polish girls attracted the eyes of the airmen.

It was while watching this occasional passing show that several condensation trails were seen to rise vertically into the northern sky. The speed and trajectory ruled out any kind of known aircraft. The trails were obviously those of some kind of rocket. Quickly distance, angles and bearings were calculated by the Kriegies and the information sent to London. It is debatable whether it was in time to do any good, but at least those in England would have an idea where the rocket-testing base was located and the Kriegies felt that even though confined, they were 'doing their bit'.

The army prisoners had noticed the bearing of the RAF. These RAF NCOs, they thought, were a trifle disturbing because of their disdainful attitude to the Germans. The army men really did not like their routine disturbed. Many of them had good contacts through working parties outside the camp and obeyed the discipline maintained by their senior noncoms. The fact that the RAF men would only accept directions from Sgt Deans, a man inferior in rank and length of service to their sergeant majors, mystified them. Technically all were under the control of the senior army NCOs but Deans stood between the RAF and the army, maintaining his quiet control with his usual tact and diplomacy. The ribald language that greeted a sergeant major's orders were calculated to bring on apoplexy.

HUNGARIAN HITCH

War takes its participants to some strangely named and remote places. When the crews of 178 Squadron Liberators were told that their target was a transport airfield at Szambathely, they had to search for it on the map of eastern Europe. About 100 kilometres north-east of Lake Balaton, it is just over the Austrian border in Hungary.

It was as well that the RAF Liberator crews were alert on their flight from Foggia for they were expected. Near the target, nightfighters were already in the air waiting. Flight engineer Mike Ludlow felt his aircraft shudder several times on the bombing run. An accurate attack damaged the nose of the Liberator, starting an uncontrollable fire. Flames streamed aft beneath the flight deck, extinguishers were useless and the aircraft doomed.

As Ludlow and Bruce, the wireless operator, raced forward, they looked into the open door of a furnace. The Liberator was hit a second time. A shattering explosion near the starboard inner engine threw the aircraft bodily sideways. Ludlow crashed to the floor as 'Lofty' Hamilton, the mid-upper gunner, scrambled from his turret and pointed towards the bomb-door whilst groping for his parachute. He had obviously heard the order to bale out. Praying the hydraulics would still operate, Ludlow reached for the emergency bomb-door operating lever, just forward of the door frame. The bomb-doors opened sluggishly, then jammed when there was a gap of just two feet.

Ramming on his parachute, Ludlow realised that he, the wireless operator and the mid-upper gunner were standing in the flames streaming past them and fanned to a blow-torch intensity by the roaring gale rushing in through the shattered nose. Outside, beneath the open door, was an unbroken stream of flame. Looking down, Mike Ludlow hesitated for a fraction of a second, but Hamilton made up his mind for him with a hefty shove. Hamilton had been shielding Ludlow from the source of the flame. Ludlow went head-first through the small gap. As he fell, he realised that his parachute pack was smouldering and immediately pulled the 'D' ring. Forgetting all the warnings, he looked down just in time to meet the pack on its way up, receiving a solid whack on the forehead. In the midst of violent action one rarely has time to remember the blackboard rules and cautions of the classroom.

Ludlow had left his aircraft at about 14,000 feet and opened his parachute immediately. It meant that for some time he found himself in the middle of the flying flak, coloured tracer and the rocking blast of a nearby exploding aircraft. He watched the glowing remains falling away in an arc. Throughout his descent, Ludlow called out loudly for 'Lofty' Hamilton and Bruce, but there was no reply.

Ludlow could detect differences in the shades of darkness below and saw that he was drifting towards a thick wood. He was lucky, his parachute snagged on branches at the edge of the wood but he was on the ground. Unable to free the canopy, he set off across a field to distance himself from the parachute. Several aircraft had been shot down in the area and *Volkssturm* groups were searching for survivors. Ludlow ran across an open stretch of heathland, into a lane. Hearing shouting in one direction, he turned to the other, and was almost level with the gate when two men stepped out shouting '*Hände Hoch!*' Ludlow had run into a guard post. A blast on a whistle brought more men from the hut and an officer came racing up the lane on a bicycle. Throwing the cycle down, the officer shone a torch in Ludlow's face and also started blowing a whistle. Soon, Ludlow was surrounded by a score or more of *Volkssturm*, led by the officer in steel-rimmed spectacles. Ludlow thought the officer looked as though he had stepped straight from a film set.

In the early morning, Ludlow was taken across fields beside a stream. In different circumstances, he would have considered it a very pleasant walk to the village. Inexplicably, a small, seven-year-old girl met the party and insisted on holding Ludlow's hand for the rest of the walk. At a small cottage, the wife of one of the guards shared their breakfast with him and produced ointment to smear on his smarting face. With his hair almost singed away, his blackened and scorched face and clothing, Ludlow imagined he must have looked like Laurel and Hardy after the stove explosion.

After a journey on a wood-fired, gas-generated milk float, Ludlow spent the night in a small Austrian town which seemed to him to be run by British Army prisoners-of-war. It was hard to believe. The British soldiers were apparently carrying out most of the town maintenance and repair work, and some were walking around with women. Several of the army men came to visit him in the town jail that evening, and brought him a towel, razor and some soap. Ludlow learned no more about this place but concluded that the prisoners here were 'on to a good thing'.

At a *Luftwaffe* station near Graz, Ludlow was locked in the guardroom with two German rankers, one of whom spoke English and delighted in telling him that he too was a prisoner.

The next day, German bureaucracy took over. It was decided that the airman must have come down on the other side of the border and would have to go to Budapest.

The train passed through glorious country until it reached a border town, where Ludlow was passed to a waiting Hungarian officer. They settled in the club coach of another train, when a passing gang of young *Wehrmacht* soldiers on the platform glimpsed the RAF man through the window. Crowding into the car, they squeezed the few Hungarian civilians and the escort into a corner. At the Hungarian officer's protest, a large, humorous-looking *Soldat* wagged his fist in the escort's face, putting paid to further protests. From the German's attitude it was obvious that there was little mutual friendliness between those allies.

Ludlow was surprised by the friendly spirit of the young, raw soldiers. At the station restaurant they filled their water bottles with Schnapps, which they shared with him throughout the night. Their 'leader' spoke understandable English and told him they were destined for the Eastern Front, were very proud and looking forward to fighting the Russians.

In the early hours, the train passed through the industrial outskirts of Gyor. One side of the track was lined with factories, belching smoke and apparently unharmed, while on the other side great areas of housing had been devastated. A Hungarian, unable to contain his fury, rushed along the coach towards Ludlow, waving his arms, pointing to one side and shouting '*Fabrica*' and then to the other shouting '*Kinder – Kaputt*'. The German 'gang leader' leapt to his feet, grabbed the Hungarian and forcibly propelled him back to his seat, decisively settling the possibility of any further disturbance.

The night passed quickly. Ludlow was glad of the company of the German lads and was almost sorry to leave them when he was handed back to his escort at Budapest, especially as the Hungarian civilians did not appear to be well disposed towards aircrew prisoners.

In a first visit to any city there is always someone who enjoys showing a visitor the sights. Two men, whom Ludlow described as 'Peter Lorre' types, collected him from the station and after a roundabout sightseeing tour of the cities of Buda and Pest, they escorted him to the last sight of all, the city jail. In a deep dungeon, with an American Mustang pilot shot down on his first mission, he waited anxiously for morning.

He was surprised when next morning he was taken in a bus to a large hotel, in the centre of the city, from which four RAF aircrew men jauntily appeared. They were laughing and chatting in a friendly manner to a couple of guards as if on a continental tour. The paradox puzzled Ludlow. The other aircrew had been housed in a five-star hotel while he and the American were deep in a medieval dungeon.

Any light-heartedness ceased at the large state prison outside Budapest. The inmates were mainly political prisoners, and the sight of them in their striped prison garb, and the stories heard about them, struck a chilling note.

A section of the prison had been set aside for the aircrew. Each man was put into a 'solitary' cell, furnished with a bed and a bucket. They were left alone, except for a visit by a striped-uniformed inmate who placed some potato soup and bread on the floor of the doorway. A guard stood beside him and, at the slightest whim, the guard hit the prisoners with his truncheon.

Every few days, interrogators entered the cells and adopted an air of shoulder-shrugging resignation at the name, rank and number routine, declaring meanwhile that the Germans and English should be allies and fighting together against the rest. Finally, the interrogators tired of Ludlow, told him that they knew all about his squadron, the commander's name and station, and showed him a list of aircrew, with his name starred in red. Then he and 24 American flyers were packed into a box-car wagon which, between interminable waits in sidings, was hitched to any train travelling north. The journey to Stalag Luft 4, Gross Tychow, took a miserable, diarrhoea-ridden week.

FINGER OUT!

Pilot Officer Edgar 'Eddie' Poulter was well into his second tour of operations when, on 13 August 1944, his Lancaster was shot down by a Junkers 88. Jumping from four miles high into the bitterly cold night air, Poulter had the bad luck to land on the roof of the only farmhouse in the vicinity. His parachute canopy snagged on the roof, and Poulter found himself suspended just two feet from the ground. Hitting the quick-release, he dropped out of his harness and reached up to pull the parachute down. The parachute canopy was draped over an upstairs bedroom window. Poulter gave up trying to retrieve the parachute as children in bed screamed with terror.

Walking into a vegetable garden at the back of the house, he buried his 'escape money' and lit a cigarette. Was this Germany or Holland? He was not sure and, as a man came out of the house 30 yards away, he thought it best just to sit, keep quiet and weigh up the situation. Despite the dark, he could see that the man held something that was either a gun or a stick. For half an hour they just looked at each other, until finally Poulter thought it time to make an approach. The man seemed quite friendly towards the Allies and Poulter assumed he must be in Holland. Nevertheless, it was not long before an armed policeman arrived and marched him to the local police station. Poulter revised his opinion of his location. He was most definitely in Germany.

On the same night, Pilot Officer Denis Fry, second pilot of a Halifax, also was shot down. For that operation Fry had been seconded to fly with the 640 Squadron CO, Wing Commander Maw DFC. The crew were strangers to him. When he was in solitary confinement at the interrogation centre at Dulag Luft, Denis Fry was startled when a German officer strode into his cell and announced:

'We've got Harris.'

That meant only one thing to Fry; disbelieving, he asked, 'Who? Air Marshal Harris?' The German officer gave a snort and replied, 'Ach, No! Not 'Butcher' Harris, you know who, your flight engineer.'

Denis Fry shrugged his shoulders as the door slammed shut. Sitting alone, he wondered how the German knew one of the air marshal's nicknames.

It was some time before Fry discovered that the flight engineer with whom he had flown that night was a P/O Harris. The German officer, mused Fry, must think him the biggest idiot he had encountered to imagine that the air marshal had been captured.

Every camp has its characters. One such was Wing Commander Roger Maw, about whom stories were legion. Inventive, industrious, clever and unconventional, Maw was known as a morale-building tower of strength. His room at Sagan was predictably known as 'round the bend hall'. Always in the lead when arrangements were made for escape, he was prevented by his disabilities from attempting escape himself. Other activities and inventions caused amusement and interest. There was, for example, a clock which would open the window at a predetermined time, so that foul air in the room could be expelled. He constructed an elastic, screw-driven submarine, which was supposed to submerge and then surface, when the conning tower would open and Adolf Hitler emerge at the salute. It worked well on his bench but, when it resurfaced in the fire pool, it promptly sank – to hilarious hoots from the assembled Kriegies.

On another occasion, Roger Maw had his tools out of their hiding place when a 'ferret', creeping about under the hut floor, was indiscreet enough to push an exploring finger up through a hole. Maw saw the finger and brought his hammer down on it with a hefty swipe. There followed a muffled yell of pain from beneath the floorboards. The sore-fingered German reported immediately to Lager officer, *Major* Pieber, but Roger Maw had been busy. The hole was invisibly repaired, and his tools safely hidden, before Pieber, now angry in the way only a German officer can be, 'tore a strip' from the guard for making him crawl into the grubby space beneath a hut and wasting his time.

THE DARK UNKNOWN

When dropping 'Joes' into occupied Europe, it was the job of the aircrew to establish with certainty that the signals received from the reception party on the ground were the correct signals. The 'Joes' could otherwise be dropped to possible capture and execution.

Flight Sergeant Bromley's crew were warned that the signal, on the night they were to drop four 'Joes', would be a 'V' of fires. Two and a half hours after take-off the Halifax was over the Drop Zone (DZ). Everything was ready, the jump-hole was open, the first two 'Joes' had been hooked up and were sitting in their jump suits, with their legs dangling in space, when the bomb aimer shouted 'Stop!' He asked the crew to look again at the signal. They saw below, not a clear 'V', but one with an extra light, which looked like a bad 'V' or a bad 'W'. 'I don't like it,' the bomb aimer decided.

The crew agreed and the drop was abandoned. It was later learned that the DZ had been discovered by the Germans but, unable to establish the correct signal, they had tried a combination. This time it had not worked and four brave men lived to jump into the dark unknown another day.

UNJUST ACCUSATION

On 18 August 1944, Lancasters of 103 Squadron, Elsham Wolds, were briefed to make a daylight attack on flying bomb sites in the Pas de Calais. The squadron was still smarting from an unjust accusation of bombing short on British troops trying to close the Falaise Gap. Sixteen Lancasters started the short journey across the Channel. At briefing they had been told to expect light cloud, and that they would meet a fighter escort as they crossed the English coast. Only at their own discretion should they bomb below 10,000 feet, but fighters would be there to protect them. It was an old and tragic story; as the Lancs crossed the French coast, no fighters had arrived and the cloud was an impenetrable 10/10ths.

Most of the Lancaster crews took the decision to drop below the cloud base. Navigator Sergeant Phil Potts plotted his aircraft on to the target and, as the Lancaster came out of the cloud, the flying bomb site lay dead ahead. The bomb aimer took over the run-in just as light flak opened a concentrated barrage. Within seconds, a burst had started a fire just inboard of the starboard inner engine. A second burst smashed through the side of the Lancaster, killed the wireless operator outright, took out the navigator's plotting table and tore a huge hole in the roof of the aircraft.

The crew completed their run, dropped the bombs and took the photograph but, by then, the fire had taken grip. The Lancaster was doomed but the pilot still had some control. He gave the order to bale out, instructing his crew that it was to be done in an orderly fashion through the front hatch. All the crew members acknowledged. Potts told the skipper that the wireless operator was dead and waited until the mid-upper gunner appeared over the main spar before jumping. The gunner followed him out.

As Potts floated down, he searched the sky for the other two men who should have followed him. He saw the aircraft circling below him in what appeared to be an attempt to crash land, and was forced to side-slip his 'chute to avoid coming down too close.

The Lancaster levelled out, as if to touch down, but suddenly exploded in a mass of flame, ammunition zooming off in every direction. Long before he reached the ground, Potts realised that nothing could be done to save the two men who were still alive when he left the aircraft. They had all acknowledged the bale-out order. Why had they not jumped? It was to puzzle him for years.

As he tumbled to earth, Potts knew exactly where he was. Although 10 p.m., it was still light. Potts had heard that the Pas de Calais area was crawling with *Wehrmacht* so he was surprised when the first person he saw was a French girl. She quickly gathered up his parachute and ran off, pointing in the opposite direction as she did so. Finding a small ditch, Potts thought he could, perhaps, hide until darkness, but was quickly surrounded by searching *Luftwaffe* men from the flak batteries that had shot down his Lancaster. Sgt Potts was a prisoner of war.

After Dulag, Potts was sent to Bankau (Stalag Luft 7) and the 'rabbit hutch' temporary huts, eventually moving into rooms intended for twelve Kriegies.

Bankau was like all Luft camps where RAF men were congregated. Aircrew were an unruly lot when they felt inclined and were prone to extraordinary and unpredictable actions that baffled the German staff. After one *Appell*, and before dismissal, the men of room 13, block 2 quite suddenly marched across the parade ground, in front of the astonished and speechless German camp officers, and into the lavatory opposite. After an interval, during which the Germans were having near apoplectic fits, the party silently marched back and resumed their places in the parade.

On another occasion the Germans decreed that twelve men in the camp were not NCOs and would be set to work. Reluctantly, the Kriegies agreed that twelve men would work – but not necessarily the twelve in question. There was mayhem when those selected turned out to be the twelve most difficult Kriegies in the camp. A hut was to be erected in a compound near the main gate. After the Kriegies had put in four days of hard work, the compound was full of holes for the foundations, but most of the hut had found its way into the Kriegies' compound for use as firewood. The Germans never repeated the work experiment.

Yet the vigilance of the guards was as marked as that of the other Luftwaffe camps. After an air-raid alert, when US Liberators and Fortresses had passed over on their way to bomb the Romanian oilfields, a Canadian airmen left his hut just before the 'all clear' had finished its steady wail. Without hesitation, a guard shot him dead.

HIMMLER'S GRIP SLIPS

The escape of 76 airmen from Stalag Luft 3 and numerous other attempts in the east served Himmler's purposes well. He persuaded Hitler that escapers might foment uprisings among the six million foreign workers within Germany's borders and carry out massive sabotage attacks. Hitler ordered that, from 1 October 1944, the camps were to be under the complete control of the *SS* and the *Gestapo*. Himmler was delighted, but when news of the order leaked out, it caused worldwide concern. *Waffen SS Obergruppenführer* Gottlob Berger was put in charge but Berger was cautious and restricted *SS* and *Gestapo* control to outside the wire. Berger saw how the war was progressing, was concerned about German prisoners in Allied hands and did his best to dissociate the *SS* from the prisoner-of-war system. In any case, overburdened bureaucracy failed to pass down the necessary instructions and so spared the Allied airmen prisoners the brutalities normal in other camps administered by the *SS*.

In early October, *Oberst* von Lindeiner, *Hauptmann* Pieber, *Hauptmann* Broili, seven other ranks and a civilian appeared before courts martial and were sentenced to twelve months' confinement in one of Germany's many gloomy fortresses. *Oberst* von Lindeiner was no fool; he knew that he could expect little mercy from an appeal to Himmler, so he did as some Kriegies found it expedient to do – pretended to be ill and played for time. By October 1944 time was running out for Germany and von Lindeiner knew that, with luck, the higher echelons would be too occupied with saving their own skins to bother further with an elderly and failed Lager *Kommandant*.

On a mid-December afternoon in 1944, Ken Campbell was one of the long-term, wounded officer prisoners to be allowed on the third and last escorted walk beyond the wire at Sagan. On their return through the pine plantations to the camp, they diverted to the POW cemetery. There before him was the nearly completed vault which was to contain the ashes of the 'Fifty'. With limited tools and materials, the working party had constructed the magnificent vault with love and respect for their lost comrades.

During the walk Campbell enjoyed the massive relief of being outside the wire for the first time for nearly three years, the almost overpowering smells of the woods and the delight of listening to the murmuring of a moving stream. The sensations mingled into one glorious feeling of the wonder that freedom could bring for which fifty of his friends had died.

A PARTY OF SCARECROWS

Stan Booker did not find the entry into Stalag Luft 3 quite so uplifting. Certainly the clean clothes and food were very welcome but he was unhappy at their reception. It seemed to him that many of the prisoners from Buchenwald automatically became second-class citizens in the camp. On arrival, their shaven heads, their wretched state, the filthy conditions of themselves and their clothes and their months of necessarily neglected personal hygiene made them feel unwanted pariahs. A toothbrush was a forgotten memory. They had never seen a Red Cross parcel, or even thought about receiving a letter from home, and no one at Sagan seemed to want to know anything about the dreadful experiences that they longed to pour out.

In fact, the officers' compound at Sagan appeared to Booker to be similar to an overseas officers' mess. Everything was so organised, uniforms were worn and he found it difficult to become used to being spoken to in a civilised manner instead of being continuously shouted at in coarse German. The ugly memories of Fresnes and Buchenwald hung over him like a dark shadow. Perhaps, he thought, the ex-KLB men were suffering from an inferiority complex, owning absolutely nothing and envying the others photographs of their loved ones over their beds, clean clothes and their contacts with home. Booker felt, too, that the Buchenwald men's attitude to their first Red Cross parcel put them in a bad light with the other residents. To a man, they sat on their beds and methodically devoured the lot.

An entry in the log of a Canadian Kriegie, written at the time of the arrival of the men from Buchenwald, describes them as a party of scarecrows, an objectionable and unsociable lot. Few efforts were made to understand the agonies of body and mind that these men had suffered or the help they needed to settle to the social and complacent life that had grown up among many in Stalag Luft 3.

ESCAPE FROM APELDOORN

Just before 8 p.m., on 5 October 1944, Halifax 'G' George had set off on a 'drop' in Holland. Crossing the coast, the Halifax went down to 50 feet above the plainly visible surface of the North Sea. Fifteen miles from the Dutch coast, the pilot put 'G' George into a steady climb. When almost over land, the Halifax, with the stick well forward, crossed into Holland in a flat-out dive, until once more the altimeter showed less than 100 feet. By the light of the rising moon the crew of 'G' George identified their last turning point and a course was set for the Dropping Zone, just south of the Zuider Zee.

All had gone according to plan, there had been no flak or searchlights and they were dead on track and ETA. There their luck ended; nowhere was there a sign of reception committee lights. Tensely they circled, until the skipper decided to fly away for a few minutes, so that too much attention would not be attracted to the area, especially as another DZ was lit just over a mile away.

On their return, there were still no lights and the twenty minutes allowed in the area had almost expired. The skipper was turning on to a course for home when flares were dropped behind the Halifax. Suddenly distracted, he either pushed the stick forward or side-slipped on the turn. Within seconds the wireless operator remarked, 'Aren't we getting a bit low?' The shouted reply of, 'By God we are!' was followed immediately by the port wing striking a tree top, badly damaging the props and engines.

With a deafening screaming and crashing, the engines tore themselves to pieces, and above all the shattering din was the ominous sound of the undercarriage warning horn. The shudders and vibrations made F/O David Ward swiftly decide that the crash position in the centre of the aircraft was the place he should be. He found the navigator and wireless operator already there. Almost immediately, the Halifax crashed, the port wing broke away and blazed furiously 100 yards from the rest of the aircraft, and the starboard wing was burning by its side.

All the crew were able to walk away from the wreck without a scratch, although the rear gunner had to be cut from his turret after vigorously shouting, 'Lemme out!' Like others before him, the name 'Lemmy' stuck.

The crew decided to attempt to contact the group whose DZ they had previously sighted and, with the help of the stars and a small compass, they began walking slightly west of south. They had walked for some three miles when Mac, the rear gunner, pointed out three men nearly 100 yards away. The crew had also been spotted and one of the men, carrying a menacing-looking Sten gun approached. As soon as the *Maquis* was mentioned, they were treated like long lost brothers and soon they were fed and bedded down for the night in a Dutch farmhouse.

For seven days they wrestled with ways of getting back, trying to sort the truth from the 'duff gen' that was brought to them. The Dutch *SS* were in the village, German soldiers were being billeted on all the farms and the *Organisation Todt* was searching for workers. The airmen knew they were being hunted; the wrecked Halifax was less than five miles away and no bodies would have been found. It was a nerve-racking time for all, and their hosts were not sorry when the crew were moved on to their next hiding place. Later, David Ward and the navigator were moved again.

At a little after ten on a Sunday morning, they and two Dutch guides, all dressed in civilian clothes, were cycling along a main road. A

German NCO walked into the road ahead and held up his hand for them to stop. With pounding hearts, three of them watched as one of their guides supplied the German with a light for his cigarette and was then waved on.

On 18 November, an enlarged party began the critical last lap of the journey, on a calm starlit night. They would have preferred the pouring rain of the previous night to cover their movements. By 10 p.m. they were within three miles of the Rhine.

The cry of halt from a German sentry scattered the party; some halted, some ran. Although the sentry did not fire, he raised the alarm, and many of the men who had been ahead of Ward had disappeared when he almost walked into a second sentry who opened fire with a Schmeisser. Momentarily Ward saw the flames from the gun barrel, dived towards the ground and felt bullets hitting him in the back and heel. The excruciating pain was only eased by an RAMC lieutenant who had been with the party. Two shots of morphia put him out for twelve hours.

In the military hospital to which he was carried, Ward was well treated and his wounds were healing. In December he began planning to escape. His transfer to a hospital in Apeldoorn confirmed his fitness. Part of the hospital was run by captured RAMC personnel and, reconnoitring during a daily rubbish disposal job, Ward concluded that escape from there would be easy. By mid-January, plans worked out with a Major Gordon for the escape of three prisoners were complete.

Only two guards were ever on duty. They sat at the head of the one flight of stairs near the doors of the prisoners' rooms but, unless the guards moved, they could not see the door of the first-floor room from which the men planned to escape. Some wounded *SS* and parachutists were also in rooms on both floors. Most of the windows were barred but, for some unaccountable reason, there were a few rooms where the windows lacked bars, One of these was chosen as the escape exit. The window was seven feet from a balcony that ran for twenty yards along the side of the block. The escapers planned to go along this balcony, then up six feet to another balcony, across a corner to another, then down ten feet to a small ledge, from there a further six feet down on to the top of an air-raid shelter, and thence to the ground. When, on 18 January, a list was issued of those who were to pack and get ready to be taken to Germany, the trio knew it was now or never. Zero hour was set for 10.30 that night. Originally, another officer captured at Arnhem was to make up a trio of escapers, but he was still unfit when the decision to 'go' was made. An American sergeant, who was keen to get away, took his place.

The escape went like clockwork. Everything that could be carried they took with them – food, medical supplies, clothes and two blankets. The American even took the wristwatch from one of the members of his crew who was 'out' after a minor operation.

Within an hour, they were a quarter of a mile from the hospital, the only mishap occurring to the American sergeant, who had wet feet after falling in a dyke. They had an address to make for, fifteen miles to the north, and hoped to arrive there before the end of curfew at 4 a.m. Each time the party came to a turning, Major Gordon would kneel and, with a blanket draped over him, strike matches and consult a map. All went well until the lane they followed petered out into fields. By 3.30 a.m., after ploughing through ice, slush, floods and dykes, they knew they were lost. The four hours of walking through difficult terrain had exhausted them. They decided to find an isolated farm and make themselves as comfortable as possible in a barn until the next evening.

Their resolution to stay in the straw was abandoned by 9 a.m. The cold wet of the night had changed to snow. They had the choice of freezing or taking a chance that the farmer would be sympathetic. Gordon spoke a little German and was sent to see the farmer. They were lucky; the Dutchman gave them food and hot drinks and, more importantly, allowed them to sleep in an unoccupied pig-sty. When they went, they left a blanket in payment.

By 4.30 p.m. the trio had set off again. Despite broad daylight, no one appeared to notice their uncamouflaged uniforms. They reached their goal before the curfew became operative, with a little time to spare.

After spending four days with their host, they moved further north and farther from the Rhine. The *Gestapo* had suddenly become active to the south, arresting many members of the escape organisation. The hopes of an early return home were dashed. The fugitives had to stay put. For two very long months they stayed in houses a few hundred yards apart, peeling potatoes, sawing wood and watching the RAF shooting up German transports. Less than a quarter of a mile away, the *Organisation Todt* was urgently throwing up defences. The trio discovered that, although the house was well into the town, they were the thirteenth, fourteenth and fifteenth members of the Allied forces who had been guests there. David Ward was anxious to get back into the fray; he had been in Holland for five months.

On solid-tyred bicycles they started off again. Familiarity had brought complacency, the journey held few terrors. They were convinced that soon they would be on their way home. The three airmen, now with two guides, all in civilian clothes, set off one fine Sunday morning, Gordon on one cycle, the American a pillion passenger on a tandem, and Ward on a carrier behind a guide.

The ride was uneventful until a guide, who had gone scouting ahead, reported that Dutch Nazis were checking all papers. The guides were discussing alternative routes when two German soldiers were seen walking towards them. Immediately ordered to walk back the way they had come, the fugitives neared another side lane and saw two more German soldiers coming towards them the other way. As they turned about, not knowing whether they had been seen, Ward suggested to Gordon, who spoke a little German, that he should tell the soldiers that the two other Germans had stolen their bicycles. It was a common daily occurrence.

It was not long before the soldiers overtook the escapers and asked them what they were doing. Gordon stuck to the story he and Ward had arranged. When it was not believed, he offered, with much gesticulation, to show them the men who had stolen their bicycles. Marched off with a machine-pistol a foot from their backs, they pointed out the two Germans when they were about 100 yards away. Their captors walked on, the two prisoners did a casual about turn and once, out of sight, turned into the woods and ran as if the devil was at their heels.

Rejoining their guides, they decided that the main road was the best route. Ward's cycle broke down but the others waited for him in a safe house. The road was packed with German soldiers, who showed little interest in the down-and-outs passing by. There was a shock when the escapers learned that all crossings had been stopped and it was necessary for them to stay in a safe house until the Allies overtook them.

Six days later, there was not a German in sight. On 15 April, the trio heard the rumble of artillery in the direction of Arnhem. The next morning, tired, dishevelled and dejected *Wehrmacht* men were retreating along the road outside, their only transport the occasional bicycle or horse.

Later that day, the only Germans in the vicinity were the crew of a 20mm anti-tank gun travelling away from the front. Ward and Gordon were discussing the advisability of trying to contact the Allied forces when they saw two men walking towards them. Friend or foe? Ward was puzzled by their strange, unfamiliar uniform, until the men spoke. They were SAS officers who had been told of the escapees' whereabouts.

A brief, grateful farewell to their hosts, a walk of about a mile and they were with the main force. Two days later they were home.

USTACHI!

Lieutenant Frank Lock, pilot of a 5 Squadron South African Air Force Mustang, flew from Fano in Italy to attack German trains and vehicles withdrawing from Greece to central Yugoslavia. From low level, he attacked a train carrying flak guns. His attack and the simultaneous fire from the flak train both rammed home. Lock's aileron controls were severed and the Mustang's radiator pierced. At 600 feet he was forced to bale out. His flak-holed parachute had barely opened when he landed heavily, causing his left leg to fold at the knee. He realised immediately that it was broken – yet he was thankful to be alive.

His relief disappeared when he saw a band of men running across the ploughed field, firing their rifles from the hip. Unable to stand, Lock watched helplessly as the fierce-looking guerrillas approached. From the large 'U' on their caps Lock guessed that these were members of the then pro-Nazi *Ustachi*. He could not imagine worse captors; their reputation for the ill treatment of prisoners, starting with emasculation, was notorious.

Lock's fears were lulled when two of the men helped him to hobble to a farmhouse, where he was given a hot drink, then placed on the back of a mule and taken to Doboj, where he was handed over to a German garrison.

Frank Lock was not sure what had saved him from the customary barbaric treatment. Perhaps it was the evident retreat of the Germans. Atrocities at that stage would have made retribution more severe. The fact that he was completely helpless, and that the German garrison was nearby, probably influenced the *Ustachi* decision, or perhaps they were rewarded for surrendering him. Whatever the reason for this out-of-character leniency, Lock was very glad to be handed over to the Germans.

Within ten days, Lock was in a three-bedded room in the *Luftwaffe* hospital at Hofgastein. *Luftwaffe* NCOs were in the beds on either side and, although nominally enemies, they developed a not-unfriendly relationship. Lock's knowledge of Afrikaans, with its similarities to German, helped communication.

On Christmas Eve, carol singing was heard in the corridor outside their room and, a little later, the door opened. An elderly lady, carrying a large basket, walked over to the first bed and presented the occupant with bottles of white and red wine. Then followed biscuits and other comforts, all with a cheery Christmas greeting. The same procedure was followed at Frank Lock's bed and that of the third occupant.

No sooner had the door closed again than the two Germans roared with laughter. A printed card with the gifts to each bed expressed sympathy that the recipient was in hospital, and hope that he would soon be restored to health to 'resume the struggle against the common enemy'. It bore the signature of Adolf Hitler.

Lock took no chances on the mistake being discovered. A knife borrowed from one of the *Luftwaffe* NCOs soon opened the bottles and the three polished off the contents. There were no enemies in the room that night.

Early in the New Year, Lock was transferred to Hohemark Hospital near Frankfurt. The train journey took five days and the last mile, on icy roads, had to be walked. Slow on his crutches, he was glad to relinquish his bundle of a few possessions (including Hitler's card) to a 'sympathetic' guard, who disappeared before the gate was reached, never to be seen again.

"Have you been here long?"

PART 6

1945

BAITING AND BARRACKING

The New Year, 1945, began with uncontrollable and accelerating panic among Germans. They had good reason. The *Wehrmacht* was fighting losing battles on all fronts. Germany had lost the war but the killing was far from over. The last great gamble of the Ardennes offensive had been blunted, with huge losses of men and materiel on both sides. 'Operation Nordwind', the attempt to recapture Strasbourg, had been unsuccessful, but the Allies still had the Rhine to cross before the Germans suffered defeat on their own soil. The Nazi hierarchy was not yet ready for 'unconditional surrender'. Confidence in victory was not felt by all the Allied commanders – General Patton, shaken by the Ardennes attack, wrote in his diary, 'We can still lose this war.'

Inside Germany, the situation was very different. Much of the *Wehrmacht*, particularly the *Waffen SS* units, was determined to fight to the end. Deserters were summarily executed by the *SS* but, increasingly, the *SS* became isolated units to be avoided by all. In the east, ethnic Germans were being expelled or were fleeing from Poland, Czechoslovakia, Hungary, Romania and the Baltic States. Ten million refugees, of all ages and conditions, were trudging westward through snow blizzards. RAF Kriegies were again quick to sense the extreme switches of mood among their guards. There was no middle course now; it was either shoulder-shrugging resignation or fierce, trembling-trigger-finger hatred.

The attitude of RAF Kriegies to their guards had also undergone a further change. They had always been wary, but the 'grapevine' or 'latrine gen' had carried from camp to camp. The inhumane events of 1944, the cold-blooded shooting of the Sagan escapers, the chaining of prisoners at Lamsdorf and other camps, the grim *Masuren* and *Insterberg* Baltic voyages,* the deliberately malevolent and savage brutality of the 'run up the road', and the subsequent treatment at Gross Tychow, all added to hundreds of other incidents that had hardened their attitude to their captors.

The Kriegies' attitude was stiffened further on Sunday 15 January, a bitterly cold winter day. At Fallingbostel and other camps they were harshly roused, very early, by the shouts of the *Feldwebel*. '*Morgen – Fertig*

---

* *Not All Glory!*, pp. 145–6, 150–2

Machen! - Aufstehen! - Heraustreten Raus! - Raus - Raus! Roughly turned out of the barracks by guards with fixed bayonets, the Kriegies shivered outside for hours as squads of Germans brought out every stool, table and palliasse from the huts and carried them from the compound. The Kriegies were to be left with nowhere to sit or lie down and no table on which to put what little food they had. Any cooperation with the Germans was now finished. There had been precious little before, but now there was nothing to be cooperative about.

'Dixie' Deans tried to defuse the dangerous situation. He was in full agreement with the non-cooperation policy but the Germans remained the armed captors of his men. The sight of the United States Air Force roaming at will overhead during the day, the Royal Air Force's nightly bombing and the squeezing in of their forces from every direction had made the German guards nervy and trigger-happy, whereas the Kriegies were becoming over-confident. They had 'baited' and 'barracked' the guards mercilessly. But, while the Germans were armed, they were in charge.

For many hours, as the bitter north wind blew, the Kriegies huddled together for warmth. When the guards had taken the last item from the huts, a *Wehrmacht* officer marched into the compound, accompanied by a *Soldat* carrying a wooden box. Placing the box in front of the Kriegies, the *Hauptmann* mounted it and began in a loud bellow: 'Our men who have become prisoners and been taken to a camp in Egypt have not been treated in accordance with the Convention of Geneva. The German High Command have been forced to take reprisals...'

His voice died away, the Kriegies had turned their backs and walked to the far end of the field. Renewing his effort, the *Hauptmann* roared to them to return, but their backs were to him and he was ignored. Climbing down from his box, the *Hauptmann* strode over, making his way through the assembled Kriegies, climbed on his box, faced them and started his harangue again. But they had already turned their backs once more, and were walking away to the other end of the compound, talking among themselves as if the German did not exist. The *Hauptmann* tried a couple more times, with the same humiliating result. Deflated, he gave up. The Germans would never understand their prisoners.

'DID YOU BOMB COLOGNE?'

On the night of 24 February 1945, Flight Sergeant Reg Gould, bomb aimer on a Halifax 3, was on a flight to bomb Lens, then only 40 miles beyond the front line. Seconds after he had been asked by the pilot to obtain a 'fix' on GEE, flak had peppered the Halifax. Gould had just gone forward, removed his parachute from the stowage rack and put it on his seat next to the navigator to give him extra height, when the order was given to clip on the parachute packs.

Within seconds, the navigator had cleared his table of maps and gone back for his parachute, and Gould had the seat folded up and the bottom escape hatch open. As no other member of the crew was ready to leave, and the aircraft wings were blazing, Reg Gould jumped. The powerful slipstream jammed him against the back edge of the escape hatch. Gould looked up for help, but the navigator had his back to him and was speaking to the wireless operator. A huge explosion blew Gould into the blackness of space.

As he fell, Gould felt for the 'D' ring rip-cord of the parachute, but there was nothing on his chest. For a moment he thought that the parachute had been ripped off during his dive from the plane. A long fall to earth and sudden death faced him but, looking up, he saw that the pack with the unopened 'chute was above his head and still attached to the harness straps. Reaching up, Gould hauled the pack down and pulled the 'D' ring. Inconsequentially he remembered the instructor's warning that five shillings would be deducted from his pay if the 'D' ring was not returned.

Horrified, he saw that, although the parachute had come out from the pack, it had not opened. He could see the shroud cords twisted all the way up to the still-collapsed canopy. In desperation, Gould began to climb up the harness and shroud lines, but he had dislocated his right arm when he had been rammed against the escape hatch. He could not lift it above his shoulder. After a climb of three feet, pain and exhaustion forced him to let go. The jerk pulled the canopy upward and it ballooned open.

Gould now started to rotate as the shroud lines unwound. He was unable to stop the movement. He could see the flashes of the front-line gunfire, and could also see that he was drifting into a wood that had been set on fire by a crashed aircraft. He was still unable to reach the cords, the parachute was still unwinding and he was still unwillingly rotating. The suddenness of an emergency parachute landing was always a surprise; one moment Gould was watching the gunfire and the next he was falling backwards in a ploughed field, 100 yards from the burning wood.

Amazed to find himself on the ground and alive, Gould quickly disposed of his parachute and Mae West and headed away from the fire. About 300 yards on, he could see in the moonlight another wood which would give him cover, enabling him to sort out his compass and escape kit. Gould did not realise that, by crossing the field instead of going round it by the edge of the woods, he had been silhouetted against the skyline. He pretended to ignore the first shout in German, hoping that the challenger would take him for a local, but the second was undeniable. He was captured and marched at bayonet point towards a village.

Ripping off his bomb aimer brevet, Gould tossed it into a ditch. With kicks and cries of '*Schweinhund*', Gould was made to stand facing a brick wall. For twenty minutes he stood, hands on head, every moment expecting a bullet in his back. He was interrogated by an officer who wanted an answer to just one question. Through an interpreter, Gould was asked, 'Did you take part in the bombing of Cologne? Answer yes or no'.

Gould could see the officer was in a temper and thought it sensible to answer a straight 'No'. He was told later by the interpreter that a 'Yes' would undoubtedly have meant a swift execution by the officer, recently brought back from the Eastern Front to bury all his family, who had been killed in a raid. Flt Sgt Gould was lucky to have eventually found himself in Stalag 7A near Munich.

DIE PROMINENTEN

The '*Prominenten*', those prisoners whom the Nazi party thought might be useful as bargaining hostages, were collected together in the concentration camps at Sachsenhausen and Flossenberg. With the wretched remnants of the prisoners who had been evacuated from the camps to the east, Sachsenhausen now contained about 50,000 gaunt, starving and dying souls. Prisoners from camps at Chelmno, Sobibor, Maidenek, Belzec, Auschwitz, Stutthof, Treblinka and Ravensbruck had been evacuated and marched slowly to the west. The few survivors of the shootings, gassings, starvation and freezing swelled the numbers at Sachsenhausen*.

As winter passed into spring, the rumble of the Russian guns grew louder until the Red Army reached the Oder, when it became like thunder. On 3 April, 'Wings' Day, 'Jimmy' James and Sydney Dowse, survivors from the Great Escape, were awakened in the early hours and told they were leaving. Quickly all residents of the *Sonderlager* were loaded into two buses and driven to Oranienburg station. There began a slow, clanking journey to Flossenberg. They had exchanged one concentration camp and one company of *SS* for another. During the Kriegies' stay at Flossenberg, *Admiral* Canaris, *General* Oster, *General* von Rabenau and Dietrich Bönhoffer were executed, together with dozens of others. The favourite slow, strangling and agonising 'piano wire' hanging was reserved for those considered traitors. The others were shot.

On 15 April, the Kriegies were again called out for a move. For 24 hours their wood-burning trucks chugged south until they stopped at yet

* *Not All Glory!*, p. 204

another concentration camp, new to them. They were near Munich and the camp was known as Dachau.

On 17 April, they were on the move again, this time stopping at Reichenau, where their numbers were increased by several *Prominenten* and their families, bringing the party up to nearly 140 worried people. Included were the industrialist, Fritz Thyssen, and his wife; ex-Austrian Chancellor, Dr Kurt von Schuschnigg, his wife and young daughter; former Chief of Staff, *General* Franz Halder; former Commander-in-Chief in Belgium and France, *General* Baron von Falkenhausen; the ex-Prime Minister of France, Léon Blum, and his wife; Fabian von Schlabrendorff, a surprising survivor of the 'July' plot; and Captain Payne-Best, the English intelligence officer who had been kidnapped in Venlo, Holland, before the outbreak of war, by Walter Schellenberg posing as a resistance agent.

An ominous note was struck when the escorting party of 30 men, led by *Hauptmann* Stille, was joined by a detachment of 20 *SS*, led by a *Leutnant* Bader. Bader was an executioner whose job was to visit the camps to reduce their populations. Although junior in rank to Stille, Bader was a killer, skilled and ruthless in his grisly trade. When 'Wings' Day planned an escape, Payne-Best counselled extreme caution, fearing for the lives of the rest of the hostages at the hands of Bader and his killers.

With April's sparkling, clear skies and nature's mountain beauty masking the tenseness among them, the *Prominenten* and the RAF men bussed slowly up to the Brenner Pass. Later, when the buses halted in the darkness, the *SS* men merged into the outside shadows, leaving the prisoners wondering about their fate. Was it to be a fusillade of shots from the roadside, or hand-grenades tossed into the crowded bus, or were they all to be taken out, stood against a wall and machine-gunned? Every possibility seemed a probability.

After a night of almost unbearably taut nerves, the *SS* men and their officers returned and, in the cold dawn, the convoy moved off again, past the frontier post and into the Italian Dolomites. They were in partisan country, with always the chance of an ambush in the narrow passes, especially now that the buses had used up all their fuel and had come to a gasping, chugging halt.

Their progress had been noted by the unseen resistance fighters and one approached who was mistaken by the *SS* officers to be a messenger from the local *Gauleiter*. His offer of accommodation for the prisoners was immediately accepted by *Hauptmann* Stille, who soon after proceeded to get drunk. Plied with more liquor, Stille was soon incapable of knowing that his wallet had been quietly removed. Inside it the prisoners found an order from Himmler containing simple instructions to the

SS – should there be any danger of the prisoners falling into Allied hands, they were to be executed, if possible making it appear as if they had been killed in an air attack.

The *SS* men were in fatalistic mood and drunkenness was fuelling their recklessness and their maudlin despair. One told Payne-Best that the prisoners were to be taken next morning to an hotel where they would be shot and the hotel burned down. But the high-ranking German officers among the Prominenten had organised a detachment of *Wehrmacht* to relieve the *SS* of their command. The *SS* men did not like it but Stille and Bader could see that the end was near and they drove away. Their *SS* uniforms proved to be a death sentence. A short way along the road the partisans hanged the *SS* men from telegraph poles.

'Wings' Day was itching for action. He wanted to arrange for the rescue of the *Prominenten* and to get home. When an Austrian resistance leader, Tony Ducia, warned that partisan groups were moving into the area and there was great danger to the *Prominenten*, 'Wings' decided that they had better get word to the advancing Americans as soon as possible. The only way was for him and Ducia to walk or hitch their way south. Never one to hesitate, 'Wings' set off. By 'procuring' a succession of cars, 'Wings' and Ducia reached the American forward units and were then passed back to various headquarters, where 'Wings' told of the plight of the *Prominenten* and their need for urgent, safe rescue.

With the departure of the *SS*, the tension among the prisoners eased, although the danger was still great. The *Wehrmacht* platoon had been withdrawn and in the surrounding woods there were plenty of deserters who, to quote 'Jimmy' James, 'would have slit your throat for a suit of clothes or some food'.

On 4 May, exhausted American soldiers, looking as though they had driven all night, arrived. 'Wings' and Tony Ducia's message had been heeded. For James and Dowse it was almost over. Their years behind the wire were at an end.

'Wings' Day was flown back to England, passing over the white cliffs on 13 May 1945, five years and seven months from the date when, with a scorch-blackened face, he had parachuted down at Langweiler.*

ON THE MARCH

For days there had been tension at Fallingbostel and much speculation by the Kriegies as to their fate as the British Army pushed towards them. They were ready to sell their lives dearly if the Nazis were to decide that

* *Not All Glory!*, pp. 14–15

the 'final solution' applied to prisoners-of-war. Malnutrition over recent months had taken its toll and many dreaded being forced to march in their weakened state.

Early on 6 April, 'Dixie' Deans relayed the orders of the *Kommandant*. The Kriegies were to march eastward; their value to the Germans now was as hostages. It was understood that the Germans envisaged the creation of a redoubt in northern Germany or Denmark where the hardliners would hold out.

Stan Reed found the evacuation of Heydekrug the previous summer a valuable training for the march. He was dressed in a variety of army and RAF clothes under a French infantryman's blue greatcoat reaching to his ankles, Foreign Legion style. A scruffy, knitted woollen hat and army boots topped and toed him. Around his waist was a belt from which hung sundry tins and cans. Carried across a shoulder was a dirty army kitbag. Apart from the clothes he wore, Reed carried a spare shirt, razor and soap, two pairs of socks and a paperback book to use as toilet paper. Reed was typical of the men around him in the unending variety and mixture of European and Asian uniforms.

STANISLAUS AND *HERR 'DOKTOR'*

Reed was marching on one of the first columns to leave the camp, on 6 April 1945. High spirits, brought on by the thought of being outside the camp, were soon dissipated by the heat and the weight of the packs. Already footsore, he discussed the chances of dodging off the column with his friend, New Zealander George Barclay, known to all as 'Boothill'. They had no compass or map and very little food but, at a bend in the road, Boothill disappeared unnoticed into the trees. Stan Reed followed and soon lay panting on the ground among the pine needles, listening to the sounds of the column passing twenty yards away. There were no shouts, no sign of pursuit – they had 'made it'. Shaking hands, Reed and Boothill set off westward.

Next morning, they were back near Stalag 357 and discussing the possibility of getting into the camp to await the arrival of 'Monty's' tanks. It seemed a strange idea but had some attractions. When skirting the camp, however, they could plainly see that the area was now jammed with masses of German troops and their transport. From where they were, Reed and Boothill could see no sign of any prisoners and the *Posten* boxes were unmanned. Fallingbostel, they decided, was no place for them. The wiser course was to keep moving west, towards the fighting front and the intermittent sound of the guns. (In fact, the German troops were probably marshalling into the vacant camp prisoners of many nationalities who had been on the road for months.)

Should they be challenged, they would pass themselves off as French or Polish prisoners. Boothill prided himself on his French. Reed hoped it was better than his self-proclaimed prowess as a medical man. Boothill said he had been a medical student; Reed called him a horse doctor. Their strange mixture of clothing was a problem. They could be taken for Gypsies, and Reed remembered hearing that the Germans had a way of disposing of Gypsies.

With cans rattling on their belts, they dashed across a wide *autobahn* into woods. Gaining confidence, they strode through the shafts of sunlight cutting through a wood of tall pines and silver birches, their steps silent on the carpet of pine needles. Strips of foil 'Window', dropped by the RAF on night raids, festooned the pines like tinsel on giant Christmas trees. That night, well satisfied with their progress, the pair spent a comfortable night in a haystack.

Next morning, forced to keep to lanes, Reed and Boothill rounded a bend and found themselves walking past an 88mm flak battery. Three guns, with tractors and trucks, were covered with camouflage netting and the crews were heating drinks over a fire. Prattling on in their best German and resisting a wild desire to bolt, the two Kriegies fixed their eyes firmly to the front. With pulses thumping in their temples, they safely rounded the next corner.

Their next meeting was with Polish POW farm workers, who advised them to keep away from Walsrode, a small town ahead, which was bursting with German troops. The Poles had no news of the British advance and thought the troops were held up near Osnabruck. Their chief concern was that the Russians, whom they feared, might make a big push into their area of north-west Germany. Told that the Poles had not seen any British prisoners, either in a column or on the loose, Reed worried that the Kriegies might have been massacred.

Pieter, a Czech woodsman, gave them food and a map from a school atlas. He, too, warned them to avoid Walsrode at all costs. They thanked their Good Samaritan. They walked on, to the edge of the woods. Suddenly, there below, was Walsrode.

The town was to be avoided but, on the outskirts, the River Böhme lay glistening in the sunshine. It looked cool and inviting to the hot, dry pair. The area seemed deserted, so they decided to risk a dash to the shadow of a small road bridge for a quick wash, drink and a refilling of the water-bottles. They planned to dart back into the woods afterwards and give Walsrode a wide berth.

The wash and drink were refreshing, but a harsh voice roaring in German from the parapet above brought them out in a cold sweat. Looking up, the RAF men were aghast to see a German soldier wearing an *Afrika Korps*-type long-peaked cap peering over the parapet. Beside him was a *Hitler Jugend* uniformed boy of about fourteen years old. Crestfallen, the two could only crawl up the bank. Luck had deserted them. To be caught by a detestable member of the Hitler Youth rubbed salt into the wound. Boothill was cursing as Stan Reed whispered, 'You'll have to talk us out of this.'

'Who are you, where are you going and where have you come from?' the puffed-up child shouted in German. The soldier, his arm in a sling and a rifle over his good shoulder, remained silent. Boothill rose to the occasion. In German, intermixed with execrable French, he told them that he was Lieutenant Paul of the French Army and that, sadly, he was a POW. Waving a piece of wood with his POW number, he indicated that Reed was his batman. The Hitler Youth was so thrilled at having captured two French prisoners that he did not bother to look at the tag. Boothill gathered confidence, assured the youth that he had been taken ill on a long, long march to Walsrode, and that his faithful batman had remained by his side throughout. Reed was impressed, especially when Boothill asked the boy for directions to the camp.

Preening with self importance, the Hitler Youth declared that POWs were not permitted in that area on their own, that the camp was in Walsrode, and he would escort them there. The wounded man said not a word. The Kriegies decided it wisest to wait until they reached the POW camp before taking any action. As they neared the railway station, they passed an enormous long-barrelled gun on its own carriage, and were happy to see that the whole train had been shot up from the air. Beyond the station was the familiar sight of a POW camp complete with barbed wire and *Posten* boxes. At the main gate, the escort had the usual shouting match with the sentry, who eventually opened the gates and shepherded the RAF men in, then went off to find out what he should do with them.

Repeating 'Tommy' over and over, grinning French prisoners gathered around the RAF men, who quickly noted that the *Posten* boxes were unmanned and there were no German sentries in that part of the camp. A prisoner who could speak some English pushed his way forward. He told the airmen that they were in a working camp, an *Arbeits Kommando*. He did not want to hear their story; it was sufficient that they were English POWs on the run in Germany. The Frenchmen, he said, were proud to help them. While the German sentry was away, querying what to do with his new charges, French prisoners collected sausage, bread, margarine and cigarettes, plus a small amount of German money. Handing it to Reed and Boothill, their new friend said, as he escorted them to the still unlocked gate, 'You must go quickly; don't worry about the Germans, we'll look after them.'

The Kriegies left, rejoicing at their extraordinary good luck. They had been in the French camp for five minutes from arrival to departure As they passed the shot-up gun in the railway yard, and the busy *Wehrmacht* men loading and unloading lorries, nobody took the slightest notice of them. The Frenchman had described the quickest route out of the town and into the countryside. There was no motor or horse-drawn traffic and the few civilians ignored the scruffy pair. Anxious to leave Walsrode as rapidly as possible, they turned into a lane, heading west. They walked 'slap bang' into a party of soldiers, in khaki uniform, working on earthwork defences. High bushes had screened their approach, so that eyes met with mutual surprise. For the Kriegies to bolt would be suicidal. There was nothing for it but try to brazen it out again.

Sweating, Stan and Boothill stopped as two soldiers stepped into their path. One began the usual questioning in German. 'Who are you and where are you going?' As Boothill began his French officer story, Stan Reed noticed the soldiers' lapel flashes. They were members of the *Organisation Todt*, engineers, not infantry. He was slightly less concerned, until the soldier mentioned the *Hauptmann* and led the way. Boothill, confident as always, whispered from the corner of his mouth, 'Don't worry, I'll soon have us out of this.' But Reed was unhappy. For the short time they had spent in Walsrode they had been under armed escort. It was apparently an important place. No wonder the helpful Poles and the Czech had told the Kriegies to give the town a wide berth.

Waiting apprehensively outside a house, surrounded by busy *Todt* workers, the Kriegies were dismayed by the appearance of the *Hauptmann*. Tall and upright, he descended a few steps and stood looking down at the nondescript pair. Very much in charge, he indicated his disbelief of their story. It would be difficult to fool this worldly man in his forties and, when he addressed them in fluent French, Stan Reed's heart sank. But Boothill was never nonplussed. Reed, following the conversation as best he could, thought Boothill was laying it on a bit thick with his repeated '*Mon Capitaines*'.

Suddenly the *Hauptmann* reverted to German: 'What an atrocious accent you have, where did you say you came from in France?'

'Bordeaux, *Herr Hauptmann*,' Boothill replied.

'Strange,' said the *Hauptmann*, 'I spent several years before the war in Bordeaux on business and your French is nothing like that spoken in Bordeaux.'

Reed thought the *Hauptmann* had a point; he knew Boothill had never been anywhere near Bordeaux in his life; but Boothill was not to be outdone.

'I was born there, *Herr Hauptmann*, and spent my early years there,' said Boothill, with the assurance of an accomplished liar, 'but my father was in the diplomatic corps and we lived for most of my youth in New Zealand where my father was stationed.'

'So,' replied the *Hauptmann*, 'that accounts for your accent which sounds more like an English one.'

Stan Reed, holding his breath, thought how right the *Hauptmann* was and desperately hoped that Boothill had reached the end of his inventions. But he went on:

'It could be, *Herr Hauptmann*, my English is quite good.'

Standing at Boothill's side, Reed could feel the sweat coursing down his back. Following odd words of the conversation, he was dreading letting the side down, but Boothill seemed imperturbable. They were not asked for proof of identity, which would have called their bluff. Boothill had apparently assured the *Hauptmann* that they had taken a wrong turning at the railway station, that they had been walking all day and were in need of the food and rest they would get at the French prisoner-of-war camp. The *Hauptmann* was satisfied. He was a busy man, with better things to do, so he decided to get rid of the pair by sending them back to the camp in Walsrode – under armed escort. Boothill thanked him and the Kriegies left, expecting that they would have to sit out the war in the French camp. Reed thought it not such a bad idea. The last few days had been hair-raising, mentally and physically exhausting.

To their surprise, half a mile on the road towards the camp, their escorting soldiers stopped, told them where to go through the town and warned them not to wander about. The pair plodded on while their escort was still in sight, and then congratulated themselves on such an unexpected escape. They were about to dash into the country when a German civilian policeman raised his hand for them to stop. Boothill trotted out his French officer story again, adding that they had been directed to the camp by the *Hauptmann* of the *Organisation Todt*. The policeman was convinced, warned them about wandering in the town against orders, and directed them back to the safety of the camp.

They desperately wanted to get out of Walsrode but seemed fated to have to return to the French POW camp. As they walked away, the policeman leaned on his bicycle, watching. They plodded on, but the policeman soon climbed on his bike and rode off. They turned swiftly down a lane to the left and made for the open country. By 4 p.m. they had entered the woods and found a spot that was dark and cool. The young trees had branches reaching to the ground, making a screened, enclosed space. At last they felt free of Walsrode and could speak in English instead of 'pidgin' German and Boothill's unidentifiable French. Yet Boothill's French had saved them; he had talked them past the revolting Hitler Youth with his brief shorts and dagger, talked the *Todt Hauptmann* into sending them away, and bluffed the policeman into letting them go.

Throwing their blankets and greatcoats down, and taking off their heavy boots, the airmen settled down for a welcome rest. 'Boothill, I was really sweating while you were talking to those Germans, especially the *Hauptmann*,' gasped Stan Reed. 'You weren't the only one,' replied the apparently unruffled Boothill, 'but it was damn rough luck encountering a German who not only spoke reasonable French but had also been to Bordeaux.'

'If we are stopped again and your French is questioned,' queried Reed, 'do you think you could find some less well known place to be born in?'

They had done well for food from Pieter, the Czech, and at the French camp, but water was a problem. Stan Reed rubbed the vegetables as clean as possible on the grass and leaves, threw in a couple of pieces of sausage and soon had a stew of sorts bubbling away on a fire.

A long 'Pssssssssttt' made them sit up in amazement. Stan Reed had only known such sounds described in comics by skulking Slavic men in long cloaks carrying a smoking object marked 'Bomb'. The well-built young man who parted the undergrowth and entered their clearing had the right furtive air. He wore a kind of black-belted, khaki uniform and a form of skull-cap, with ear-flaps that folded upward and buttoned over the crown. In German he asked, 'Are you Englanders?'

He was obviously not German and, at Reed's reply, came forward with outstretched hand. 'Russki,' he said proudly, 'a POW like you.' Pumping their hands, he repeated, 'Englander good, good,' and then, indicating the fire, he said that it must be put out immediately – it was too dangerous in that area. There were Germans all around who would see or smell the smoke. The Russian then demolished the fire, treading and crushing the embers deep into the dust.

Boothill was the first to regain his composure. 'Who are you, where do you come from? Are you living in the woods?' he asked urgently.

'I am Mischa, I am Russian and have run away from the farm where I was working,' replied the man and then, with a rush of words, 'You must come to meet my comrades, we have a place much deeper into the woods. Come quickly, before the Germans come here and catch us,'

Reed and Boothill were worried; they had thought themselves reasonably safe away from Walsrode but now they seemed to see Germans behind every tree. Quickly they decided to go with Mischa. As they hurriedly relaced their boots, Stan Reed asked Mischa how he had discovered them.

'I smelt smoke,' he said, 'and when I came to see who was foolish enough to light a fire so close to the Germans, I heard you talking in English.'

Hurrying them, he said that he wanted to get away from their hiding place. He was sure that the Germans would arrive at any moment.

Leading them into the darker recesses of the forest, Mischa suddenly stopped, cupped his hands and gave a low call, which was answered by a soft whistle. 'My comrades are just ahead,' he said. At the top of a tree-lined hillock stood a man and two women of about Mischa's age.

'This is Karl, a Cossack,' said Mischa proudly, indicating the fierce-looking, black-haired man with a scar over his right eye. A large black moustache bristled on his upper lip and another long scar marked his right arm. In his right hand he waved a Luger pistol.

'This is Nadi, who is Karl's woman,' Mischa said, bringing forward a slim, dark girl. Reaching for the hand of the second woman, he said, 'This is Varli, who is mine.'

While they absorbed this startling information, Stan Reed introduced Boothill as George. The Russians were very impressed to know that he came from New Zealand and that both men were flyers. Added to that was Boothill's sudden promotion of both Kriegies. Boothill had a habit of elevating them in rank, realising that rank often carried the day.

Mischa had been captured, defending Moscow, in 1942. He and Karl had run away from farms. The women, also from nearby farms, had readily agreed to join them in their escape bid. They were desperate characters, all aware of their fate if caught. Stan Reed did not fancy staying with them very long.

Boothill asked how they managed to make their uniforms last three or four years. The sobering reply was that their uniforms were replaced from dead comrades. Supplies were frequent. The women were dressed peasant-fashion, with heavy skirts made from old grey blankets. Blouses, head-scarves and heavy boots completed their ensemble, nothing at all feminine.

'Washing and cooking is not possible,' Karl informed them. 'There is only a little cold water to drink, and it is far too dangerous to start fires. Tomorrow, before dawn, Mischa and I will obtain some more food, which we will steal from the Germans before they are awake. You must look after the women while we are away. Your turn to get food will come.' Boothill and Stan Reed exchanged glances; this turn of events was not to their liking.

Karl and Nadi had lined a spot with bracken, two thin army blankets and a couple of greatcoats. Mischa and Varli had a similar nest, which took up most of the remaining room. Boothill and Reed had no alternative but to settle down for the night beside them. The Kriegies, although used to sleeping rough, and exhausted by the day's adventures, found that sleep would not come. Their Russian friends chatted quietly. They said the Germans did not move around much at night; nevertheless, the escapers must be as quiet as possible and careful with matches and smoking. That, and the thought that the Germans surrounded them, as the Russians claimed, gave the RAF men a desire to push on and get away from their new friends early in the morning. They eventually slept. It had been a long Sunday.

The forest's dawn chorus awakened the airmen and they saw that the Russians were already up. Dressing consisted of pulling on their boots. The shortage of water ruled washing out of the question. Boothill looked dark and villainous with his two-day growth of beard. As they brushed each other down, removing the bracken and pine needles, the airmen agreed that the Russians, despite their warnings, spoke very loudly. This reinforced their desire to get away.

In their *lingua franca*, a form of Stalag German, Boothill told Karl that they were going off in a south-westerly direction to meet the British Army. Karl immediately opposed the plan, certain that they would not get very far. The area was swarming with German troops. Seeing that the pair were adamant, Karl reluctantly agreed, and gave them bread and sausage for their journey. Wearing their greatcoats, and with all their gear hung around them, the Kriegies set off. Karl was to accompany them to the edge of the wood. Now he insisted on absolute silence. It was Monday and people were likely to be about.

Stan Reed had just looked at his watch – it was 6 a.m. – when Karl, who had been leading the way, stopped and held a warning forefinger across his lips. On a track below them four German soldiers, in a well-camouflaged light, Jeep-type vehicle, came into view. Following them came two three-ton canvas-covered lorries. Karl grinned at the RAF men as if to say, 'What did I tell you.?'

The sun was obscured by the trees, so that ascertaining directions was difficult, but deep in the woods they trudged on, with Karl in the lead. Half an hour later, Karl stopped again, with a finger to his lips.

Beckoning the pair forward, he pointed to a large clearing ahead. It was full of lorries, Jeep-type vehicles and masses of young-looking German soldiers teeming around small tents and cooking fires. Karl reckoned they could be marines, but whatever they were, they frightened Boothill and Reed. They had not the stomach for a confrontation with an overwhelming number of soldiers of an armed active service unit. Those men in the clearing were not Hitler Youth, one-armed soldiers or *Organisation Todt* men, but front-line fighters who would give them very short shrift. The airmen accompanied Karl back to the camp, which they reached before 9 a.m. They felt shattered but heartily relieved to be in the comparative safety of the clearing. They concluded that they would just have to get used to spending their time with the Russians while waiting for 'Monty' and his men. Mischa, Varli and Nadi welcomed them back as if it was a homecoming.

The constant struggle to keep one step ahead of the Germans, and talking themselves out of trouble, during the three days that they had been on the run, had drained the airmen's nervous and physical energy. For six months they had subsisted on near-starvation rations. Only good luck, quick wit and courage had kept them going so far. It was impossible to gauge how much longer they would have to survive in these conditions of hunger and ever-present danger. Reed and Boothill reckoned the Russians needed them as much as they needed the Russians. Boothill made a sudden decision; he would take command.

Stan Reed was interested to see what rank Boothill would assume. So far, he had adopted rank according to the person with whom he had been dealing. It had varied with the Germans, French, Poles and the Czech. Boothill called a pow-wow. Reed named it a 'Small Three' conference of England, New Zealand and Russia. Boothill appointed himself spokesman. As he was the most senior in rank, had the greatest experience, had commanded an aircraft and possessed the greater knowledge of languages, he was willing to assume command. His master stroke was to throw in that he was a doctor. The Russians were impressed. Boothill did not elaborate on his being a mere second-year medical student.

The Kriegies were concerned about the Luger pistol that Karl waved around so freely. It seemed a miracle that someone had not already been shot, and the RAF men were sure that Karl meant it when he said he would use the Luger if the Germans found the camp-site. Their fate after such an action could be easily visualised. Karl had to be separated from the gun.

It proved surprisingly easy – but there was a price. Accepting Boothill as the leader, Karl pointed out that the airmen had wristwatches, whereas neither he nor Mischa possessed one. Boothill must have the pistol because of his rank and qualifications, but perhaps, as a gesture of goodwill, the airmen would give them one of the watches in exchange. This was agreed and Boothill decided that Reed's watch was inferior to his own and should be handed over to a delighted Mischa. Furthermore, Boothill declaimed, with reckless hyperbole, that the Russians were collaborating so well that King George in England would give them each a medal when the war was over.

The Russians were pleased but Karl had one other amendment to add to the agreement. He made it absolutely plain that the arrangements excluded the women. If the airmen wanted a woman, they had to go and get one for themselves. He did not elaborate. The airmen swiftly assured Karl that such thoughts were furthest from their minds, that their only wish was to return home to their loved ones. Look-out watches were arranged during the daytime, two hours on, four off. That way, there would always be two maintaining a look-out, while the others kept low and out of sight. Boothill ordered that complete quiet was to be maintained; there was to be no more wild Russian singing and dancing. His authority was accepted without question. Stan Reed thought Boothill full of 'bull', but very likeable and born years out of his time. He should have been a pirate or bandit and, indeed, looked the part. With some affection, Reed reckoned him the ideal partner for such a perilous adventure. So many of his hare-brained schemes came off.

Boothill next sorted out the food situation, persuading Karl and Mischa to go out next morning to seek more food, craftily mentioning the two medals again. Stan Reed was to collect water from the brook, with Mischa as look-out. The women were to distribute the daily rations. Boothill, in the loneliness of command, did not seem to have much to do.

First names were now used, Reed became Stanislaus and Boothill Georgi, or *Herr Doktor*, which pleased him greatly. Reed was suffering severely with burst blisters on his feet. *Herr Doktor*'s prescription was to avoid wearing boots in the camp.

The camp-site was bigger than it first appeared. It was some 30 feet across and heavily covered with bracken and young firs, behind which an area was set aside as a latrine. In front was a large clearing with a wide track from where would come any impending danger. Guns could be heard again and Typhoons frequently passed overhead, much to the delight of the Russians. Their hate for the Germans was very apparent. A special watch was made for the approach of a searching Fieseler *Storch* which was, luckily for them, noisy and slow. A commonsense warning came from Boothill not to leave any gear, greatcoats or blankets where they could be seen. Everything was to be hidden under the bracken.

The sun rose bright on the crisp Tuesday morning, rapidly clearing the slight mist that hung around the trees. Karl and Mischa had been out before dawn and had returned with two loaves and a tin of meat which the women said was horse. It was a welcome diet addition. Mischa had gone out again as the airmen were pulling on their boots, the only piece of apparel they removed at night. A low whistle signalled Mischa's return. To everyone's surprise, he was accompanied by a tall, thin man with a scraggy black beard. Holding the man's hand was a small boy of about ten, who appeared terrified. Boothill studied the man's face. He was in his forties and almost as scared as the boy. He was dressed in a long black overcoat and a matching black trilby.

The man could see that his new hosts were extremely interested in a small suitcase he was carrying. Reluctantly, and to forestall any violent appropriation attempt, the man hurriedly unlocked the case with nervous fingers. It was stacked with packets of cigarettes which, reluctantly but liberally, he passed to those around. Karl relieved the trembling man of the remainder.

The newcomer spoke a strange language that none of the four understood, but their basic German proved sufficient. Breathlessly, the man told them that he was an Estonian, and had been working in a *Wehrmacht* canteen at Nienburg. His wife had died two years before; now he was running away because the fighting was drawing close. He was making his way towards Walsrode, where he knew someone who might take him in.

Boothill and Stan Reed did their best to reassure the petrified boy but he knew no German. Mischa agreed to escort the man and boy to the edge of the woods, but Karl warned the Estonian that if he mentioned their presence in the woods – there he stopped. A finger drawn significantly across his throat was sufficient to convey his meaning.

The next morning was warm and deceptively quiet, only the birds made any noise or moved in the sun dappled peace of the wood. Between their tours of duty as look-outs, the four took the opportunity to rid their clothes of some of the accumulated body lice. It was during a watch by Mischa and Stan Reed that the sound of motor transport was heard coming from the east, towards the clearing below. Apprehensive, the two other men crawled through the bracken to see. A *Wehrmacht* jeep was followed into the clearing by a truck towing a long-barrelled gun on a trailer. Another radio truck followed, towing a four-barrelled anti-aircraft gun. Soldiers poured from another jeep and manhandled the big gun, an 88mm, into position, set up the four-barrelled gun and parked the vehicles under camouflage netting. The escapers lay watching this action 200 yards distant, as quiet as their laboured breathing and pounding hearts would allow.

The tense waiting stiffened everyone, as more distant guns started to shake the area. Then there was frenzied activity around the guns below. Six Typhoons circled round the area and the 20mm gun took up the action. Then the Typhoons dived in line astern out of the sun, firing rockets and cannon, their roundels, squadron codes, invasion stripes and characteristic chin air-intake clearly visible. This was the famous Typhoon 'cab rank' in action. Stan Reed resisted the urge to stand up and cheer. As the rockets left trails of smoke and missiles whistled and thudded into the ground, the escapers buried their heads. The four-barrelled gun opened up but the Typhoons were too low and too fast for either gun to follow them.

The four men in the secret clearing watched spellbound, despite missing some of the action while their heads were down. As the aircraft roared across the treetops and climbed away, the thick smoke over the gun area started to clear. The watchers were disappointed that the guns appeared to be undamaged, although there were plenty of craters and some bodies spread around them. The incident had taken no more than 60 seconds.

The Germans hurriedly packed up their equipment, raised the guns on to the trailers and drove the vehicles out of the trees to link up. The dead and injured were placed in the lorries and, within minutes, all had disappeared.

That night Reed and Boothill were excited, for the day's action, the noise of the guns getting nearer and the thought that freedom was almost within their grasp, made sleep among the bracken difficult.

Their rest was also disturbed by a sudden cry of masculine anguish. Karl's back had fixed rigidly in such a position that he was unable to move. It was an emergency job for *Herr Doktor*. Boothill leapt to his feet, shouting to Reed to come and help. Amid much howling from Karl, the airmen managed with massage and quackery gradually to ease Karl's pain. Quiet eventually returned to the dark forest clearing.

The rumble of artillery in the distance shivered the still morning air as Boothill and Varli took their watch on the clearing below. The sunlight suddenly felt cold, and the watchers froze like statues as an eight-strong *Wehrmacht* patrol stole in single file into the woods, not 50 yards away. All were young men with a formidable appearance in their long-peaked caps, black jackboots and black leather equipment. They carried efficient-looking machine-pistols and were led by a hook-nosed, old-sweat *Feldwebel*, the kind who would stand no nonsense.

Boothill signalled the others. They all lay low, scarcely daring to breathe. Reed felt sure that the patrol was looking for them; this was the nearest Germans had been to the camp-site. The only sound from the furtive four peering through the bushes was the thumping of their hearts.

A quick look around, then the patrol ran from the clearing, leaving the four shocked and drained. They agreed that, if they were discovered, they would make a dash in different directions for the woods behind. Survivors would meet after dark near a large oak.

Boothill and Varli were suffering severely from dysentery and Stan Reed's heels were desperately sore. Although none was seriously physically ill, they realised that their mental resources were dangerously low. The next few days were spent in anxious and painful waiting, no one moving except to go to the latrine behind the site. In one way, Reed was thankful that nobody was eating; at least he did not have to go with Mischa to steal food.

Sunday 15 April dawned bright and sunny, but only Mischa and Stan Reed stirred from their blankets, the others felt too ill to move. Small arms and automatic fire was heard a couple of miles away. The fighting front was coming closer. It was decision time.

There was nothing for it; if the Germans fell back and overran their camp-site, Mischa and Stan Reed would have to run and leave the sick four to their fate. Reed felt a deep stab of regret at the thought of leaving Boothill. They had been through a lot together but there was no point in staying behind. Mischa and Reed thought they might be able to manage something between them. They decided to go for some water and have a look around.

Mischa, as always, led the way. Once at the track, he peered carefully in both directions. He retreated quickly. '*Soldaten!*' he hissed. '*Deutsche?*' asked Reed. Mischa nodded and Reed looked up the track. Ten soldiers stood around a machine-gun on a low stand, about 200 yards away. It was difficult to see their uniform colour, but it did not appear to be the usual grey-green. There were many different uniforms in the forces fighting for the Germans, but the helmets did not look right. These were shallow, steel helmets with twigs and leaves stuck into camouflage netting. Then Reed saw that the soldiers did not wear jackboots but had canvas anklets above their boots, and they wore battledress. They were British.

Excitedly, Reed told Mischa and jumped on to the track, frantically waving his arms above his head and shouting wildly in English. Mischa had stayed crouched in the wood. Reed stopped, petrified, when a burst of fire whipped over his head. He raised his arms and looked round for Mischa but he was out of sight.

'Halt – then come forward.'

Reed did as he was told and called out, 'Don't shoot, I'm British, I'm a Royal Air Force prisoner-of-war.'

'Keep coming,' ordered the soldier.

Reed went towards them. Sten guns were pointing at him. The lieutenant in charge of the group looked at Reed with astonishment.

'You can't be British, dressed like that,' and was unimpressed until Reed produced his identity discs and other proof.

Wild excitement seized Stan Reed. He wanted to dash back into the wood to pass on the good news to those at their camp-site, when he remembered Mischa. Turning back to the British soldiers, he called, 'Don't shoot the man hiding in the bushes, he is a good friend and speaks no English.'

The soldiers, Royal Scots of the 7th Armoured Division, reassured him. They, too, were happy and delighted; Sgt Reed was the first British prisoner they had encountered but the lieutenant interposed. 'We now have to lock up Russians' he said quietly. 'They have been murdering, raping and pillaging among the German population. I'm afraid your Russian friends will be detained.'

There will be no medals for them now, thought Reed.

Quickly calling a jubilant Mischa out to safety, Reed led a party of four soldiers and the lieutenant to the hideout in the woods. There was no sound from the camp, but Boothill peered from beneath his blankets. 'What's up then?' he asked blearily.

As Reed's news sank in, Boothill rapidly came alive and resumed command. The Russians hugged each other with delight, while the soldiers stared in amused amazement at the bedraggled appearance of the Russian women. Their few belongings were gathered up and the lice-ridden blankets left behind, hidden.

For the first time, Reed looked closely at the soldiers. They were in high spirits, their morale at a peak. They had fought their way across Europe since the Normandy landings, and knew they had conquered. The Germans were on the run, fighting their last despairing battle.

Back at a farmhouse in a clearing, Jeeps and Bren gun carriers, carrying the invasion star on their sides, were parked all around. Bodies lay under blankets and several wounded, grey-faced and shocked *Wehrmacht* men, some very young, lay flat on the ground or sat propped against the walls.

Knowing they would not see their Russian friends again, Reed and Boothill said a fond goodbye to them and were taken back to an advanced field dressing station, a collection of tents flying a Red Cross flag. The Kriegies then told of the masses of troops and defences they had seen in Walsrode on 7 April, of the flak gun positions, the huge gun on its own railway wagon, the French prisoner-of-war camp, where they had been so well treated, and finally of the concentration camp at Bergen Belsen.

After delousing, Reed and Boothill were taken to a medical officer who was then attending a sixteen-year-old boy on a stretcher. The boy was crying and continually calling for his mother. The words, '*Mutti, Mutti*' sounded piteously across the area. The MO told the Kriegies that the boy had been hit by small-arms fire as he scrambled from a slit trench, one bullet entering his body through the rectum. Sadly, he said, 'I very much regret there is nothing more I can do for him but to give him a stiff shot of morphia to put him to sleep.' Those words burned into Reed's mind, leaving an indelible memory.

An *Unteroffizier* with a terrible stomach wound lay on another stretcher nearby, blood oozing from a heavily stained shell-dressing. To Reed the man appeared conscious but he made no sound. He just lay watching, with great eyes staring from his grey face. As he prepared another syringe, the MO muttered, 'There's nothing I can do for him either.' Calling orderlies over, the MO told them to take the two victims to another tent, where they would be allowed to die in peace. Suddenly, the ex-POWs felt that the dysentery, starvation and all the suffering they had been through seemed trivial.

ON THE RUN

Danger surrounded those who stayed with the columns and those who 'sloped off'. On the spur of the moment, John Broughton and four friends decided to run. They had no clear plan or knowledge of the direction to take but thought anything better than the interminable wandering across north-west Germany.

They nervously passed a platoon of German troops who, to their relief, completely ignored them. The police and armed residents of the next small village, however, did not. They were aggressive and intimidating. The surrounded Kriegies were in danger of, at best, a beating and, at worst, a lynching. They tried in vain to explain that they were prisoners-of-war who had become separated from the main column and were lost. The situation was explosive until Broughton remembered the name of the last place at which the column had stopped. It was Salem and the villagers were partially convinced. They allowed the Kriegies to go, pointing in the direction they should take.

Broughton's group decided at this late stage that, in his words, 'discretion really was the better part of valour'. They found and rejoined the Kriegie column.

Wally Bradley and Doug Endsor did not act on the spur of the moment but had planned an attempt to escape from the moment that a march from Stalag 357 was rumoured. They were in the second batch of 200 prisoners marched eastwards at 6 p.m. on Friday 6 April.

Quickly reconnoitring the situation in their column, they saw the opportunity to steal away as they traversed a causeway with bushes at intervals and a ditch beyond. They most feared the guards at the rear of the column, two with sub-machine guns and two with dogs. At about 10 p.m., they exchanged signals, then quickly slid into the ditch, out of sight. The column moved on and no one missed them.

Now on their own, they knew the Germans had orders to kill escaping prisoners on sight. They walked until 4.30 a.m., when they laid up under a hedge in a field. Three hours later, they were awakened by a horse neighing and looked up to find a German officer on horseback gazing at them. He took no action but they tucked into some of their food in case he sent the local home guard to find them.

Nothing having happened, they set off again at about 9 o'clock that night. There were scares. Once they met a five-man guard coming off duty and bribed their way with cigarettes. They walked round a tank-repair depot that was heavily guarded. At first light, they found a copse in which to spend a furtive day. Again at about 9 p.m., they decided to move on. They could hear gunfire some way ahead. Reaching open country, they found a barn in which to shelter. It was now Monday 9 April, and they stayed hidden in the barn for three days, without food or drink, while there was activity all around. At one stage a German officer was signalling with pistol shots the advance and subsequent retreat of a large number of heavily armed infantry. He was only the thickness of a plank from them.

In mid-afternoon on Friday the 13th, a smoke screen appeared ahead. When it cleared, the fugitives saw British tin hats whose owners were digging slit trenches, covered by four armoured vehicles. When activity ceased and the armoured vehicles had gone on, Endsor and Bradley tied a white handkerchief to a stick and showed themselves. Reaching the troops, they explained who they were and were taken to see the commanding officer. They were the first prisoners liberated by the KSLI 11th Armoured Division. The major told them that he had intended to demolish the barn in which they had been hiding, but he had been knocked 'base over apex' by his traversing gun.

The two music men were free. They were on the fringes of Lüneburg Heath and, after a night in the sergeants' mess, they were taken by jeep to Celle. On the way, Endsor went through the windscreen when the steering failed. From Celle they continued on to Brussels in a Dakota. Endsor took the controls for a time but, after four years in captivity, baulked at landing the aircraft. After a brief stay in Brussels, they were flown home in a Lancaster.

Like Bradley and Endsor, Lancaster pilot Flight Sergeant Ray Gulliford slipped away from the column on the first night out from Stalag 357. In the darkness he had become parted from his 'combine' and, with another Kriegie, steadily made his way westward towards the sound of the guns. Meeting some Russians, Gulliford and his friends were told to hide themselves quickly, high in the fir trees. They had hardly done so when German troops arrived and began digging defensive positions. It was hours before they were able to descend and break from the trees, followed by air bursts from British 25-pounder guns. The shellfire forced the pair to throw themselves into a trench already occupied by a German soldier. Loath to miss a chance of finding food, they asked, '*Haben Sie brot?*' Receiving a negative reply, they hurriedly left and made their way into the next village. It was a mistake, for the village had recently been shot-up by marauding Spitfires and the locals were angry. When a villager saw the wings on Gulliford's tunic, he and others weighed in, fists flying, until the airmen were rescued by a contingent of German marine grenadiers.

Returning them to the camp at Fallingbostel, with a newly captured 'Tommy', a German marine commented, 'You were lucky it was us, an *SS* group just over there is shelling the British troops with an 88mm gun and are not taking prisoners.'

THE BEATEN MAN

The morning of 10 April was another sunny day. Vic Gammon awoke to the sound of men talking, preparing drinks and splashing at a standpipe labelled '*Kein Trinkwasser*'. He pushed back the straw, wiped the frost from his eyebrows and stretched after the finest night's sleep for weeks. Boots were retrieved from deep in the straw where they had been hidden, then, working his way along the queue to the standpipe, he had the first reasonable wash since leaving Fallingbostel.

That day he, together with Leakey and Hamilton, decided to explore the immediate area to search for food. Instead, they found a

Kriegie who had received a merciless beating. He had been caught stealing another's meagre ration of meat, his second such offence. Against the wall of a barn and among bales of straw, the man had been pummelled until he had fallen semi-conscious and defenceless. Again and again he had been lifted up and beaten until his face was a swollen, almost unrecognisable mess. Hunger had pushed the beater, and beaten, to extremes.

Looking closely, Gammon identified the groaning figure among the straw bales as a talented musician who had entertained in the camp. It was a tragedy of fierce emotions fanned by circumstance. Opening a puffed eyelid, the man saw that the three Kriegies standing around him were friendly and understanding. They knew too well the pressures that hunger can bring. As they helped him to his feet, he said groggily, 'I know where the farmer has some potatoes, do you want some?' They took them gratefully. But they were seed potatoes that had been chemically treated to prevent them rotting in store and only added to their stomach ailments.

BACK TO 357

At a prearranged signal, a diversion was set up by Kriegies in the column, who openly wandered away so that the guards were forced to chase them and shout for their return. Others suddenly surrounded guards and asked irrelevant questions. Arthur 'Chester' Morris, Jack Carey and Jack Kearey, a German speaker, wrapped in dark blue blankets, had thrown themselves into roadside ditches and remained undiscovered in the evening gloom. Morris, lying face down, felt that his back was ten feet wide and expected at any second to hear the click of a rifle bolt. Eventually Carey and Kearey answered his soft call and at 10.15 they turned back to the direction from which they had come. Next afternoon they heard footsteps coming towards their hiding place in a copse. A teenage lad, led by a dog, walked unerringly up to them. The lad told the group he was sure that his father, a German farmer, would be willing to help, and suggested that they stay where they were until nightfall, when he would return.

When the boy had gone, the trio moved from their hiding place. Why should the Germans help them? Suppose it was all a ploy, a trap to keep them in a place where they could be rounded up or shot? As darkness fell, the boy returned with two men wheeling bicycles. The Kriegies, tentative and cautious, stepped out to meet them. The men were the lad's father and uncle and were eager to help. Their farm was near but could only be reached by passing a German guard-house standing back from the road. It was planned that Kearey would walk with one man, laughing and chatting, while Morris and Carey would each push a bicycle, with the other men walking beside them. With luck their uniforms would not be recognised in the fading light. They hoped to give the guards the impression that the party had been for a night of carousal and were returning home slightly inebriated. With beating hearts and sweating palms, the airmen set off with their new friends.

As the guard-house drew near, the Germans called out jocular greetings which drew a cheerful '*Gute Nacht*' in return. As they passed, Morris felt trickles of cold sweat course down his back and sides.

Led into a big farmhouse kitchen, they were greeted by a red-cheeked *Hausfrau*, the mother of many children. After a meal they all talked of the war, Kearey interpreting. The family was violently anti-Nazi and the woman told of a Nazi farmer nearby who had fed his pigs with surplus milk when she had been unable to get food for her children. Brandishing a Luger pistol she cried out, 'When it is all over that Nazi swine is mine.' Morris was convinced that she meant every word.

For six days, as the gunfire drew closer, the three hid under the hot roof in the rafters of a barn, being fed by the lad, who, they learned, had deserted from the *Wehrmacht*. On 15 April the trap-door to the loft was suddenly thrust upwards by a French NCO who told them that the area was clear of German troops and they were free. Writing a letter of thanks for the German family, the trio left for the assembly point for prisoners of war. It was Stalag 357.

At Fallingbostel there was not a German in sight but the population of the camp was now of every nationality and had swollen by thousands during the time they had been away. Sleep, for many in the ransacked camp, was to be in the open. Paul Hilton and Don Boutle, with hundreds of other sick Kriegies who had been left behind, saw the return of the last parties to leave. They had been cut off by the fighting and marched back. Russian, Serbian, Polish and French prisoners had poured into the camp until it held 6,000 hungry and desperate men without food, water or electricity.

TOO MANY TO MURDER

Sergeant Johnny Smith was impatient and hungry. The guards had left Stalag 357, the *Posten* boxes were empty. Only the wire was between him, food and freedom. A young cockney army private felt the same. Together they marched out of the unguarded camp main gate and down towards the outskirts of Fallingbostel, on a foraging mission. Happily clutching a loaf of bread and a bottle of milk each, they turned back to Stalag 357, taking a path through the woods. The afternoon was very hot, so stripping off their singlets, they tied their booty in them, pushed sticks under the knots, then walked with the parcels over their shoulders like a couple of tramps.

A challenge in German stopped them in their tracks. Forty armed *Wehrmacht* men stood solidly in their path. Smith recognised some of them as former camp guards. Roughly grabbing the two prisoners, the Germans forced them to the ground with their backs to a tree. A *Feld-webel* in charge made a quick decision and barked orders to his men.

'What's he saying, Smiffy?' asked the private. 'What's he saying?'

Smith knew enough German to understand the *Feldwebel.*

'Shut-up you fool, they're going to shoot us,' Smith answered, and watched warily as the *Feldwebel* detailed men for the execution. Smith was desolate. Now, at the tail-end of the war, his last moments had come.

The private looked on in disbelief and then suddenly announced, 'They're not going to shoot me on an empty stomach.' Grabbing his singlet, he pulled out his loaf and began eating ravenously.

A sudden commotion in the woods a few yards away distracted their *Wehrmacht* captors. Four Kriegies, who had earlier scrambled from the marching column, emerged from the trees at gun-point. There were now six Kriegies. The *Feldwebel* decided that there were too many to kill in one go. With a wave of his gun as a warning to the prisoners, he signalled his party to leave. Smith breathed deeply and turned to look at the cockney private. He was still eating.

When an American column caught up with marching Kriegies in the Magdeburg area, Warrant Officer Ray Hedley thought that at last he was going to leave the fighting line. 'We've got to take that village,' said an American officer, 'then we will get you home as soon as possible.' He left a radio car and crew with them. But a Hitler Youth company had other ideas, fiercely attacking the newly released Kriegies, just as they were feeling safe. The radio crew, assisted by released soldier-Kriegies, fought back and American artillery shelled the village. Eighteen hours of explosion and fire ensued, until the Kriegies were rescued and eventually taken to the aerodrome at Hildesheim. As the senior man of the group, Hedley was put in charge of 24 soldiers taken at Dunkirk, who promptly dubbed him 'major'. The 'major' was heartily glad to be relieved of this responsibility when they boarded a Dakota for RAF Wing. There, being the only RAF man to disembark, he was immediately seized by a waiting group captain and a WAAF and escorted to the mess, where a large plate of bacon and eggs was placed before him. Hedley did his best to retain the rich food but it ended up on the concrete outside.

A BRUSH WITH THE *WAFFEN SS*

Flight Sergeant Graham Hall and Sergeant Stanley 'Cherub' Lang had been on the run from the Stalag 357 column out of Fallingbostel for ten days. They were exhausted and ravenously hungry. At dawn they crawled cautiously to the edge of the wood in which they had been hiding. A short distance away was an isolated farmhouse. It looked deserted, but they watched for signs of life until 11 a.m.; then, feeling desperate, they decided to break in. Naturally reluctant to make a violent entry, Hall first knocked at the door. To the pair's dismay it was opened, and the man who enquired what they wanted was dressed in the black uniform of an *Oberst* of the *Waffen SS.*

The *Oberst* quickly guessed that the men at the door were prisoners-of-war on the run. He invited them into the farmhouse. Graham Hall felt that Lang and he were entering the lion's den but they had little choice. The *Oberst* was friendly. When he discovered that his unexpected visitors were hungry, he called his batman and ordered a good breakfast for them. Hall and Lang tucked into the bacon, eggs, bread and butter, wondering what the outcome of this odd situation would be. Was it to be the last meal of condemned men? Hall eventually summoned the will to ask the *Oberst* his intentions.

'Well, there is going to be a big battle in this area,' replied the *Oberst.* 'In the woods over there I have 400 of the world's finest fighting men and the British are over there,' he said, pointing to the west. 'The best thing you two can do is to make your way to your own people and, once there, you can watch the battle from a safe distance.'

Hall and Lang were staggered by his friendliness, but the German had not finished. Calling his batman again, he instructed him to take the Kriegies in his jeep-type vehicle to a crossroads, from where they could make their way safely to the British positions. Wishing them luck and shaking their hands, the *Oberst* saw them on their way. At the crossroads, the batman dropped them, pointing to the direction in which they should head.

With the 'good luck' wishes ringing in their ears, Hall and Lang hurried off, hardly believing the happenings of the last two hours. The road opened up ahead and before them was Stalag 357. It was 16 April 1945; the 8th Hussars, 7th Armoured Division of the British Army, was in the process of liberating the camp. Hall and Lang were free. From a vantage point they saw and heard the battle that ensued between British and the entrenched *SS.* In that strange way that one can feel in war, Hall and Lang hoped that the *SS Oberst* survived.

SONDERLAGEREN

Oflag 4C Colditz, just over twenty miles south-east of Leipzig, was a little unusual as a prisoner-of-war prison. It was a castle, not unlike that at Spangenberg, but there any similarity ended. Here in this *Sonderlager* the bad boys, the persistent escapers and troublemakers, the constant nuisances the Germans wanted to keep under close watch, were more securely caged.

It was inevitable that Douglas Bader would, sooner or later, join them, though the loss of both legs effectively prevented his escape. He could neither run nor move quickly – an absolute essential to some part of an escape – and he was immediately recognisable. Bader never regarded his lack of legs as a disability; disabilities were, in his view, made to be overcome, but it was a constant frustration. What he lacked in mobility he more than made up for in courage and cussedness, but his chances of a successful escape from the confines of Colditz were minimal. The walls of the 'escape-proof' castle had been breached earlier by Pat Reid, Airey Neave and others, but Bader was there to stay until 13 April when, after a noisy battle, American troops freed the prisoners.

THE FLAGGING COLUMN

Each time a potato clamp was seen by the side of the road, a surprising number of Kriegies decided they needed a '*Pinkepause*', during which the clamp was hurriedly opened, potatoes extracted and pockets and trouser legs filled. Trouser legs were always tucked into socks, ready for such an emergency. Battledress blouses were also a useful hiding place for the occasional neck-wrung chicken.

Foraging was the only way to survive. As the already lax discipline of the guards loosened further, the Kriegies became more daring, prospecting farther from the column and almost openly living off the land. The perimeter, patrolled by guards, and then dogs, was too large for them to control effectively. Livestock on the farms was in great danger from hungry Kriegies. Although pigs disappeared and were slaughtered at one stop, about a hundred chickens at another, and dozens of eggs and stones of pearl barley went into Kriegie stomachs, there were few full bellies among the thousands on the march.

Body lice were a problem for many who had been unable to clear them completely from their bodies and clothes since the winter marches. Little water was available, so many Kriegies spent their nights in a torment of irritation. Rats and mice added to their misery.

The occasional rest day brought relief, not only to aching limbs, but also for the chance to clean themselves. Cecil Room found a cold river in which to wash from head to foot. He shivered but felt reasonably clean for a while. Some of his clothes were discarded and the lice with them. He then spent the afternoon slinking into a garden to steal some rhubarb sticks, and making a pie with a little flour. His combine ate in style.

At a nearby *Luftwaffe* aerodrome, Spitfires and Typhoons shot up stationary aircraft and buildings, Messerschmitt 109s took off and an exciting combat screamed and roared above the Kriegies' heads. As a 109 plummeted to earth in flames, Cecil Room said that 'a bloody great cheer went up'. When the battle was over, the Kriegies emerged from their hiding places in barns, bushes and wood-piles.

That night, Room was louse hunting again. The morning dip seemed to have done no good at all. By next day, Room and his friend Jack had just about had enough. They had nearly reached Ebstorf, where they had boarded the box-cars after the infamous trek in arctic conditions from Gross Tychow*. Somehow it seemed as though they had turned full circle, it was all so very stupid. It was time to go. 'Left turn,' Room whispered urgently, prodding Jack's back and turning into a farmyard at a moment when the guard's attention wavered. Sweating and trembling, they darted into a cattle shed and swiftly burrowed under straw. There they lay still until the sound of the column died away. Then they discovered that they had been followed into the farmyard by a disaffected *Unteroffizier* Marz. The three lived comfortably on the farm until the Germans in the vicinity had retreated and the British arrived.

The march shuffled on, tedious and slow. There were still enough trigger-happy armed guards and ferocious dogs to make escape attempts risky, and there was some comfort in numbers. The thousands in the columns staggered on, but a few Kriegies were disappearing whenever opportunities arose.

On the evening of Saturday 14 April, RAF Sergeants Bob Trett and Ivor Norris met a Dutch worker on a farm. He told them that the Americans were only twenty kilometres away. It seemed unlikely, as this was a sector where British and Canadian troops were advancing, but it was worth taking a chance. That night they would prepare to go at the first opportunity in the morning. Trett had noticed that the guards who had been on duty during the night marched eagerly towards the day shift as soon as they saw them approaching. For a couple of minutes, the dogs were away and the Kriegies unguarded.

Trett and Norris picked their moment. Gathering up their few belongings, they ran across the road, over a field and into a spruce wood.

* *Not All Glory!*, p. 201

The wood was thin so, bent double to make a smaller target, they dashed on to another wood, where branches of taller spruce trees reached the ground, with enough room beneath to stand. It was a natural bell-tent. Bob Trett gasped thankfully, 'An army could hide in here.'

That night they bedded down in the wood, remaining as quiet and as carefully concealed as possible. A German, accompanied by a Russian prisoner, had been seen in the woods and the RAF men were still apprehensive.

On Monday they awoke to distant artillery fire, and heavy machine-gun fire nearby. They had not realised the fighting front was so close. Trett, wearing an army battledress, decided that it blended into the background better than RAF blue and decided to 'risk a wander' to find out what was happening. To his surprise, he found five Kriegies who also had left the column and were hiding in the wood. One of them was very ill from drinking contaminated pond water.

Tuesday was another fine day. They had seen no rain since leaving Fallingbostel. In the early afternoon, one of the other party in the wood came to find Trett and Norris and told them that the sick man was much worse, that they were going to take him out and risk meeting a German patrol.

All was quiet for a while, and then Trett, shaken and shocked, saw eight soldiers walking straight towards him. Certain of recapture, his hopes were dashed until he saw that the soldiers were wearing webbing gaiters, not leather like *Wehrmacht* men. The British Army had arrived. Bob Trett was so excited that he jumped out, shouted and waved with joy. He was lucky not to be shot but the soldiers had been forewarned by the men who had taken out their sick comrade.

As they left the wood, Norris and Trett saw that the woods on either side had been burnt to the ground. There had been opposition and flame-throwers had been used to flush out the Germans. The RAF men were happy that the opposition had not come from 'their' wood.

Back at the headquarters base of the 11th Hussars, the chef, splendidly arrayed in check trousers, white coat, sweat scarf and white hat, prepared a snack for each of the escapers. It consisted of a huge slice of white bread and butter, topped with six fried (foraged) eggs and washed down with a large army mug of strong, sweet, hot tea. They were back among civilised people and 'had the recently captured, very arrogant ex-Hitler Youth not spat in my face,' Trett says, 'I would not have hit him – but a lot of hate went into that punch.'

As the columns moved on, the shrinking of the German pocket around them brought the danger of the prisoners being involved in the last-stand battle among the German defenders on the wrong side of the Elbe. It was an unpleasant prospect. Bob 'Smudge' Coles was another who decided that he must quickly leave the column; the river was too close for his liking.

On the morning of Sunday 15 April, the column passed a military aerodrome covered with burnt-out front-line aircraft. In other parts of the airfield ground staff were drawing aircraft together in groups and burning them in spectacular and noisily explosive fires. Pilots they still had, but there was no fuel to get the planes off the ground.

As the column threaded its way through a pine plantation, Coles looked round for his partner, Bob Hale. Jerking his head to indicate the woods at the side of the road, he calmly strolled away into the trees. Hale joined him, and then they ran. Only one German had seen them go, a friendly guard who looked about him to make sure that no other guard had noticed their disappearance. When the pair had reached what they thought to be a safe distance from the column, they threw themselves down to ease their pounding hearts and gasping breath. That night they slept exhausted on a bed of bracken and pine needles.

Next morning, they discovered an 80-foot fire observation tower high on a hill. From the top they could see that their position was strategically poor. The Americans were pushing along the Elbe towards Lüneburg, which was four miles to the north-west; the British were presumably fighting their way to the same area, having by-passed Hamburg. The spot where the airmen were encamped seemed almost certain to be the site of a fierce battle. To go forward in a south-westerly direction would be the quickest route to Allied troops, but the huge Lüneburg heath, although offering cover, would be swarming with the enemy. There would be guarded bridges and railways to cross, escape roads would be stuffed with retreating *Wehrmacht*. There would be gun posts and mines. The runaways decided to wait and assess the situation.

On Wednesday morning, they were awakened by loud earth-shaking detonations. They raced up the hill to the observation tower to see what was happening. Small-arms and machine-gun fire rattled across the area. A pall of smoke covered the river. Were the Germans blowing up bridges? They could see twelve miles in every direction but there was no-one in sight. It was ghostly – just the spasmodic gunfire and bird song to be heard. Across the countryside to the south, patches of smoke covered large areas, marking the road to Uelzen. The tower was now obviously unsafe; although only their eyes appeared above the parapet, they could be seen by anyone with binoculars.

Back on the ground, they waited, tense and expectant. At 3 p.m., a file of German soldiers ran along the road, dodging in and out and hugging the trees. Some carried anti-tank *Panzerfaust,* others sub-machine-guns. Machine-gun fire was now within half a mile of the Kriegies in their hide-out. They watched German soldiers flogging exhausted horses as they tried to speed their retreat, and groups threw themselves under cover as searching Spitfires flew low. More gunfire made soldiers run away from the road towards Coles and Hale. It was getting too hot. Diving into a trench, the airmen bent low as a German soldier dashed by at a half-run. They could hear him sobbing for breath and see the fear in his eyes. When the German had passed, the pair threw themselves into a dug-out they had mentally noted for an emergency. As shells whined over-head and bullets ricocheted among the trees, they knew they were in the midst of a desperate battle. There was also the fear that a retreating German might throw himself into their dug-out. The Kriegies knew he would shoot first and think after. But, as a shell burst near, Bob Hale was laughing. 'I'm dead scared,' he gasped, 'but I'm happy.'

'Smudge' Coles was happy too. 'Well, son,' he said, 'there's no need to conserve that bread any longer – cut me a slice and don't stint the marge.'

The action moved away. As he munched his bread, Coles peeped over the ridge of the dug-out. British tanks and trucks were passing a few hundred yards away. The red berets of airborne troops could plainly be seen as they clung to the trucks, Tommy-guns under their arms at the ready. They appeared casual and carefree, scorning steel helmets. After a brief halt, the British tanks moved on, leaving the road as quiet as before.

The airmen dared not show themselves yet; Germans were still in the woods around and neither relished the idea of a bullet in the back after the years of waiting. Both were prepared to wait another day until, they assumed, the infantry would roll up. But within twenty minutes, when another British armoured column appeared on the road, they decided to run for it. Leaping out of the dug-out, bounding across the field, stumbling over the furrows, shouting and waving their hats, the Kriegies saw the crew of an armoured car leap out, drop to their knees and cover the runners with their Tommy guns. Arms held high, the airmen quickly slowed to a walk. As they neared the soldiers, Coles and Hale shouted, 'Hello, Tommy! we're British!'

The stern, wary faces of the soldiers split into grins. The Tommies seemed as glad to see the Kriegies as they to see them.

ALOFT AGAIN

Len Clarke's 'combine' of four discussed the right moment for a dash from the column, always bearing in mind the warning from the Germans that those dropping out would be shot, and the real danger from vengeful civilians who had been evacuated from bombed cities. But there was no guarantee that staying with the column meant a safe and permanent release from the Germans.

One of the 'combine' quite suddenly began to show the extreme effects of privation. He stopped, slowly lowered himself wearily at the roadside and swore that he could go no further. Pleas for him to carry on had no effect. Warned that he could be shot, he merely whispered hoarsely but vehemently, 'Sod it, I don't give a damn.'

The exhausted man could not be carried and would not try any more. The column had to keep going with their useless trudge to nowhere. A guard spoke to the exhausted man and, to the relief of the watchers, was seen to shrug and move on.

That night, as the group pulled straw around them and settled down for the night, a guard advised them to get a good night's rest as it was their intention next day to cross the Elbe, about 30 kilometres distant. This then was the moment to make their getaway. Once across the river, it would be impossible to get back. The three burrowed deep into the straw and next morning emerged when everyone had left.

As they were brushing away the straw and collecting their few belongings together, a soldier armed with a rifle strode through the barn door. It was exactly the kind of encounter the airmen feared, but their reply to his query that they were sick and had to rest satisfied him. To their relief, he shouldered his rifle and left.

Keeping to paths and by-roads, the three plodded through country which seemed strangely empty. Aircraft wheeled overhead and Len Clarke reckoned the Allied forces were only a few miles away. The group's biggest danger was of meeting retreating German troops, to whom a few more bullets and bodies about the area would hardly be noticed.

On the road they joined a party of sick prisoners, some walking, others carried in a horse-drawn cart, who were making their way to Melbeck, a small village just south of Lüneburg. The party stayed at a farm that night, watching the close glow of fires. It was 17 April, the end was obviously very near and commonsense told them it would be wise to stay where they were.

White flags were hanging from the windows in the village the next morning when the sound of tanks was heard. The Kriegies ran to the road and there, coming with a roar, were tanks and trucks with what seemed like hundreds of British soldiers. It was a scene of delirium; soon the Kriegies were surrounded by a milling mob of men of the King's Shropshire

Light Infantry, and their pockets were being filled with cigarettes and chocolate.

A soldier invited Clarke to go with him to check houses in a search for hiding *Wehrmacht*. Pushing their way into a house, they found the occupants cowering and frightened. Clarke did not like to see these trembling people, now completely at the mercy of their conquerors, expecting fierce retribution. These same people, though, had probably had no qualms when their own troops were marching in triumph across occupied countries.

At Rheine, the airfield was a scene of utter destruction. Clarke had just missed the last plane back to England and was looking at destroyed German aircraft, studying a Dakota which had tipped into a bomb crater, contemplating the white flags and the waste of war, when a Canadian pilot asked him how long he had been a prisoner. On learning that it was five years, he said, 'Heck, I guess you'd like to get back then. If you don't mind riding on crates, I'm just leaving for Wing, one of the POW reception centres.'

Within seconds, Clarke was in the aircraft wondering how he would feel about flying again. It was just three weeks short of five years since he was last in an aircraft, and from that flight he still had the smell of cordite, spilling oil, glycol and smoke in his nostrils. But, as the Dakota lifted, all the sensations of flying returned and he leaned back on a crate, wondering if the last five years had really happened. His dirty khaki battledress blouse was sufficient to remind him.

As he left the Dakota at Wing, he called to the Canadian pilot, 'Thanks for the ride.'

The pilot laughed, 'That's OK,' he called, 'but don't stay away so long next time.'

CROMWELLS AND CHURCHILLS

For many marchers the strain was proving too much. On 17 April a small party was sent back the way they had come. A slow journey by horse and cart ended that evening at a barn with a large Red Cross flag draped across the roof. The exhausted men gratefully settled down in straw and slept.

At first light, the Kriegies were awakened by the sounds of battle all around them; aircraft roared low overhead, shells screamed above and bullets ricocheted. There was nothing the men could do but literally keep their heads down. At 11 a.m., everything stopped. The quiet now could almost be felt. For an hour nothing happened. Peeping outside, the Kriegies waited, fearful and hopeful. At noon, RAF planes flew overhead and a Cromwell tank rumbled along the road towards the barn. The British

Army had arrived! For Sergeant John Knott the overwhelming joy of that meeting will forever stay in his memory.

Sergeants Moffat and Bartlam dodged off the column and spent four days in the woods. French workers told them that the Germans had said they would leave the prisoners behind when they retreated. And so it proved. When the local *Bürgermeister* heard that British ex-prisoners were around, he insisted on surrendering the village to them. Moffat and Bartlam accepted the surrender and handed over the village to a column of British tanks that evening. The commander of the tank squadron radioed the release of the Kriegies back to his base, from which it was relayed to Britain. Four hours later, Moffat's mother knew of his release.

NIGHT OWL – HOMING PIGEON

On 8 May, Flight Lieutenant Phil Middleton waited with several hundred RAF officers at Lüneburg aerodrome for Lancasters to take them home. The aircraft arrived next day, after the Kriegies had been celebrating half the night.

The pilot of the first Lanc looked with distaste at the creased, unkempt, ill-dressed and unruly-looking mob waiting to board his plane. He pointed to Middleton and called, 'You sir, here!' Middleton was allowed, rather reluctantly, to push through the crowd and climb the steps. 'Seat for you up front, sir.' Middleton did not argue and went forward. It seemed that he was the only one in the motley mob to be wearing a rather battered but still recognisable officer's cap. Packed in the rear of the aircraft were wing commanders and squadron leaders, perhaps even the odd group captain.

Flt Lt Middleton was provided with a helmet and intercom and soon found that their destination was Dunsfold near his home at Redhill. He explained to the pilot that he would love to see if his home was still there. The pilot glanced at Middleton's observer brevet and agreed to allow him to map-read him from the Thames estuary. Middleton knew the south-east intimately; it was no problem for him to approach his road, Woodside Way, as if on a low-level bombing run.

Down the centre of the road he could see a line of tables. The children were having a VE Day party. Middleton guessed his wife was down there among the helpers. He was relieved to see that the last house on the left, his home, No. 2, appeared to be unscathed.

Once clear of the reception at Dunsfold, Phil Middleton dashed to the telephone. He and his wife had not heard from each other for several months and were thankful that they were both alive. She told him that a darned great big bomber had buzzed the estate celebration tea party that afternoon. Some of the kids were thrilled and others alarmed. Middleton was pardoned by his wife, but the Kriegie officers in the rear of the Lancaster were not amused at the 'G' involved on their gentle cruise back to 'Blighty'.

ONE MORE DAY TO LIVE

Fort Zinner, a Napoleonic stronghold near Torgau, had been a *Straflager* and a *Wehrmachtgefängnis*, dreaded as a punishment camp for Kriegies and German servicemen who had transgressed military law, as a holding prison for political prisoners and as a place of execution. When flight engineer Sergeant Norman (Bill) Panter was sent there from Stalag 4B in early April 1945, he joined twenty prisoners-of-war who were to be court-martialled by the Germans. There were also 200 Germans, military and civil, who had been sentenced to death, were filled with foreboding and just waiting.

Huddled together in the cells, the prisoners sat, quiet, petrified, until, at four o'clock each afternoon, those who were to be shot next morning were informed. Heavy footsteps thumped along the corridor, as guards moved from cell to cell, calling out the names. If the guards passed a cell, the inmates sank down slowly or collapsed exhausted, believing they had at least one more day to live.

With the usual chaos, the Germans marched the Kriegies and the 80 German political prisoners who remained, out of Fort Zinner. After 25 kilometres, they were turned back by the proximity of heavy gunfire, and were then machine-gunned by US planes.

On 23 April, the prisoners awoke to find only one guard remaining in the fort. He had orders to shoot them all before they were overrun, but that was beyond his capabilities and desire. The next day the Americans arrived: the torture was over.

COOKS ON THE MARCH

Brian Walley was on the cookhouse staff at Stalag 7, Bankau. Men volunteered for the job for various reasons, some merely to keep themselves occupied and fit, others because they were entitled to feed themselves a little better than the rest of the Kriegies, and some because they wanted to be of service to their fellows. Most cooks in the forces come in for heavy criticism and so it was in prison camps. The cry of 'Rackets!' often was less jocular than it sounded.

The forced march from Bankau began in the early morning of 19 January. The previous night, Russian bombs had put out of action a temporary airfield near the camp and some of the bombs fell frighteningly close. The cookhouse staff led the column, manhandling a heavy sledge loaded with camp records as well as cooking supplies. The sledge went smoothly enough along the snow-covered country roads, but when the column reached Kreuzberg, Walley and his group found the streets had been cleared of snow. Heaving the sledge along became a desperate struggle, and at Konstadt a wagon was commandeered from a local farmer and the sledge left in exchange. 'We made a right mess of reloading the camp records,' Walley recalls. 'Many of them took off with the wind.'

The cookhouse staff were certainly worth any salt they could find, for after the day's march in temperatures sometimes 15 degrees Centigrade below zero, they had to set to and try to feed almost 1,500 exhausted and very hungry men. On the first night, Walley was one of 100 men housed in a tiny schoolroom. There was not room enough to lie down in their sodden clothing. On the following day, the march started at 5 a.m. The cookhouse staff had had enough of dragging the wagon and decided to abandon it. The German guards rustled up a horse and used the wagon to carry the sick, of whom there was a growing number.

By 10 a.m. the marchers had added another 12 kilometres to the 28 marched on the first day. They had reached Karlsruhe and were pushed into an abandoned brick factory and provided with two field kitchens, which were capable of providing for 200 men. The cookhouse staff did the best they could, 'made everything into the proverbial soup and doled it out, half a cup per man'. This army certainly was not marching on its stomach.

The column left the brick factory at night and in arctic conditions covered 42 kilometres. They crossed the Oder, despite attempted delaying tactics in the hope that the rapidly advancing Russians would overtake them. Once they were over, German sappers blew up the bridge. They halted at Schonfeld, where they were herded into a walled farmyard. Each man received 100 grams of biscuits, to which Walley & Co could add but half a cup of ersatz coffee. Walley and others who had the experience went to work and milked the cows on the farm to the last drop. Despite the promise of a two-day break, the Kriegies were roused at 1.30 a.m. and those who raised objections were soon brought to heel with rifle butts. On the fourth day, 31 men too sick to march were evacuated and it was found that another 33 had quietly left the column. These managed to contact the Russians and eventually reached England by way of Odessa. The column moved on and that day, 22 January, reached Jankwitz, 34 kilometres on. Rations of meat, barley and peas enabled the cooks to provide one-quarter of a litre of soup for each man.

On 25 January, they crossed paths with a column of Kriegies from Stalag 8B who seemed to Walley to be 'in worse shape than us'. But the meeting somehow gave them all a fillip. Next day the camp cooks were able to provide soup twice, as well as coffee. The march went on. Rations were skimpy and more sick had to be evacuated. In just over a week more than 80 men could not continue.

From town to town they marched, often at night. From Pfaffendorf to Standorf, to Peterwitz, which was reached at 4 a.m. after a march of 22 kilometres. Walley writes: 'This was undoubtedly by far the worst section of the whole debilitating trip, carried out under blizzard conditions and in darkness.' When they arrived, the exhausted marchers were left standing in a freezing wind while the guards looked for secure accommodation. Walley found himself in a barn. He had already rubbed snow on to a frost-bitten ear to try to restore circulation. Now, when he tried to take off his boots, he discovered that his socks were frozen to them.

Transport was promised for the remainder of the journey, but then the Kriegies were told that first they must march to Goldberg, a further 20 kilometres. They were all desperately hungry and some of the men broke into a cellar in a farmyard. They found sacks of dehydrated potatoes which they mashed with hot water to make a belly-filling meal. Some men fought over sugar-beet tops and were violently ill. After a two-day break at Peterwitz, the column pushed on to Prausnitz, a distance of 12 kilometres. They remained there for four days, until 5 February. Dysentery, or the 'squitters', as it was inelegantly called, was rife and volunteers were called for to dig trenches for latrines. The offer of double rations produced enough volunteers. The tools were supplied by the Germans.

On 5 February, the column took to the road for the last time and soon covered the 8 kilometres to Goldberg. They almost, but not quite, wished that they could continue marching, for the train journey was a nightmare. Travelling in the usual cattle trucks, 55 to a wagon, the men could not lie down, but they organised themselves into rows with each man, except for the first row, who had their backs to the wall, sitting between the outstretched legs of another. That was the best they could do. It was 35 hours before they were given water to drink. In Walley's wagon a former London pastrycook described at great length the making of chocolate éclairs. 'He wouldn't stop,' Walley recalls. 'One chocolate éclair after another – to this day I just can't stomach them.'

For three days they sat in their own mess and the showers at Luckenwalde came as a great relief. Interestingly, those who had been incarcerated for several years stood up to the ordeal of the march and the train journey better than those captured more recently, probably, Walley believes, 'because we had had time to become adjusted to poor living and so were mentally and physically better able to cope with the horrendous conditions'.

RESTRAINT ON FREEDOM

The prisoners at Luckenwalde knew that the Russians were getting close. Still suffering the effects of the long forced marches from Lamsdorf and Bankau in terrible conditions, they felt a deep sense of relief rather than excitement. The Red Army's inexorable advance, no more than a distant rumble earlier, could now be heard distinctly as a series of explosions. They were about 15 kilometres distant. The Kriegies decided that, for their own security, a constant watch should be maintained. P/O Les Poole drew the 1 a.m. to 2 a.m. shift and, as soon as the sentry passed the block, Poole scuttled across the open space to the *Abort* and perched by a glassless window. In the direction of Jüterbog an incredible firework display had him riveted. Flares, markers, Very lights, gun flashes and huge fires lit the horizon. By morning the German guards had disappeared.

The news spread through the camp like a bush-fire and Kriegies poured through the gate into the Vorlager. They discovered an arsenal. There were machine-guns, rifles, hand-guns, bayonets and knives, even some ceremonial swords. Everything was taken back into the camp. The Kriegies were apprehensive. A Russian barrage might descend upon them; the Germans might launch a counter-attack. The reappearance of German soldiers in the camp was greeted with dismay. The *Wehrmacht* officer in charge demanded that the arms be returned immediately; otherwise he would order a field-piece to fire on the camp.

The Kriegies staggered under the weight of the guns and ammunition they carried, but instead of returning them, they dumped them in a pond some 200 yards outside the wire. There was no reprisal. On 23 April, the Russians arrived and the Kriegies were nominally free. But the Russians were in no hurry to release them. The joy of liberation was dissipated as the days passed and the Russians stubbornly prevented their leaving the camp. American lorries arrived and were sent away, the Russians firing over the heads of Kriegies who tried to board them. That there was a political motive and the Kriegies were in effect being held hostage was obvious. It was 21 May before the Russians took the Kriegies in trucks to the Elbe at Wittenberg. There they were made to leave all their belongings before crossing the long, undulating pontoon bridge to the American side of the river.

Much to the fury of the Red Army officers, many of the Kriegies had found their own way home. They felt that they had been pitched from the German frying pan into the Russian fire. Unwilling to continue in spurious captivity, Sergeants Jim Palmer and Brian Walley, with about a dozen others, broke out of the camp in the early morning of 5 May. They soon caught up with a company of 100 or so Russians who were conducting mopping-up operations in the woods. The status of the Kriegies did not concern them and they raised no objection when Walley's group tacked on to the end of their column, behind a horse-drawn dray loaded with gear. Some women soldiers were perched on the top.

The column was ambushed by German soldiers, who still had fight left in them. The Kriegies dived for the ditch, deciding this was no longer their war. Within seconds the Russians also had taken cover, before regrouping and launching a relentless counter-attack. The Germans were routed. One very frightened officer was spared so that he could be interrogated; the rest were shot. The Kriegies went their own way, making good time to reach Treuenbrietzen the same night. Next day they reached Wittenberg, having hitched a ride with an American who, for some odd reason, was driving a horse-drawn dray. The group, now numbering just three aircrew Kriegies, stopped to rest at one point and found themselves by the roadside grave of some Russian soldiers. A German soldier lay dead in a ditch; for him no grave had been dug.

That night, 7 May, they found beds in a foreign workers' camp. French, Belgian and Yugoslav inmates, men and women, prepared a splendid feast and produced a bottle of peach brandy which had been buried under the floor. On VE Day the three Kriegies got a ride on the bonnet of a jeep and crossed the Elbe on the pontoon bridge. They were among the last to cross before the border between the Russian and American zones was sealed off.

ABOUT TURN!

It was 8 May, Ted Chapman's fourth anniversary of sailing his SAC boat 'into Boulogne High Street' – as he described his attempt to rescue a Messerschmitt pilot in the sea off Boulogne, which ended, ironically, in his craft being attacked by Messerschmitts and his being captured*. He was fed-up. The number of Russian guards in the camp was double that of the Germans, they were still mopping up in the area and their general was insisting that the Kriegies would eventually be sent home via Odessa.

Chapman knew the Americans were to the west, and looked for a chance to run. His duty that day was as gate guard with a Russian-speaking Pole, which allowed him to converse with the Russians. Luckenwalde

* *Not All Glory!*, pp. 33–5

camp had been a work-commando and a woman arrived with her teenage daughter, who had been raped by Russian soldiers. She said that she wanted to return a khaki jacket belonging to an Irish sergeant who had worked on her farm. Ted Chapman believed he would be shot if he permitted the woman to enter the camp, so, feeling rotten about doing it, he deliberately caused a commotion. The Russian guards gathered round the Pole to hear what the fuss was about and Chapman slid away down the road.

Well clear, on a road banked several feet higher than the fields on either side, Chapman saw a jeep approaching. Sure that it was Russian, he determined to put on a bold front, expecting the worst. The jeep slowed down and, to Chapman's surprise, he saw that the driver was a coloured American sergeant, who was as astonished as Chapman and, on learning that he was heading for the Russian lines, horrified.

The sergeant, rapidly turning the jeep and offering Chapman a ride, told his story. With three other coloured colleagues he had taken four German women to a derelict farm. In the middle of the night, a party of Russians stormed into the farm, shooting and killing everyone except the driver, who had been knocked down in the mêlée and left for dead beneath the bodies of the others. Lying still for several hours until the Russians had left, he went outside and was amazed to see the jeep still in the farmyard. He had driven off quickly, apparently in the wrong direction.

Chapman told the sergeant that he was a British officer, and when they came across a party of Americans, he praised the bravery of the soldier who, he said, had saved his life. The Russian guards at the eastern end of the Elbe pontoon bridge were hopelessly drunk so that their shooting at the American party was wildly inaccurate. Joining the last party to cross the bridge, Chapman reached the west bank and was free.

THE HERO'S RETURN

Appearances undoubtedly do have a marked effect on the way one is treated. The healthy, robust figure usually commands respect, whereas the invalid or under-nourished is often disparaged, as Warrant Officer Paul Hilton was to find out. He had just returned home after being a prisoner of the Germans for three years. He was in one of the first batches to be released and consequently arrived at RAF Cosford before they were expected. Senior NCOs were sent on home leave wearing airmen's tunics and greatcoats and without badges of rank – not that they cared much for that, but those things seemed to make a difference in a somewhat class-conscious society. The clothing stores had done their best, but Hilton was not easy to fit anyway. He had spent most of the previous winter in the camp hospital, suffering from chronic bronchitis and pneumonia. That, combined with a poor and meagre diet, meant that his 6ft 2in bone structure weighed a mere eight stone with a haunted expression to match.

Carrying his new kit and as much of his old kit as had survived the delouser, Hilton deposited his collection at Victoria station services left luggage office. He decided to visit the hairdresser in the catacombs beneath the station before continuing his journey. A proper haircut was long overdue and 'these things were important then'. He settled in the chair and it occurred to him that he would have to kiss several female relatives so, on completion of the haircut, Hilton suggested a shave. The barber stroked Hilton's soft 23-year-old chin contemptuously with the back of his hand and said, 'You don't need a bloody shave.'

Unshaven, he sauntered back to the left luggage office to retrieve his bags.

In the train, he had to listen to an ATC officer's sad tale about a young clerk who had recently been jailed for masquerading as a wing commander, complete with DSO and DFC, and giving thrilling lectures to factory workers and ATC squadrons. It was considered a huge joke and a pity the poor lad was jailed, and the authorities lacked a sense of humour. Hilton could not comment; he had known too many real senior officers, mostly now dead. If anything, he felt sick. In a way he dreaded his home-coming, for he knew that both his parents had been taken by the Japanese. He huddled further into his featureless greatcoat until the train arrived at Haywards Heath, where he shouldered his kit and crept quietly home.

Months were to pass before Paul Hilton learned that his father had survived in Changi jail but that his mother had died in Sumatra.

Index